Lionello Perera

An Italian Banker and Patron in New York

Diego Mantoan
University of Palermo, Italy

Series in World History

VERNON PRESS

www.vernonpress.com

In the Americas:
Vernon Press
1000 N West Street, Suite 1200
Wilmington, Delaware, 19801
United States

In the rest of the world:
Vernon Press
C/Sancti Espiritu 17,
Malaga, 29006
Spain

Series in World History

Library of Congress Control Number: 2022936678

ISBN: 978-1-64889-441-1

Also available: 978-1-64889-442-8 [Hardback, Premium Color]

Cover design by Vernon Press. Cover image: Arturo Noci, *Portrait of Lionello Perera*, 1933, oil on canvas. (Courtesy of the Perera Family Archive)

To Giulia and Angelica
my little big world

Table of contents

List of Figures

Chapter 1

A Postcard as a Foreword

Leo Collier

My name is Lionello Collier, born in 1938 in Washington D.C. I am the maternal grandson of Lionello Arturo Lopes Perera, born in Venice in 1871. My grandfather died on April 26, 1942, on a train to New York City after visiting my family in Falls Church, Virginia, shortly before my parents went to La Paz to join the US Embassy in Bolivia as diplomats. He had come to wish his daughter Nina and her family goodbye.

This story started in 2012 when I received from my cousin Carol Perera Weingeist a copy of a postcard found in the possessions of her father Charles (Fig. 1.1). The postcard shows Palazzo Foscari in Venice, a beautiful palace on the Grand Canal from where many famous paintings were executed. This card sent me on a quest to learn more about my grandfather, who graduated in July 1889 from the Venetian Regia Scuola Superiore di Commercio, today Ca' Foscari University of Venice, Italy. He graduated before emigrating to New York to work in the Cantoni Bank owned by his maternal uncle Salvatore Cantoni, whose family it was told had also supported his studies in commerce and banking. After losing both his parents as a teenager, he left five sisters in Venice –Rosa, Olga, Clary, Clelia, and Alice– for whom he felt deeply responsible.

I contacted Ca' Foscari University in Venice asking its Alumni Association if they had any records of Lionello as a student, and to my amazement, I heard back from Marco Cosmo that indeed they still held records showing his enrolment, address, and report of studies, and eventually even his graduation documents. Thereafter I travelled to Venice to visit the house where Lionello and his five sisters had lived, at the address found in his enrolment papers. It was most likely owned by the Cantoni family who helped Lionello and his sisters after the death of his parents. At his alma mater, I met Marco Cosmo and his then-director Diego Mantoan who received me warmly. They also had a great interest in learning more about Lionello Perera's life, especially after he left for the United States and became famous as a banker, philanthropist, and a patron of the arts and music. On that occasion, I visited the now famous balcony to the main study hall where no doubt Lionello had courses, admiring the Grand Canal during his classes. The visit led to the inception of a six-year search through our family archives, to assemble all the possible information about my grandfather, with the hope that one day a complete biography could be written about the life and accomplishments of this great person.

While I was only four years old when my grandfather visited us in Virginia, throughout my childhood and teenage years, his influence on my life was considerable. First, he had eighteen grandchildren and had left funds to pay for their university education. In my family, Lionello's great interest in music, Italian musicians, and conductors was deeply felt. With the help of my grandmother Carolyn Perera and concert violinist Yehudi Menuhin, my mother Nina Perera Collier founded Young Audiences, firstly in Maryland to bring classical music into the public schools and to expose young pupils to concert performances of many well-known musicians. Eventually, Young Audiences became a nationwide organisation, which still operates today. The legacy of classical music has stayed with me throughout my life, and I can well remember Yehudi Menuhin practicing in our house in Maryland, as well as giving a private concert in our living room. Every year, at different times, each of us five children would be invited to visit Lionello's widow in her comfortable apartment on 91st Street, to have around me many Old Master paintings and to sometimes hear my grandmother played the violin.

The warmth of the Perera family was amazing to a country boy like myself, and I learned little by little about the incredible life of Lionello, his success as a banker, a leading person in the Italian community, and a backer of the arts, music, and musicians in New York during the first half of the twentieth century. My great thanks go to Diego Mantoan for researching and writing the story of Lionello, my grandfather, for future generations and his family, as well as for scholars and his home university to learn more about his life and deeds.

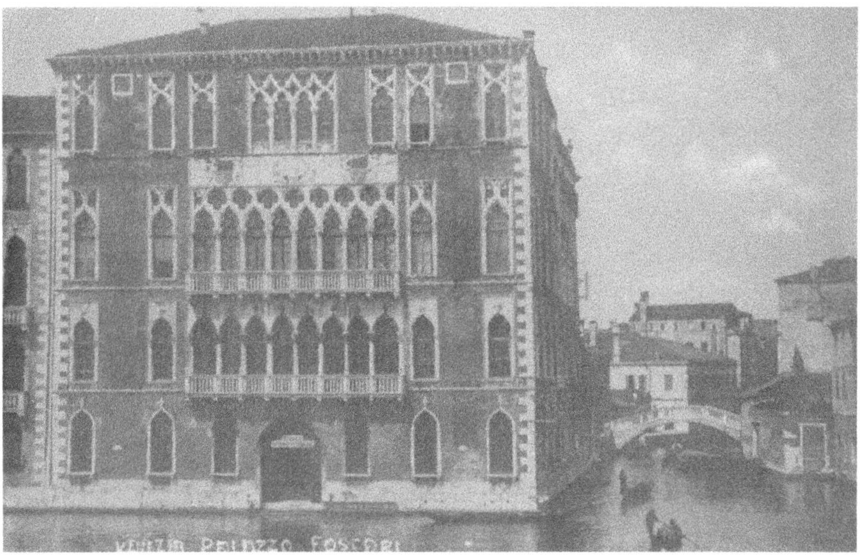

Figure 1.1: Postcard of Ca' Foscari in Venice, Italy

Probably dating to the late nineteenth century showing a sign on the canal entrance door of the building saying "R. Scuola Superiore di Commercio", plus a handwritten note on the lower edge stating "Palazzo Foscari Venezia". (Courtesy of the Perera Family Archive)

Part I:
Retracing a Venetian Connection

Chapter 2

Prologue to a Lost Biography

As much as I am reluctant to write scholarly contributions in the first person, the prologue of this book needs to be addressed in a lively manner, since the story of Lionello Perera struck me to the core when I first heard it. Sometimes in academic life you come across episodes, traces, materials that immediately light up ideas in your mind and anticipate a fruitful research path. Such an intuition was perhaps obvious in the case of Lionello, as I will allow myself to call him in a familiar tone given the deep confidence and sympathy with his biography derived from years of in-depth study. His story is that of a Venetian immigrant arriving to New York City at the end of the nineteenth century and destined to be the East Coast's most successful Italian American banker, later even participating as Vice President in the foundation of today's Bank of America. Certainly, little acumen is needed to understand the value of such a man, who further acted as philanthropist to his countrymen trying hard to make their way in the United States, as well as being an eager art collector and generous patron to many musicians in the early twentieth century. However, getting beyond this preliminary curiosity, there must be a coincidence of factors to trigger a proper research project. An elective affinity between the researcher and his study topic must quickly arise, I dare say, or the initial interest would inevitably wane. I still remember the very moment I was first told of Lionello Perera and his remarkable achievements. It was in early November 2013, while on a research trip to Berlin and my phone rang right after unmuting the mobile device upon leaving the library. At the time, I was serving as the Director of the Alumni Association at my alma mater, Ca' Foscari University of Venice in Italy, thus, with my colleagues and collaborators we were in the rush of organising a big yearly reunion later that month. It was customary to open this event with a short theatrical reading on the biography of famous alumni, hence we were constantly looking for interesting stories and digging into the university archives for useful material. As compared to many European universities with century-long tradition, Ca' Foscari was founded only quite recently, in 1868. It was the first Italian business school and later also an institute for foreign languages, but given its disciplinary focus, its Alumni soon excelled in international trade, diplomatic affairs and literary studies.[1] Indeed, in 2012 we had unearthed the history of Maria Rimoldi, the first woman to graduate in accounting and economics at Ca' Foscari in 1904, as well as the first one in Italy to do so, and we had imagined her life being particularly challenging as the sole female in the classroom, living apart from her family who stayed in Milan.[2] The audience's reception at the alumni reunion had been good, therefore we were thinking of delivering another stunning biography at the 2013 meeting. When my colleague Marco Cosmo called me from Venice, that distant day in Autumn, he sounded quite excited. A usually laid-back person, Marco told me euphorically he had been contacted by an American living in England, Leo Collier, presenting himself as the grandson of one Lionello Perera, who apparently was a graduate of our university, in order to find information on his grandfather's study period in Venice. We soon retrieved some information based on enrolment papers in our archives and Lionello was proudly featured even in the alumni bulletins at the turn of the twentieth century.[3] His elegant photographic portrait was accompanied by a short caption describing him as a private banker in New York (Fig. 2.1). His profession and place of activity sufficed to arouse our curiosity and we immediately asked Mr. Collier for as much information as possible on Lionello's life after university. Soon a few newspaper clippings and short biographies followed, articles that had been published in America some seventy or eighty years ago. Despite the lack of materials, the picture was clear enough. After leaving Venice, Lionello Perera set forth to step into his uncle Salvatore Cantoni's shoes in New York, taking over the family business and developing it into a successful private bank –the biggest savings bank of the city– that served the Italian American community.

Doubtless we had found the main character of our next alumni meeting, but first and foremost, I was convinced a lot of work remained to be done to uncover every detail in the life of a man who even was a dear friend of star conductor Arturo Toscanini and an early supporter of political leader Fiorello La Guardia. This book comes at the end of an intense period of research and public dissemination originated from this initial encounter, thus it offers the unique opportunity to present the remarkable and, so far, lost biography of Lionello Perera. Although literally unknown today, he was the principal financier, art collector and philanthropist for the Italian American community in Manhattan at the beginning of the twentieth century. Indeed, in 1928 he participated in the foundation of Bank of America together with another banker of Italian origin, the California-born Amadeo Peter Giannini whose life and deeds in the West Coast's financial world are well known, particularly his role in the fortune of Walt Disney. Besides starting the major Italian American bank of New York, Lionello gave support to many immigrants of the East Coast founding and funding welfare societies as well as public hospitals. As will be unravelled in the coming chapters, he also acted as a patron of the arts, supporting many artists and musicians, such as Toscanini, who had to resettle in America. Eventually, Lionello used his prominence among Italian Americans to help La Guardia's political success, particularly in his run for the office of mayor of New York. Regarding his artistic passion, he counted among the most refined collectors of Venetian Settecento and financed the building of the only known one-family Art Deco mansion in Manhattan, besides being an eager drawer and collector of caricatures. What nurtured my personal obsession with Lionello's biography was precisely the fact that so little was known about him, although as a successful entrepreneur and generous philanthropist he had evidently contributed to the development of the Italian American community of New York, even participating in relevant turning points in the city's economic and political life. The idea that such a rich personal history had remained solely the memoir of his closest family members truly tormented me, and I was eager to dig deep into his life to disclose as much as possible. If I had been a screenwriter, I would have immediately featured Lionello in my next script, devoting a movie or an entire series to his remarkable achievements, and sometimes adventurous life, which were paralleled only by the love and caring he reserved to all his relatives, especially to his wife Carolyn Allen Perera. As I am a scholar, after the mentioned alumni reunion, I embarked on a long journey that would allow me to further research Lionello's biography and subsequently reveal part of the discoveries made in different formats. It thus became a long-lasting project spanning from plain historical scholarship to the history of the arts, though at the same time situated in the field of public humanities and fuelled by two principle means of research. On one side, I relied on the documents and recollections of the extended Perera family, whose commitment and passion really proved instrumental in retrieving materials to be vetted historically according to best scholarly practice. On the other side, various sources were drawn from in-depth research into digitised documentary archives that have been made available across the United States, resulting in an essential collection that spans from judiciary documents to penny press articles chronologically ranging back to the mid-nineteenth century. Hence, this book is based on rich documentary evidence gathered over almost a decade thanks to the collaboration of the extended Perera family and the incredible richness of digitised American archives, thus providing material that has never been disclosed before. Therefore, I also made it one of my aims to provide all papers this book is based on in an online and open access repository. This shall allow future scholars of various disciplines – banking historians, Italian American culture experts, art historians, musicologists, and many more– to dig even deeper into this peculiar biography that is just a tiny part of a much broader picture of American history and New York's cultural life.

Despite the considerable amount of time needed to discover the traces of Lionello Perera's professional, social, and cultural activities among online datasets –a task that was crucially eased with the assistance of Rosie Perera and Carol Perera Weingeist, in particular– my research efforts were constantly accompanied by a lure for openness as is now customary in the domain of public humanities. From my perspective, attempting to disseminate Lionello's biography at every step was decisive, keeping interest alive among his relatives, who would provide more and more accounts and sources. It further allowed getting in touch with a growing audience, much beyond the sole scholarly community. Sometimes, I must confess, early disclosure came with some inaccuracies that later findings would again correct. At the beginning, for instance, it seemed that Lionello had been among the cofounders of today's Citibank, while in truth, he had merged his activity with Bank of America and was later subject to a hostile acquisition by Citibank's forerunner during the Great Depression. But these mistakes could be amended precisely because growing interest on the subject allowed a deeper scrutiny of sources and materials. Eventually, the book derives from an intense programme of public activities devised with the help of Ca' Foscari University and its Alumni Association. Public programmes I organised reached out to institutions of international renown such as the Teatro La Fenice, the Venetian opera house, where in May 2015 the story of Lionello was told with accompanying American arias, some by composers Lionello had hosted or supported in New York.[4] The recital was then turned into a radio drama for the Italian State broadcast RAI Radio3, airing in January 2017 on the occasion of Toscanini's anniversary, again with soprano Giulia Alberti and pianist Ilaria Torresan playing the American arias already performed at La Fenice, as well as with playwright and actress Chiara Clini's reading about the friendship between the Italian Maestro and Lionello.[5] Shortly after, in February 2017, I recorded a documentary again for Radio3 on the life of Lionello Perera, which aired nationwide in the programme Wikiradio.[6] So far, every public activity was done in Italian, in order to disclose Lionello's life to his countrymen, but I always felt the story addressed topics for a much wider audience. Again, with the strong encouragement of Leo Collier who is the *primum movens* of this entire process, I thus set forth to condense all I had discovered in a book for the English reading audience. To my mind, it had to be a scholarly work, because the relevance of the subject deserved to be treated with a proper research methodology and discerned with scientific accuracy –once and for all, hopefully. Hence, this book shall offer the unique opportunity to discover the unknown biography of the remarkable Lionello Perera, situating his financial career, as well as his activity as a patron and philanthropist on the backdrop of the very fluid US banking system at the turn of the twentieth century and in the context of the fast-growing Italian American community of New York City. Indeed, in the following chapters, he will emerge as a central character in the development of banking business in America, as well as discretely acting as a catalyst of integration in the USA for the wider milieu of Italian immigrants, already before World War I and then during the politically charged interwar period offering a sense of nationhood that was alternative to the Fascist ideology. Furthermore, his refined taste for art, architecture, classical music, and opera theatre put him in touch with the Italian cultural community, turning his Modernist home in the Upper East Side into an epicentre of New York's jet set during the 1930s.

This book adopts a variety of methodologies and speaks to a range of different disciplines given the diverse aspects of Lionello's biography that need proper examination. A multidisciplinary and integrated view is thus needed to capture the complexity of his life and deeds, resorting to a wide range of approaches. A touch of business history proves necessary to unravel his activity as a successful banker and co-founder of Bank of America, while an art historical view uncovers his eagerness as a collector of eighteenth-century Venetian paintings, especially genre scenes by Pietro Longhi, which constituted the backbone of a peculiar iconographic programme devised for his carefully planned Manhattan home. His contribution as a philanthropist for Italian immigrants in New York needs a background in social history as well as knowledge of the history of Italian Americans, especially the concerns about Italian identity in the early twentieth century, between systemic discrimination in the United States and the rise of fascism in Italy. Eventually, his support to many musicians, either of Jewish or Italian origin, particularly his friendship with Toscanini, relate undoubtedly to the domain of music history. For this very reason, I resolved not to proceed in a mere chronological manner, but rather to analyse his biography from various perspectives. Thus, the structure of the book revolves around four different facets in his life taken separately. Here in Part I, to begin with, I investigate Lionello Perera's early life to study the distinctive historical, geographical, and family context he was brought up in, referring specifically to the strong network among his Jewish relatives. I further offer a deep insight in his business studies at Ca' Foscari, the elite university he enrolled at in Venice, which fundamentally shaped his competences as a businessman and his mindset as an Italian national operating for his country abroad. The second aspect I delve into, in Part II, is of course, his banking career, which started in New York alongside his uncle Salvatore Cantoni, the first Italian American banker of New York. Lionello would then take over his uncle's banking business and expand it, which was further made possible by his strong ties with both the Italian community and the Jewish bourgeoisie of New York, given the initial support of his wife's family, whose father was a reputed financier. He then reached the height of his career in the 1920s, a very volatile period for the banking sector that Lionello navigated through a series of difficult mergers and acquisitions. Another facet of his biography, analysed in Part III, is his relationship with the arts as a patron and collector, as well as an occasional cartoonist, and his relationship to his Italian kinsmen in the USA as a major philanthropist. His interest in

Venetian genre painting reveals the long-lasting bond with his hometown and turns out to be pivotal in collecting habits among New York magnets of the time, while his taste for newer architecture produced an unprecedented Art Deco family house, which constitutes a little-known landmark in Manhattan. Of particular interest is then his connection to many musicians, originating from his and Carolyn's love for music. Furthermore, I will take on his role inside the Italian American community of New York, with regard to both his social activity in favour of immigrants through the funding of hospitals and assistance projects, as well as his political activity supporting the improvement in consideration deserved by the Italian American community, which peeked with the success of La Guardia. The final part of this book, Part IV, considers the varied and rich legacy of Lionello Perera, first by addressing his late years and personal struggle with the Fascist demons that were wreaking havoc on his fatherland, and which unfortunately would close in on his close relatives. As a useful appendix to this part come the unprecedented plates of paintings, drawings, and caricatures owned by Lionello Perera, thus presenting in a unified section the first-time reconstruction of his remarkable art collection. Photographs from the family archive are instead spread throughout the book, such as to reference peculiar aspects of the banker's professional life and philanthropic activities. The rich material legacy comprising documents, letters, and photographs further complements this book through an online repository (pererapapers.wordpress.com) that provides open access to the full range of sources in his family archive for the benefit of future research. This digital collection of varied materials, which is physically scattered among the extended Perera family, is searchable online both according to the nature of the items (Drawings, Paintings, Photographs, Letters, Documents, Bibliography) and by means of thematic clusters (Formative years, Banker, Patron, Philanthropist, Italian Americans). Back to the book structure, please let me highlight the intimate foreword by Leo Collier, whose recollections about his late grandfather I believe are essential to open this long research journey with the right tone.

It will become evident that Lionello Perera is one of the most remarkable alumni of Ca' Foscari University of Venice, precisely because his professional success and social consciousness proved instrumental for the Italian American community of New York in the early twentieth century. I hope this book will cover a gap in the field of Italian American history by means of a long-lost biography, which renders justice to the relevance Lionello holds as a contributor to the social and cultural integration of Italians in the United States. Over the last three decades, a wide array of papers and volumes dealing with Italian immigration and Italian American culture flourished in the scholarly field, such as the popular *La Storia: Five Centuries of the Italian American Experience* by Jerre Mangione and Ben Morreale.[7] Among the most recent scholarly work on the subject is *The Routledge History of Italian Americans* by William J. Connell and Stanislao G. Pugliese, a collection of papers on numerous aspects across a wide chronological spectrum.[8] Another thorough insight trying to differentiate myth from reality is *The Italian Americans: A History* by Maria Laurino, which starts from the classical period of immigration in the late nineteenth century and refers to both obscure and well-known individuals.[9] These volumes added to the first monumental textbooks of the mid-twentieth century, particularly the seminal work of Howard R. Marraro and the comprehensive volume *Four Centuries of Italian American History* by Giovanni Schiavo.[10] To properly understand the context and mindset of Italians in America, this book also relies on fundamental research carried on by recent Italian scholars such as Stefano Luconi, Francesca De Lucia, Michele Strazza, and Giuseppe Faustini.[11] This shall help to offer a slightly innovative perspective that is not always focussed on by American scholarly works, which is the tight interrelation of Italian Americans, especially of the East Coast, with political and economic events in their country of origin.

On the other hand, the present recollection of Lionello Perera's deeds may further provide a useful addition to the field of early banking history in the United States. There appears to be a wide interest in the events that led to the Great Depression of 1929, which also include the merger of Lionello's venture with the newly founded Bank of America. A remarkable example of this is the Pulitzer Prize winner of 2010 *Lords of Finance: 1929, The Great Depression, and the Bankers who Broke the World* by Liaquat Ahamed, a book very much in tune with the financial scandals of our present times.[12] With regard to scholarly works, over the last decades, a number of studies highlighted the much deeper instability and immaturity that ran in the veins of US banks already in the early twentieth century, which clearly emerges also from the business history of Lionello Perera & Co. Recent analyses on banking panics and bank runs by economists like Charles W. Calomiris, Gary Gorton, Andrew J. Jalil, and David Wheelock are paramount to get a proper idea of the complex situation private bankers were facing in the United States before the Great Depression set in.[13] This book offers the opportunity to step into the shoes of a foreign banker making his way in New York City's extremely competitive finance sector at the turn of the century, thus illuminating a much bigger picture in US banking history through a particular case study. Time is ripe for a full account of Lionello Perera's life, a successful business leader, a passionate patron, a discrete and generous man that helped shaping the acceptance of Italian Americans in twentieth-century America.

Coming to the end of this prologue, I am glad to make lots of acknowledgments, since I hold this book a product of real collaborative research. First and foremost, my deepest gratitude goes to Leo Collier together with Carol Weingeist and Rosie

Perera who entrusted me with Lionello's legacy, as well as to the extended Perera family for sharing their oral history and source materials. My thanks also go to the Ca' Foscari Alumni –especially to Andrea Tomat, Marco Cosmo, and Anna Morbiato– for the support and enthusiasm provided in the early stages of this long journey. I am particularly grateful to soprano Giulia Alberti, actress Chiara Clini, and pianist Ilaria Torresan for collaborating with me on creative works to tell Lionello's biography, feeding my conviction that his story possesses an incredible public appeal. A heartfelt thanks goes to Silvia Ballarin for her support in finalising this venture, especially regarding the digital and public tools devised to visualise and share the story and papers of Lionello Perera far beyond the scholarly community. Finally, I would like to thank the Fondazione Teatro La Fenice and Rai Radio3, two institutions that provided early platforms to recount this precious piece of Italian American history.

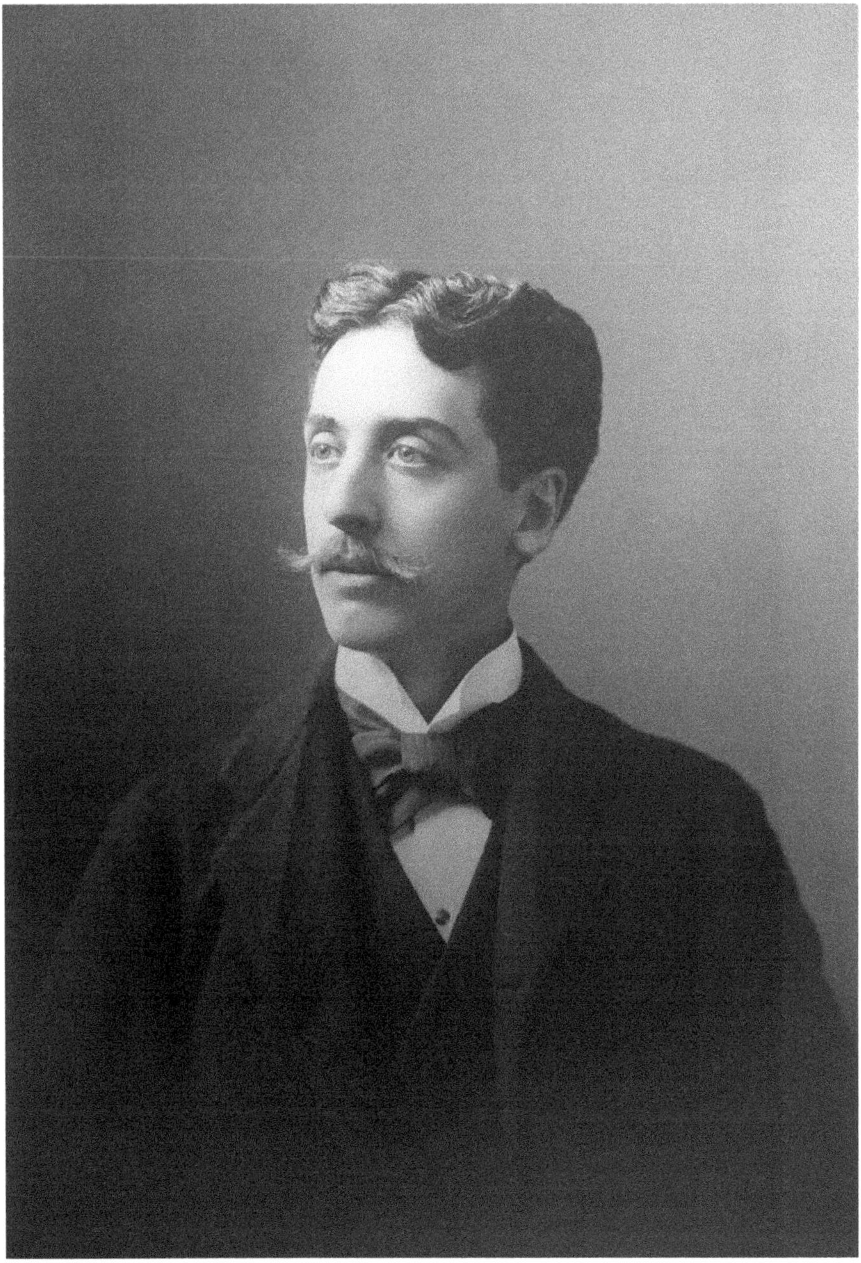

Figure 2.1: Lionello Perera as a university student (1886-89)
Probably dating to his time at Ca' Foscari University in Venice, then called R. Scuola Superiore di Commercio, where he studied commerce and banking business between 1886 and 1889. (Courtesy of the Perera Family Archive)

Chapter 3

An Errant Jewish Family with an Italian Core

Lionello Perera was born on June 25, 1871, in Venice, Italy, his parents being Cesare Lopes Perera (Fig. 3.1) and Emilia Cantoni (Fig. 3.2). This is confirmed by a series of archival documents, as well as by personal accounts and recollections published on various occasions.[1] Indeed, his American passport issued on March 27, 1924, states this date and so do several posthumous short biographies mainly based on a sketch provided by his family.[2] However, on some Italian records June 28 is set as a birth date, as on his military leave issued in 1891, which probably depends on the fact that he might have been registered three days later.[3] Curiously enough, that same Italian certificate shows a different first name and an added last name, which later was lost in the United States. Thus his full name was registered in Italy as Leone Arturo Perera Lopes, which was sometimes shortened to Leonello Perera, as can be found in the scholarship papers of his university in 1889.[4] Leonello is in fact the Italian diminutive form of Leone, his maternal grandfather's name, and it means 'little lion', but in Venice he would have been called Lionello given that the Venetian word for lion is 'Lion' or 'Lio'. At the time, the name Leone was likely to be common in the Italian peninsula, as it was the name of two Catholic Popes of the nineteenth century,[5] but it is also widespread in the Jewish tradition since the Middle Ages, both for Sephardi and Ashkenazi communities.[6] An interesting fact, which clearly discloses Lionello's ancient family origin from the Iberian peninsula, is the mistake made by the Army Captain who filled out the mentioned leave form, since at first he erroneously spelt the last name 'Pereira Lopez', only to correct himself in a footnote to the document. Pereira is indeed a widespread surname of ancient Jewish Portuguese tradition and Lopez is instead a Spanish last name, so it is likely the captain was going automatically for the name option he knew best or thought more likely.

Lionello's family had Sephardic origins on his father's side and its ties can be partly traced back to the Spanish diaspora of the sixteenth century.[7] In 1492 Jews were ruthlessly banished from Spain and again a century later, in 1597, Jewish people were expelled from different European territories controlled by the Spanish crown under the rule of King Philipp II, such as in Milan.[8] This reference is of particular importance, because as a consequence Sephardic families would disperse to several cities around Europe, for instance, London,

Bayonne, Amsterdam, Livorno, and Venice.[9] In the eighteenth century, the diaspora would further expand on the trade routes across the Atlantic and disperse Sephardic merchants from North America to the Caribbean.[10] With regard to the name Lopes Pereira or Perera, specifically, it can be found in several European cities already during the seventeenth century, for example, in Amsterdam, Dublin, and further in Rouen especially in marriage banns, in other sort of contracts or on gravestones.[11] At least from the early eighteenth century onwards, the surname is to be found also in the Tuscan port city of Livorno, where a Dayyan –a rabbinic judge– by the name of Isaac Lopes Pereira was active around 1742.[12] A few years later, in 1758, a Manuel d'Abram Lopez Perera appears on a register in Livorno, hence the name definitely existed and was common within the Livornese Jewish community at the time.[13] Interestingly, the ancestry of Lionello can be traced back to one Jacob Lopes Perera, born in Livorno around 1766-68, who was married to Allegra Chaves and their son born in 1809, still in Livorno, was called Abramo Lopez Perera, Lionello's paternal grandfather. It appears that Jacob was the son of Daniel and grandson to Manuel Lopes Perera, still in Livorno and perhaps the same person as the one mentioned above, thus, the family was probably present in the city's Jewish community already at the end of the seventeenth century. That the Pereras, among other Sephardic families, would live in the Tuscan port city has distinct historical roots, which depend on the explicit welcome policy introduced by Cosimo I immediately after the last Spanish expulsion. As a matter of fact, Jews in Livorno were granted freedom already in the seventeenth century and as compared to most European cities, they were not required to live in a demarcated area, such as the Venetian ghetto.[14] The port city profited from this openness that drew especially Sephardic families to Tuscany, and trade flourished due to the merchants' good connections both with the Orient and the Western part of the Mediterranean. The personal liberties and partial civic integration that Jews were granted in Livorno through regulations, known as the *Livorninas*, fostered a sense of open community which involved them deeply in the goods trade and money business of the area. Thus, the Sephardic merchants would develop their networks around a basic distinction in trust-building, depending on the degree of familiarity with the customer or business partner.[15] Since Jews in Livorno were allowed free trade with Christians, especially loans and money exchange, the number of clients soared and family ties were the best way to keep control over one's own business. Individual freedom in Livorno, however, was not matched by full political integration by the end of the eighteenth century, so the Jewish community had to wait until the unification of Italy in the mid-nineteenth century to finally enjoy a fuller participation in the nation's development.[16]

Trust building among close family members, as will become evident, is a peculiar feature in the case of Lionello, first and foremost when he was called to assist his uncle, Salvatore Cantoni (1842-1896), at the private bank the latter had founded in New York. But the interconnection among relatives runs much deeper and can easily be seen from the Lopes Perera genealogy (Fig. 3.3).[17] Indeed, Lionello's parents were distant cousins. Cesare, born in 1838, was the son of aforementioned Abramo Lopes Perera (1809-1870) from Livorno and Rosa (or Rosina) Cantoni (1821-1882) from Venice. On her part, Emilia Cantoni, who was probably born in 1848, was from another Venetian branch of the Cantonis since she was a daughter of Leon Vita Cantoni (1815-1888 or 1889) and Rosa (or Rosina) Cesana (1810-1884). At the beginning of their married life, Cesare and Emilia travelled to find a place to settle, probably following close on the heels of Cesare's older brother Alessandro Lopes Perera, born in 1837, who had moved to Alexandria, Egypt. Lionello's eldest sister Rosa was born on January 20, 1868, in the North African city, thus setting her parents' marriage definitely prior to that date, perhaps in 1867, but not much earlier given their mother was quite young at the time. A year after Rosa's birth, however, Cesare and Emilia returned to Italy, since their second daughter Olga was born in Venice on October 15, 1869. Together they would have another four children in Venice: Clara (or Clary) in 1870, then Lionello a year later, eventually Clelia in 1872 and Alice in 1878. The reason for Cesare and Emilia to settle in Venice likely depended on misfortune in Africa, so they oriented themselves to the possible support they could get from relatives back home. A family of Ashkenazi origin, the Cantonis were present in Venice since at least three generations and Emilia's father Leon Vita was active in the city as a commercial agent.[18] Just as in Livorno, the role of Jews in Venice had been quite relevant on a financial level in the city's history, although the community had suffered physical confinement since the early sixteenth century until the end of the Venetian Republic in 1797.[19] Especially in the last centuries of the Serenissima the Jewish community represented a separate minority group that had to affirm its own identity and steadily negotiated its position with regard to the city's ruling class, since the well-being of both was interdependent.[20] After a long period under Hapsburg rule and the consequent economic downturn, in 1866 the entire region was annexed to the newly constituted Kingdom of Italy, thus promoting the hope of a much-awaited boost in commercial activities, especially related to trade routes in connection with the opening of the Suez Canal.[21] Still a young man, it appears that Lionello's father entered the growing finance sector in Venice, probably with the introduction of his father-in-law Leon Vita or perhaps in his actual business.[22] Emilia's older brother, Salvatore Cantoni, was also in the banking system, though he had emigrated to New York already in 1860 and founded a private enterprise, which supposedly became the first Italian American bank of New York City.[23] Leon Vita might have been in close partnership with his son and he probably had good business relationships there. In fact, Leon Vita was elected a corresponding member of the American

Numismatic and Archaeological Society of New York on November 14, 1867.[24] In any case, Leon Vita was certainly in Venice in the 1870s, when Cesare and Emilia settled there, and he later became the legal ward of Lionello and his five beloved sisters, when they were orphaned and went to stay at their grandfather's home in the district of Cannaregio, one of the six *sestieri* of Venice.

Regarding Lionello's parents, the exact dates of death can be found in the Civil registry of Venice, though some details remain unclear. Indeed, as reported in two biographical accounts of Lionello's career, he was barely 15 years old when his father suddenly died leaving his wife and six children behind.[25] These biographies also maintain that his mother died just one year after her husband, literally of overwork, so the years must be between 1886 and 1887, precisely at the time Lionello was starting university in Venice. However, the death report of Cesare was registered in Venice on January 10, 1882, though it is preserved in an entry copied a decade later to ask for the correction of the deceased's last name.[26] The Civil Registration death record in Venice also states Lionello's mother Emilia died at the age of forty-two on July 3, 1892, a whole decade after her husband.[27] On Lionello's military leave certificate, issued on September 1891, he was registered as son of "fu Cesare", which means of the 'late Cesare', and of Emilia Cantoni, though with no reference to her possible death. Since the information filled out in the form was probably delivered by Lionello himself, there is no reason why he should have concealed the latter, while admitting the death of his father. If these dates are correct, it is rather strange that family recollections would instead emphasise a much shorter time span between his parents' deaths. Although it may not seem essential to reconstruct the exact unfolding of events, this moment in Lionello's personal life is particularly important, because the decisions his family took thereafter would decide his fate and ultimately allow him –or even oblige him– to emigrate to the United States in 1894. Several Italian documents shed some light on the evolution of his family status, so that a few more conjectures can be made. First come his enrolment papers at Ca' Foscari, where he passed the admission exams in May 1886, which then led to a confirmation letter signed on October 31 that same year by the School Director Francesco Ferrara.[28] On this admission form, Lionello is referred to as "Perera Leonello di Cesare", which means 'son of Cesare' at the present time, suggesting his father might still have been alive in the Fall of 1886. On a transcript of records updated at the end of his third academic year in 1889, instead, Lionello's home address seems to have been added anew and it is explicitly referred to at the home of "Mr. Leon V. Cantoni" in Cannaregio, n. 4667, which lies just a few steps off the church of Santi Apostoli, close to the Rialto Bridge.[29] So by then, Cesare must have already passed away. On that same transcript of records, a note was made in the second academic year, reporting that Lionello skipped his exams planned for Easter 1888, which he then had to take in July. Usually a diligent student, his life had probably been disrupted by some family event, either his father's death or his grandfather's one. The family history goes that Cesare's business partners, perhaps Leon Vita and Salvatore Cantoni themselves, had paid for Lionello's university period. However, documents show that, as an orphan, Lionello also applied for a public scholarship, which was eventually granted on January 9, 1889, for an amount of 100 Lire to cover the three years of his study course *a posteriori*.[30] This grant certainly was a big help, but for sure his grandfather – until he died, perhaps around Easter 1888 or a little later– and his uncle were paying for the living expenses of Lionello and his five sisters, waiting for the boy to come of age and optimise his higher education in commercial studies for the whole family. In any case, the death of Cesare and then the one of Leon Vita Cantoni suddenly disrupted Emilia's life and her six siblings'. Hence a strategy needed to be found and apparently, regarding her daughters, a swift and safe wedding was the answer. Such a circumstance is confirmed by the fact that all of them married into close relatives: Rosa married one Emilio Perera, while on June 26, 1892, Olga married Eugenio Pincherle, a distant cousin on her father's side[31], and Clara yet again a member of the wider Perera family, Giulio. Although the exact wedding dates are lost, one may suppose Lionello's three older sisters married shortly after their grandfather's death, that is between 1888 and 1892, which is corroborated by the fact that Olga's oldest daughter Emilia (or Emilietta) was born on March 28, 1893.

These conjectures are useful to understand, at least approximately, when and why the plan was arranged to send Lionello over to New York to his uncle Salvatore Cantoni. First, Lionello had to wait anyway until he was granted military leave, because otherwise he would not have been allowed to emigrate. As was customary in the Kingdom of Italy at the time, young men were expected to start military service right after their 21st birthday, with the exception of some cases, such as orphans, who would instead receive so-called third category leave.[32] In 1891, as already recalled, Lionello was summoned by the military authority for the compulsory inspection of eligibility and, because of his orphan status, he was immediately granted the "Foglio di congedo illimitato di IIIa categoria", which would exempt him permanently from military duty in Italy and allow him to expatriate whenever he liked, as stated in the certificate.[33] Hence, the military leave poses a date *post quem* the option of his emigration could effectively have been discussed. However, since his mother died a year later, plans wouldn't become concrete before 1892. At that point, an orphan of both parents and with the support of his three oldest sisters already secured through marriage, he was theoretically available as a workforce. His higher education, as will be specified, further made him a very valuable asset for the Cantoni family business. The Italian passport necessary for his emigration was issued in Venice on March 23, 1894, only a few days before he left the port of Genoa on board of the Kaiser Wilhelm II, which departed on March 27 to reach

Ellis Island on April 19, 1894.[34] Curiously, though hardly a surprise, the records at Ellis Island describe him as Lionello Perera Cantoni, probably because of his uncle's reference letters and for the simple reason that Salvatore was a renowned New York banker. To the contrary, the Italian passport went under the last name Lopes Perera and further specified that Lionello was an "agente di commercio" by profession, that is a commercial agent like his late grandfather. One can suppose he was already working in Venice, perhaps even in the family business, since he had finished his study period at Ca' Foscari in late 1889. Hence, between 1892 and his departure for America, Lionello was already earning money, probably not a lot, but it seems clear that the necessity to have him over to New York laid rather on his uncle's side. In fact, at the time, Salvatore Cantoni & Co. was almost thirty years in the Manhattan banking business. Lionello's uncle might have thought of passing over the control of his venture to someone he trusted, but he had only three daughters –Natalie, Olive, and Edna. Salvatore probably asked his nephew to come already in 1893, since issuing the passport for Lionello surely took several months, so the papers for the request had probably been arranged in advance. The most striking point, however, is that less than a week passed between the day his passport was ready in Venice and his ship boarding in Genoa, two cities which lay at least one or two days of travel apart. Basically, as soon as Lionello had the passport, he packed his luggage and jumped on a train to reach the opposite side of Northern Italy and embark on the first available ocean liner.

The urgency that goes with this departure is very telling. Apparently, uncle Salvatore was particularly eager for his nephew's arrival and, of course, money was not a problem since the ticket for the Kaiser Wilhelm II was probably bought at the last minute at the port of Genoa. Naturally, the question arises whether there was a particular reason for this hasty journey, so that the circumstances concerning Salvatore Cantoni & Co. need further investigation. In her memoirs, Lionello's future wife Carolyn Allen recalls that the young Venetian was initially held back by Salvatore's sons-in-law, who tried immediately to expel him from the bank upon his uncle's death by a carriage accident in 1896.[35] This may hint at an acrimonious relationship among Salvatore's extended family in New York even before Lionello's arrival, such that his uncle would trust only a blood relative to take over the business. Upon a closer inspection of newspaper archives a relevant clue arises that sheds some light on the tense situation in the 1890s surrounding Salvatore Cantoni & Co. As a matter of fact, only a month after Lionello's arrival a big scandal broke out involving his uncle, which hit the headlines from New York to Chicago. On June 6, 1894, *The Chicago Daily Tribune* reported that one Mrs. Elsa C. Forster had sued Salvatore claiming she had been his partner for seven years and that he was the father of two of her children, only to find out at the end of their relationship in 1892 that he was already married.[36] An immoral millionaire, a cheated wife, an abandoned mistress, two illegitimate children, a legal battle: all these elements in the Cantoni scandal made up exactly the kind of human interest stories the papers thrived on. *The Brooklyn Daily Eagle* had it as a top story on the front page and didn't hesitate to disclose all the details as reported by Elsa Forster.[37] According to her account, when she first made the acquaintance of Salvatore in 1884, she was 22 and a happy wife of Mr. David C. Brennan, as well as a mother of three daughters. Mr. Cantoni, she alleged, fell desperately in love with her and presented himself as an unmarried millionaire, persuading her to leave her husband as he promised he would make provisions for her and her children even after his death. The young woman thus filed for divorce, with expenses borne by Mr. Cantoni, henceforth living together as husband and wife under the name of Mr. and Mrs. Fortunay, at Salvatore's expressed desire. The affair suddenly broke up in May or June 1892, when Salvatore told her he had to cease the relationship abruptly, because he was already married. Subsequently, aided by his future son-in-law, he tried to send her off to California. Although Mrs. Forster would not mention the name of the young man involved, the papers noted that on October 12, 1893, a fashionable wedding took place between a Mr. de Beixedon and one of the Cantoni daughters.[38] Upon further investigation, the names of the bride and groom turn out to be Salvatore's second daughter, Olive Douglas (1874-1966), then only 18 years old, and Edward Francis Fremaux de Beixedon (1868-after 1920), who was a member of an illustrious family of the New York elite. In fact, Edward Francis was the son of a French nobleman, Francis Edouard Fremaux de Beixedon from Lille, and even the grandson of the Marquis Joucquoy, but first and foremost, on his mother Julia Augusta Rogers' side, he pretended to be a direct descendant of James Rogers, who had come to the Americas in 1635.[39] Although this claim is historically inaccurate, the family tale with regard to these ancient origins would live on, since Edward Francis Frémaux De Beixedon III, son of Edward Francis and Olive Douglas, compiled a family genealogy in 1921 entitled *The ancestors and descendants of Dr. David Rogers* which directly referenced this presumed ancestry.[40] Despite these inaccuracies, at the end of the nineteenth century, the de Beixedons were counted among the aristocratic families of highest lineage in New York, with all the privileges in terms of social acceptance that go with it, while the Cantonis rather belonged to the newly rich kids in town emerging from first-generation immigrants. Regarding the fashionable wedding celebrated on October 12, 1893, the picture is quite clear. It was supposed to be the union of two kind of American families, aristocrats and *nouveau riches*, with all the typical tensions and reciprocal suspicions between them that framed the Gilded Age of late nineteenth century. It is a societal picture that endured until well into the early twentieth century and which was later masterfully condensed in F. Scott Fitzgerald's *The Great Gatsby*.[41] In this particular case, while the groom brought an old and blazoned ancestry, the bride brought much-needed new money, resulting in a convenient agreement for both sides. Indeed, Olive Douglas was given $19,000 as a marriage gift, like her other two sisters.[42] A nice sum, but surely what really was at stake were rather Salvatore's banking business and personal estate. Hence, his love affair was not reason enough to break up the engagement, but surely it sufficed for the fiancée to intervene in person for a resolute and quick settlement of the situation, in order to avoid any sort of social embarrassment that might have ruined this prospective marriage and the reciprocal interests.

Evidently, what happened in Spring 1892 was that Salvatore's affair came to light, at least inside his inner family circle, and quite obviously, his prospective son-in-law felt this disreputable situation posed a threat to the incumbent wedding. Considering his noble ancestry, Edward Francis de Beixedon likely forced Salvatore Cantoni to end his extra-marital relationship that discredited the entire family and together, they tried to get rid of Elsa Forster sending her off to the other side of the continent. In the beginning, the plan seemed successful, so the marriage could take place without any sort of embarrassment. Soon after, however, probably in early 1894, Mrs. Forster came back and dared suing Salvatore for the considerable amount of $170,000, of which $100,000 was for the miserable condition she had been left in and the remaining sum for the service as housekeeper over a period of seven years, that is $10,000 a year. The requested sum was considerable, though it could hardly have affected Cantoni & Co. at a financial level. The real danger was posed by the scandal, if the news went public, since it would easily have disrupted the bank's reputation and that of the entire family. Furthermore, the presence of illegitimate children was an enormous threat to the estate, as they could possibly claim a share of it. The papers stated that Salvatore was given notice of the full allegations in April 1894 and that he waited until May 15 to file his answer, which was obviously a plain denial. This means that Mrs. Forster had officially sued Salvatore as early as February or March 1894 and Lionello's uncle was definitely aware that a lawsuit was under way in early Winter, when the lady had returned from California. By then, he knew that a scandal could hardly have been avoided and perhaps feared his sons-in-law might seize the opportunity to oust him from the family business for good. At the beginning of 1894, Salvatore Cantoni must have felt besieged and urgently called for his nephew in Venice to come as soon as he could to have the support of a close and trusted family member –as well as a trained commerce agent– at such a delicate moment. Indeed, the de Beixedons were neither kinsman nor blood relatives of the Cantonis, while Lionello was both. After the initial scandal, the lawsuit took three years to come to an end, which was completely in favour of the by then late Salvatore Cantoni.[43] As reported by several New York papers, Elsa Forster was prevented from appealing in any way against his estate.[44] However, the reports in 1897 are rather incongruous, particularly with regard to dates and lawsuits, but it appears that

Mrs. Forster might have sued Salvatore twice. The first time was in 1892, upon discovering he was married, but then she retracted accepting $6,000 from Lionello's uncle. Yet again, she sued him in 1894 after coming back from California. Eventually, another appeal in October 1897 against the latter decision would allow Mrs. Forster to resume her case against the late Salvatore Cantoni, although the final outcome in November was a plain break.[45] The legal challenges and this confusion about the exact unravelling of events makes it even clearer that the scandal was big at the time and it threatened both the good name and the bank of Salvatore Cantoni.

In conclusion, while Lionello and his sisters had certainly been supported by the Cantonis –both grandfather and uncle– after they were orphaned, neither payback to Salvatore nor real financial need were likely the main reasons for the young man to abruptly emigrate to the United States in March 1894. The scandal looming over the Cantoni bank was probably the strongest motive for the nephew to be summoned to New York straight away, since the dates of the Forster lawsuit and those of Lionello's hurried departure are too close to one another to be merely coincidental. Yet again, a sense of belonging, as well as the spirit of unity and solidarity among family members would lead young Lionello to abandon Italy and start a new chapter of his life in America at the side of his tormented maternal uncle. What he left behind were his five sisters, whom he would come to visit every year in Italy and support financially throughout their entire life as a true family man. In departing for the new continent, he inadvertently gave up part of his Jewish heritage. After all, in the United States, the major feature of his identity in the eyes of long-time Americans was especially his Italian nationality, not so much his faith since people would probably have taken him for a Catholic given his country of origin. Lionello arrived in North America at a time when the number of Italian immigrants was rising at exponential levels.[46] While he set forth to proudly represent and sustain the Italian community in New York at the end of the nineteenth century, back in the Veneto region, secular anti-Semitic feelings were progressively closing in on Jews. This resentment, clearly anticipated by the language used especially in Catholic newspapers of the time, showed little embarrassment in overtly pinpointing stereotypes and allowing an ever-growing malicious innuendo that departed from religious issues to become plainly racial, often addressing the supposed financial supremacy and disguised political power of Jews over the entire society.[47] Recent research shows that, right after World War I, the situation in Italy swiftly turned sour and people of Jewish origins were gradually marginalised, only to be definitively excluded and eventually persecuted at the dawn of World War II.[48] For almost five decades into the twentieth century, Lionello would struggle for Italians to integrate in America and be perceived as good people as well as hard workers, though back home, the myth of good Italians – "italiani brava gente"– simply slid away into the depth of history. As far as the scope of this chapter goes, though, it stops at a twenty-two years old Italian national, who arrived in New York City on a late April day of 1894 on behalf of his uncle, probably ignoring that he would soon become a central figure in his immigrant community.

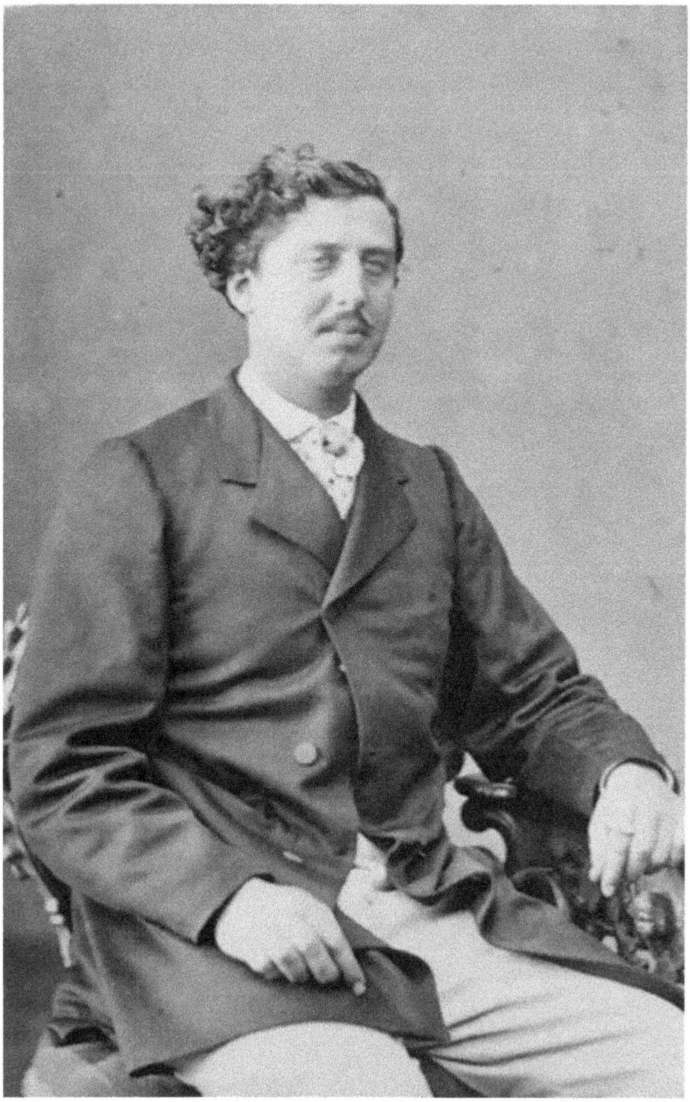

Figure 3.1: Photograph of Cesare Lopes Perera (ca. 1880)

Taken in Venice by A. Sorgato and probably dating to the early 1880s. On the back, there is a later handwritten inscription by Lionello Perera stating "Il mio adorato papà" (My beloved father). (Courtesy of the Perera Family Archive)

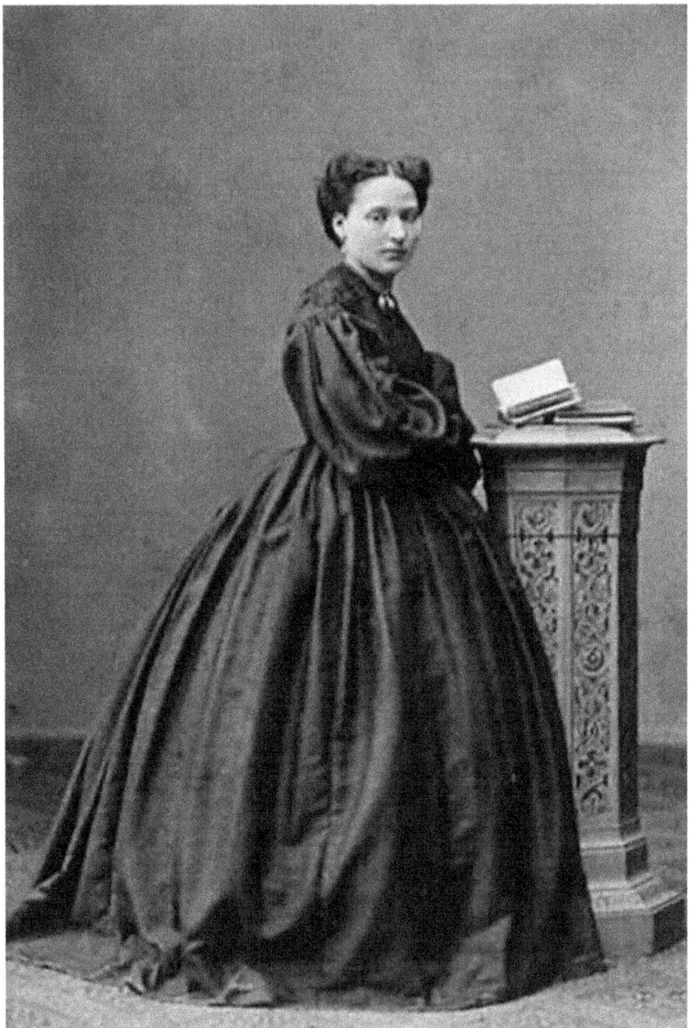

Figure 3.2: Photograph of Emilia Cantoni (ca. 1880)
Taken in Venice by A. Sorgato and probably dating to the early 1880s. (Courtesy of the Perera Family Archive)

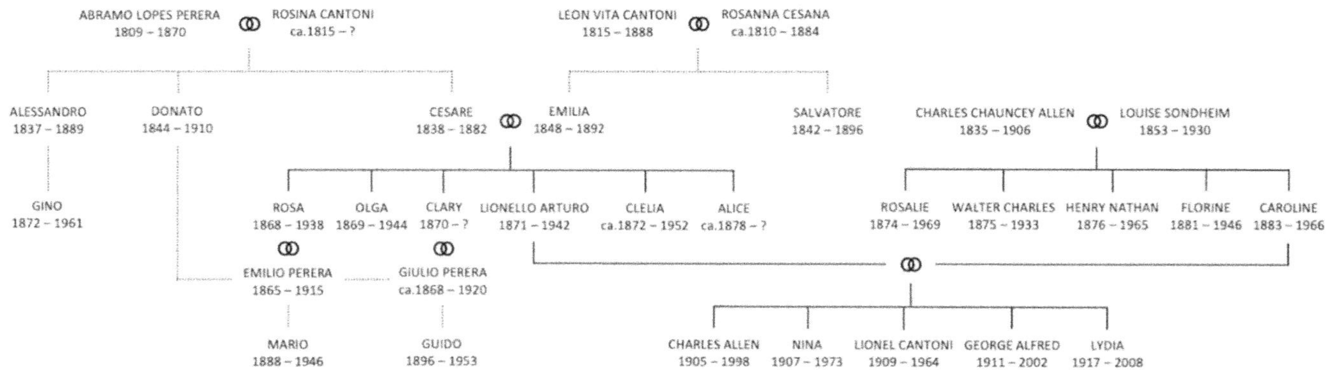

Figure 3.3: Lopes Perera family tree
Simplified genealogy of Lionello Perera's family reconstructed thanks to research done by Rosie Perera.

Chapter 4

Among Students of Ca' Foscari and its Alumni

Before addressing Lionello's new life in the United States, it is necessary to take a closer look at the kind of university training he received in Venice, as well as at the institute in which he was enrolled. This holds paramount relevance for understanding his life, not just concerning his professional success, but also with regard to his attitude towards his countrymen. As will become evident, the importance of his education between 1886 and 1889 at Ca' Foscari cannot be underestimated, because Lionello himself referred to his time at the then-called Regia Scuola Superiore di Commercio whenever possible. He was very proud of his graduation at the Venetian institute, which at this time was one of the most advanced international business schools together with Paris, Antwerp, and Mulhouse.[1] Although founded relatively recently, in 1868, right after the annexation of Venice to newborn Italy, the special programme at Ca' Foscari had a strong reputation. It was the sole Italian institute to provide theoretical and juridical courses about international commerce and finance, further offering specific training in business practice and insights with case studies, which proved particularly useful for students in their later careers.[2] Indeed, graduates of Ca' Foscari felt they had participated in an experimental as well as unique programme of higher education, which prepared them *de facto* for the economic and diplomatic progress of their nation.[3] The sense of identity from this shared experience resulted in an early alumni association, one of the first of its kind in Europe, which was launched in 1898, just thirty years after the institute's foundation.[4] With regard to the research scope of this book, both the university and its alumni hold particular relevance, because Lionello kept in contact with his former classmates by actively participating at various programmes of the graduate association from its very inception. It is thus necessary to investigate the role of Ca' Foscari in late nineteenth century, in order to show the belief system and attitudes that nurtured young Lionello's world view and business abilities, and which, in the end, led him and his fellow alumni to remain proudly united around their common university identity.

Today's Ca' Foscari University of Venice takes its name from the majestic Quattrocento palace on the Grand Canal, at the bend between the Rialto Bridge and the Accademia, which still holds the headquarters of the institute founded in 1868. The university was started thanks to a joint initiative of various public institutions –the municipality, the provincial authority, and the national Ministry of Agriculture, Industry and Commerce. It was called Regia Scuola Superiore di Commercio, which can be translated as Royal School of Higher Education in Commerce. It was the first institute of its kind in Italy and the fifth in Europe, a proper business school, thus devoted solely to the study of economic and commercial topics, which could be entered upon the completion of a senior high school exam.[5] Such European business schools constituted an unprecedented experiment that spread during the second half of the nineteenth century across the continent and later spilled over to the United States, given the growing relevance of international trade that went along with gradual industrial development and colonial expansion in the Western world. The first institute of this kind was founded as early as 1820 in Paris as a private venture and was later reformed in 1861, while in the 1850s, another two schools of higher education for commercial studies were opened, one in Antwerp in 1853 and one in Budapest in 1857.[6] In 1866 France opened another business school in Mulhouse which, although closed only five years later, constituted together with Antwerp a direct precedent to the Venetian institute. As far as the study programme is concerned, the Regia Scuola was an attempt of combining a theoretical approach with practical activities in one and the same course, structured around different disciplines.[7] The true founder of the Venetian business school was Luigi Luzzatti, a young and influential politician, who nurtured ambitious plans for his hometown after the annexation by the Kingdom of Italy. He wished the city to regain a glimpse of its glorious commercial past, though he was aware that such a plan could be accomplished only with a new generation of trained agents.[8] Since 1840, under Austrian rule, Venice was host to a polytechnic institute. Already in October 1866, after Austria's retreat from the Lagoon, it was natural to reflect on the institute's transformation into a newer kind of higher education specifically devised for the Italian nation. In fact, after the fall of the Venetian Republic, the city had shown total impatience towards the state bureaucracy dictated by the Hapsburg Empire, since the latter was technically underdeveloped as compared to the administrative tradition of the past Venetian regime.[9] Furthermore, Vienna had constantly favoured the city of Trieste as its main port on the Adriatic Sea, clearly at the expenses of Venice and blocking its historic trade routes. The idea of opening a business school was necessary to boost Venice's maritime traffic and Luzzatti considered it as important as a special customs regime, the widening of the port infrastructure, and the strengthening of the city's commercial routes along the Adriatic Sea.[10] Right after the annexation to Italy, the debate among the city's ruling class focused on quick recovery by repositioning Venice as one of the nation's principle ports, so that the Province took the lead over the business school idea. In November 1867 a plan was drafted to involve various public authorities in the foundation of this new institute: the Municipality, the Chamber of Commerce, and the Ministry of Agriculture, Industry and Commerce. Hence, Luzzatti and his acolytes were aware that such an ambitious project could not survive as a mere local initiative, but it needed instead the direct participation of the national government. In January 1868, two commissioners were sent from Rome, in order to assess the possible involvement of the Ministry of Agriculture, Industry and Commerce in the initial activities of the business school. They were Domenico Berti and Francesco Ferrara, who at the time served as members of parliament and were both former ministers. Under their supervision, in April, a joint committee with representatives of the Municipality, the Province and the Chamber of Commerce completed the master plan for the new institute, which was officially presented by Luigi Luzzatti and Eduardo Deodati.[11] At the heart of this initial project was the so-called 'banco' such as in the case of Antwerp and Mulhouse, which was intended as a practical laboratory for trade that should train students by means of carefully designed exercises and simulations.[12] Eventually, the Ministry was convinced of the innovative character of this new institute and designated Ferrara as Board Director of the business school, a post he would hold for over thirty years up until his death in 1900, so that he fundamentally shaped the elite education given at Ca' Foscari. Ferrara himself would participate at the selection committee for future students, hence his signature appears on the acceptance notice of Lionello Perera in 1886.[13]

The opening of the Scuola Superiore di Commercio was declared by law on August 6, 1868, by the Regio Decreto n. 4530, which also approved the internal statutory regime of the school. On December 3, the newly appointed professor Luigi Bodio opened the first academic year giving a solemn speech on statistics and political economics that set the tone of the new institute, thus initiating the first nine classes with five more professors hired on this occasion.[14] Meanwhile, thanks to the suggestion of Antonio Fornoni, another relevant Venetian politician of the time, and soon-to-be mayor, Palazzo Foscari on the Grand Canal had been chosen as a suitable venue, since it had been vacated by the Austrian troops formerly quartering there.[15] It was indeed a convenient place, as not only its rooms were spacious and its position very central, but the entire palace was magnificent and reminiscent of an epoch of splendour when Venice was the ruler of the Mediterranean Sea, both in commerce and warfare. The name of the building referred to an influential aristocratic family with famous personalities among its members, such as Francesco Foscari (1373-1457) who was the longest-serving Doge in the history of the Venetian state and whose rule allowed the Republic's widest territorial expansion, from the Aegean Sea to Milan.[16] Studying at Ca' Foscari with its glorious past and a stunning overview of the Grand Canal, from which Canaletto himself used to draw some of his so-called 'vedute', allowed students to step in the shoes of the once-mighty Venetian Republic and to fully appreciate the importance of maritime trade and international connections. As Europe's major business hub in early Modern Times, Venice had gained enormous wealth over the centuries and also contributed to the advancement of management practice worldwide.[17] During the Renaissance, for example, the inventor of the modern double-entry accounting system, Luca Pacioli, chose to print his pivotal treaty *Summa de aritmethica, proportioni et proportionalita* (1494) at the print shop of Paganino de Paganini, thus signalling the city's fundamental role in business history.[18] The choice of this palace was a good omen for a school set up to train the officers, traders, and consuls for the newborn Kingdom of Italy, a nation that immediately aimed at becoming a colonial power copying the overseas expansion of Great Britain, France, and Belgium.[19] Hence, Ca' Foscari was much more than a school of higher education, since its majestic gothic facade and interiors stood as a powerful monument that shaped the sense of identity of anyone who walked through its salons and studied in its classrooms. Upon entering the palace, the students selected for the Regia Scuola Superiore di Commercio likely felt they were committed to a fundamental process in the nation's growth and that they would soon play a role in the breaking dawn of a new-born Italy. It is no wonder Lionello kept a postcard with the picture of Ca' Foscari among his dearest memorabilia for his entire lifetime (Fig. 1.1).

Right from the start, the business school was divided into three courses or 'sezioni', which were established in 1871 to pursue three different career paths.[20] After a common year with mandatory lectures and laboratory work, students were divided into either a commercial course of three years or a consular course of five years, though they could also choose a third path that led towards the teaching profession in various disciplines such as economics, statistics, industry, accounting, and foreign languages.[21] Hence, depending on the course of study, graduates could become either commercial agents for private and public companies, in the industry or finance sector, or they could embark on a diplomatic career, or they could be teachers of specialised disciplines in secondary and polytechnic schools. Of these three paths, however, the true novelty was the first one, an unprecedented three-year course in business studies that needed to be developed from scratch regarding contents and methodology. The main feature would become the so-called 'banco', a set of practical exercises and business simulations that covered ten out of thirty hours of weekly teaching.[22] Students had to interpret the role of a business leader by performing all technical and legal tasks for opening a new venture or running an existing company, such as a limited liability partnership or a consortium or a brokerage firm, with the completion of all due accounting books and bureaucratic papers based on current prices for goods and services. By means of combining a complex set of tasks within a theoretical firm every student was in turn confronted with various activities that were necessary in a modern company operating at an international level. They would, for instance, do account audits, issue invoices, prepare bills of exchange, draft letters of credit, import goods, receive money from abroad, manage arbitration with foreign companies, and many other daily tasks. Interestingly the term 'banco' held a specific historical meaning in Venice and it further constitutes the etymological root of the word bank, as it was used in connection to the city's high trade traffic at the Rialto market that boosted financial activities during the Middle Ages and in early Modern Times.[23] As a matter of fact, it refers to the work bench that merchants and traders would set up in the morning to open their businesses, which was nothing more than a simple wooden plank where they would buy and sell stock from departing ships, exchange or loan money, divide stocks of goods arriving by sea and do other financial transitions. The first private 'banchi' were opened in Rialto as early as 1157 by noblemen, though they often and quickly failed, which gave rise to the definition of 'bancarotta' –bankruptcy, literally broken plank– so that in 1451 the Republic organised a state controlled stock exchange called 'bancogiro'.[24] Trade operations, accounting methods, and financial practices were in the veins of the city and were comprehensively laid at the heart of teaching activities at the nascent business school. In this regard, the research approach and the disciplinary methodology that came to characterise Ca' Foscari were influenced by Venice's ancient tradition, as interpreted and developed by Fabio Besta (1825-1922), who would soon become the most influential professor at the institute and a much-reputed business expert at an international level.[25] He held the chair in accounting systems for almost half a century and his professional standing even helped the institute to be credited as a university in 1913, while its diplomas had already been retroactively turned into proper Masters degrees in 1907.[26]

By the time Lionello Perera enrolled at Ca' Foscari, in 1886, the teaching routine was already firmly established after almost two decades, thus, his student's records offer a glimpse of the kind of education and training that was by then typical for the Venetian institute.[27] The high standards of teaching were accompanied by the careful selection made among the best applicants from all over Italy, with entrance exams that required a good preliminary preparation in a varied range of topics. In fact, the admission certificate signed by Director Francesco Ferrara on October 31, 1886, noted that Lionello came from the preliminary course of the Istituto Ravà in Venice (Fig. 4.2).[28] On May 25, 1886, he had been tested in Italian literature both orally and in written form, as well as in geography and history, arithmetic and algebra, physics and natural history, French language and calligraphy, eventually even accounting with a total mark of 78 ½ out of 100 points. He scored particularly well in mathematics (9) and foreign languages (9 ½), while all other marks were 7s and 8s, thus making him a good candidate for the first communal year. Final exams were held every July to award the elevation to the following academic year and after the first-year students were allowed to choose among three-course options. Lionello concluded his first year with 112 ½ out of 130 points and then decided to proceed with commercial studies.[29] On the second year, as already mentioned, he skipped the mid-term exams, but was granted permission by the school board to take them in July 1888, scoring 119½ out of 130. In his final year, Lionello decided to specialise in the so-called 'cassa' for his graduation, which stands for treasury and comprised all sorts of financial and accounting activities, both for industry and the banking sector. In the exams of July 1889, he totalled 137 ½ out of 150 and became the 245th graduate of the Regia Scuola Superiore di Commercio in Venice. Twenty years later, as soon as Ca' Foscari was allowed to issue official Master's degrees, Lionello applied for the validation of his diploma, which was granted by the institute's Board Director and Senator of the Reign Nicolò Papadopoli Aldrovandi as a 'Laurea in Scienze applicate del Commercio', that is business studies, on February 10, 1909.[30] The fact that he asked for his old academic qualification to be recognised as a full equivalent of the new Master's degree, although he certainly did not need it in his current profession, hints at the pride and importance he personally held in his studies at Ca' Foscari.

Aiming at a principal role as a business school at an international level, the Venetian institute immediately offered its students foreign languages and culture, which were in addition to economic courses. Such a feature had been conceived from the beginning and it was explicitly mentioned during the preliminary stages that preceded the official foundation of Ca' Foscari, when experts summoned to draft a plan for the business school argued it would be important to teach both Western and Eastern languages.[31] The presence of language teachers was again rooted in the history of Venice, a city that surged as a major trade hub for oriental goods and merchants in Europe, thus it would soon come to characterise the institute at a national level and beyond, for instance being the first university in the world to have a chair for Japanese Studies established as early as 1873.[32] What was clear to the founders of Ca' Foscari was the relevance of foreign languages and the knowledge of distant cultures to prepare young people for international trade or a consular career. The time was ripe for such international connections given that the newborn Kingdom of Italy had just signed commercial treaties with the Empires of China and Japan, but first and foremost, the opening of the Suez Canal started a new era of oriental relations.[33] Hence, the original intention of the business school was to retrieve Venice's lost role as a doorway to the Orient and the initial plan was to have the monks of the city's Mekhitarist monastery teach Modern Greek, Arabic and Persian.[34] However, at its inception, the languages taught at Ca' Foscari were English, German and French, the latter being required even at the admission exam, as prospective students were expected to develop high standards in foreign languages in order to be successful. By the end of the nineteenth century, the institute had greatly expanded its language teaching, offering classes in Greek, Spanish and Rumanian, as well as Arabic, Turkish and Japanese, while plans were made to soon have teachers for Chinese, Persian and also Amharic. The distinctive training in foreign languages and culture allowed early graduates to effectively develop an international career, even in the Orient, such as in the case of Arturo De Luciano who established his business company in Beirut and, in 1897, he even wrote a treatise on silkworm breeding in Arabic.[35] With regard to Lionello Perera, he already proved a high level of French in the admission exams and would then deepen his knowledge of Western languages during his studies. This is confirmed by the recollections of his wife, who noted in her memoirs that he comfortably spoke several languages – Spanish, English, and German too– but she was also impressed by the vast array of Italian dialects he could understand.[36] As a national *unicum*, Ca' Foscari attracted students from the entire country and Lionello had probably met classmates that came from every Italian Region speaking their own particular dialects, which later proved instrumental to interact with Italian immigrants that constituted the core-clientele of his bank in New York. In conclusion, studying at the Regia Scuola Superiore di Commercio trained him for a career in the financial sector, but also prepared him to understand the relevance of regional as well as foreign languages and culture in an international career.

The pride and affection that Lionello Perera manifested towards his alma mater was probably a shared feeling among his classmates, since the institute decided to start an alumni association precisely at the end of the nineteenth century in response to the growing network of its graduates scattered around the world. The idea was suggested by Alessandro Pascolato, who replaced Francesco Ferrara in 1893 to become director of the business school.[37] Indeed, in early 1898 Pascolato travelled to Antwerp for an international conference in business studies and took notice of several alumni associations that had originated at similar schools. Back in Venice, he involved the teaching body of Ca' Foscari in a discussion about the benefit and feasibility of launching an association for their graduates, encountering a general enthusiasm for this prospected venture.[38] Because he was the only professor who had also been a student of the Venetian institute, Primo Lanzoni was given the task to do the preliminary work for the foundation of such an organisation that had no precedents in Italy. At a conference organised at the business school on May 4, 1898, Pascolato announced he wished to found an alumni association similar to the one at the institute of Antwerp, which he referred to as 'Antichi Studenti', standing for old or former students.[39] Already a month later, on June 5, 1898, a general assembly was called for the constitution of the 'Antichi Studenti della Regia Scuola Superiore di Commercio di Venezia', the alumni association of Ca' Foscari that would last for over four decades until the eve of World War II. The gathering chose Pascolato as President of the original committee together with Besta as a Secretary, crediting him as the most influential professor at the institute, while Lanzoni was put in charge of the organisation's treasury. The association's mission was to allow a permanent liaison of all graduates, in order to keep relationships dating from the classroom alive or to build new connections among alumni. This would be beneficial for the individual members and for the general interests of the nation's commerce. Furthermore, this organisation could be employed to circulate information among its members, promote events and services, offer scholarships and even assist new graduates in their search for employment. Also, the Antichi Studenti would prove instrumental in fostering a common sense of identity among alumni, which favoured the dissemination of the institute's reputation across Italy and particularly abroad. To meet these aims, soon after its foundation, the association started publishing the so-called *Bollettino degli Antichi Studenti*.[40] The bulletin was meant as a periodical magazine that carried information about various topics of interest in commerce, economics, industry, and finance, but it also listed the position and whereabouts of the members of the organisation. Furthermore, it would regularly inform about any kind of progress of the Venetian business school, and it also contained very useful information such as job postings, announcements of selection, open teaching positions, grants and prizes, sometimes even reports regarding successful alumni.[41] The first number was printed in 1899 and its publication would last until 1971, even longer than the original association's lifetime, though at different pace –sometimes every three months and sometimes every four.[42] The bulletin was sent out to all subscribers and thus became instrumental to sustain a sense of belonging to Ca' Foscari and also to raise the number of alumni, which in fact soared in the first ten years of the association's life. Already a year after its inception, in December 1899, the Antichi Studenti had 203 members, a figure that constantly grew to roughly over a thousand in 1908.[43] Interestingly, the list of alumni was published alphabetically with all information provided by the members themselves, which usually included the job title, sometimes even a photograph, and very often the business address, thus they could be contacted by other subscribers. These lists are useful to discover the typical employment of graduates from the Regia Scuola Superiore di Commercio and their geographical distribution. This showed that thirty years after the school's foundation its alumni had effectively gained positions in commerce, industry, public offices, and diplomacy.[44] With regard to the members' origins and current activity, the bulletins highlight how Ca' Foscari's graduates easily covered the entire Italian territory –from Naples to Milan, from Rome to Genoa– and that they were expanding in important trade hubs in the Western world as well as in the Orient –from New York to Beirut, from Rio de Janeiro to St. Petersburg.[45] Apparently, Lionello Perera was among the many alumni that shared this common identity and totally supported the commitment to the new association, since he enthusiastically joined the Antichi Studenti as soon as the opportunity of membership was announced. His subscription is dated July 12, 1898, so that he was registered already in the society's first bulletin.[46] Over the years, his name would constantly appear on the pages of the subsequent bulletins bearing information about his business and once even a picture with a distinct nineteenth-century moustache (Fig. 4.1). He would present himself, of course, as the head and proprietor of Lionello Perera & Co. located in 49 Wall Street, New York. Interestingly, in one bulletin he added "comp. successore di Salvatore Cantoni",[47] which means successor to his uncle, though the abbreviated form "comp." might have a double meaning: either 'compratore', that is purchaser of Salvatore's bank, as really had been the case, or more likely 'compagnia', which instead signifies he saw himself as legitimate heir of the Cantoni company. Apparently, Lionello was proud to openly connect with his uncle's former banking activity, as it was the oldest and most prestigious in the Italian American community of the East Coast. Besides, it was a useful distinction given that he was not the only Venetian graduate in that area or in other international hubs. A bulletin of 1902 reported also a Mr. Petrocelli and one Mr. Ruffo in New York among an impressive number of other former students working around the globe –in Bombay, Buenos Aires, Istanbul, Sao Paulo, Smirne, Tripoli, Tunis, and Washington.[48] It is highly probable that Lionello eagerly read these bulletins, since it is the only way he might have heard of the opportunity to transform his diploma into a proper Master's degree in 1909. One should further consider that the mentioned School Board Director Papadopoli Aldrovandi, who signed the equivalence papers, was a member of the association too. Hence, the network among the Antichi Studenti was truly effective and the members shared a genuine pride in their common identity, a feeling they mutually held for the commercial and economic development of their country, both at home and abroad.

The strong bonding and professional awareness of these alumni, demonstrated in the graduates' association of the Regia Scuola Superiore di Commercio in its first decade of activity, show the sentiment and attitude that Lionello Perera held when he departed for the United States, in March 1894. He was not a simple immigrant looking for a better future for himself and his closest family members, leaving his fatherland for good. To the contrary, he most likely felt a sense of belonging and a responsibility towards a much bigger entity, his nation, which would develop into an ongoing commitment to the Kingdom of Italy, precisely because of his university experience. After all, he certainly was a high-profile expatriate, but it was not a question of being privileged. What mattered to him was being a trained and promising Italian national who was expected to serve his country well even in New York, which also implied he needed to care for his countrymen across the Atlantic.

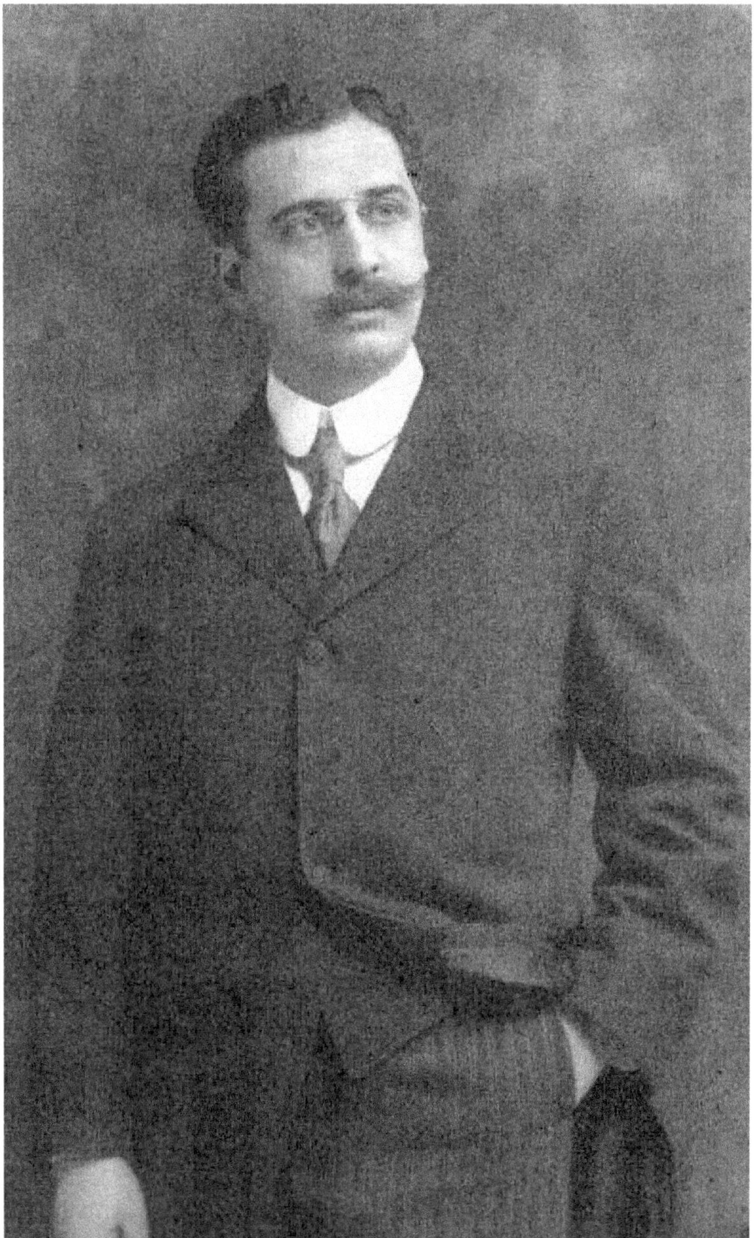

Figure 4.1: Photograph of Lionello Perera for the alumni bulletin (ca. 1900)
Probably taken in New York and dating to the early 1900s. This photograph was used in a cut-down version for the alumni bulletin of Ca' Foscari, which started to be printed in 1899. (Courtesy of the Perera Family Archive)

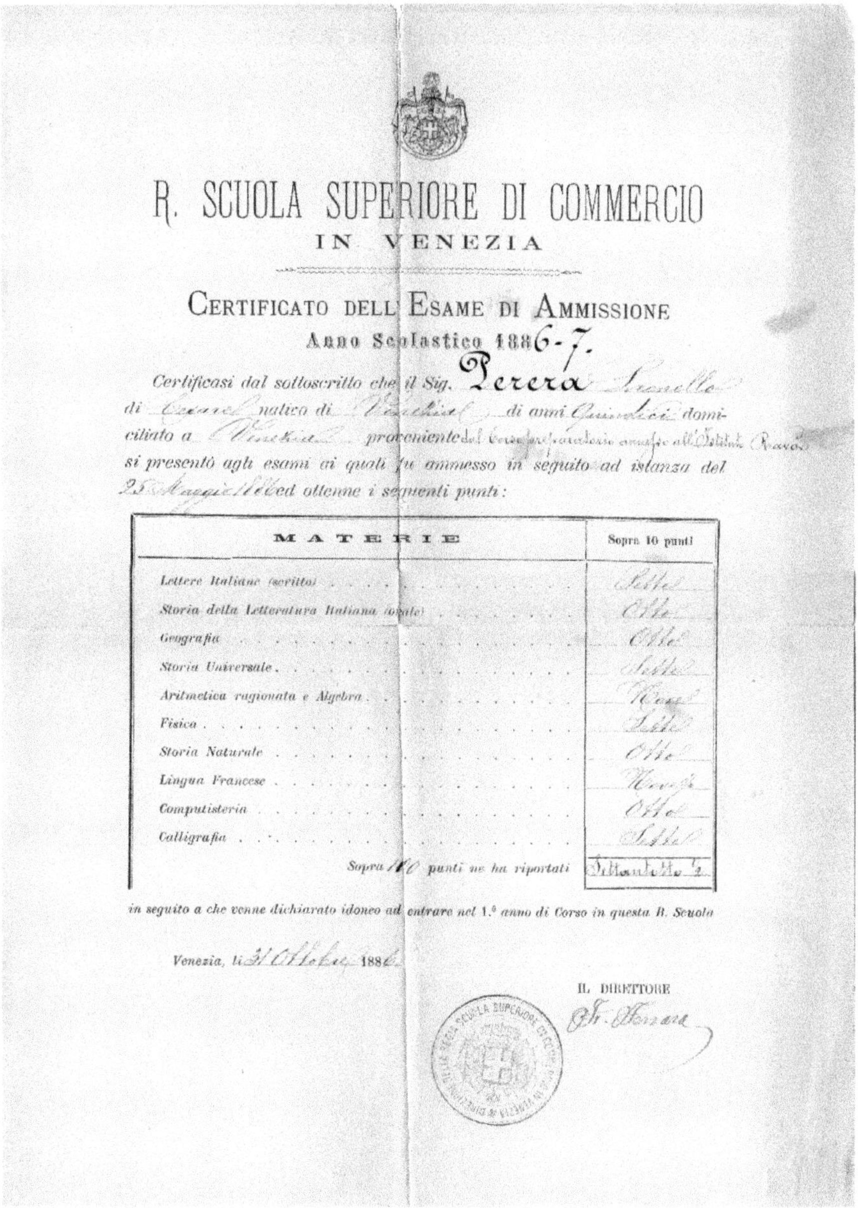

R. SCUOLA SUPERIORE DI COMMERCIO

IN VENEZIA

CERTIFICATO DELL'ESAME DI AMMISSIONE

Anno Scolastico 1886-7.

Certificasi dal sottoscritto che il Sig. Perera Lionello di Cesare nativo di Venezia di anni Quindici domiciliato a Venezia proveniente dal Corso preparatorio annesso all'Istituto Ravà si presentò agli esami ai quali fu ammesso in seguito ad istanza del 25 Maggio 1886 ed ottenne i seguenti punti:

MATERIE	Sopra 10 punti
Lettere Italiane (scritto)	Sette
Storia della Letteratura Italiana (orale)	Otto
Geografia	Otto
Storia Universale	Sette
Aritmetica ragionata e Algebra	Nove
Fisica	Sette
Storia Naturale	Otto
Lingua Francese	Nove
Computisteria	Otto
Calligrafia	Sette
Sopra 100 punti ne ha riportati	Settantotto ½

in seguito a che venne dichiarato idoneo ad entrare nel 1.° anno di Corso in questa R. Scuola

Venezia, li 31 Ottobre 1886

IL DIRETTORE

F. Ferrara

Figure 4.2: Admission Certificate of Lionello Perera to Ca' Foscari (1886)

Dated October 31, 1886, the admission certificate of Lionello Perera is signed by Prof. Francesco Ferrara, founder and director of the Regia Scuola Superiore di Commercio at Ca' Foscari in Venice. (Research purposes: © Università Ca' Foscari Venezia)

Part II: The Italian Banker of New York

Chapter 5

Banca Cantoni and an Uneasy Succession

Writing about the late Salvatore Cantoni and his banking activity in New York, in the second half of the nineteenth century, is a difficult task given the lack of primary sources and bibliographic references on the subject. One must rely on family recollections, on very few articles that appeared in US newspapers of the time, and on scant information in Italian American magazines and periodicals. However, in each of these materials, there is inaccuracy or exaggeration, thus they must be critically examined to reconstruct both the development of Salvatore's remarkable career in the United States and the uneasy succession of the family business in favour of Lionello Perera. Interestingly, the professional experiences of uncle and nephew relate to two very different moments in the immigration history of the country, particularly regarding the presence of Italian Americans. Salvatore Cantoni was active in New York roughly from the beginning of the 1860s to his death in 1896, while Lionello's banking activity covered the years from his succession until his retirement in the early 1930s. Unfortunately, official census figures referring to Italian immigrants in the nineteenth century are quite unreliable, considering that Italy was divided into many different States until the late 1860s and not all passengers were registered as Italians. For instance, those coming from Venice like Salvatore Cantoni were citizens of the Hapsburg Empire. Nevertheless, evidence shows that before the Civil War, only very few emigrated from the Italian peninsula, roughly in the hundreds per year, and mostly they were well-educated people from the northern and central parts of the country, while the numbers began to soar to thousands only after 1880 with the majority coming from the poorer southern regions.[1] At the turn of the century, Italian immigrants numbered tens of thousands every year constantly increasing until the 1920s, which inevitably gave rise to serious issues of discrimination and difficulties of integration.[2] Roughly speaking, when Salvatore Cantoni emigrated from Venice in the early 1860s and officially started his banking business for Italians, his countrymen were low in numbers, although the State of New York harboured a considerable community, with around 2,000 Italians officially residing there.[3] These figures were second only to California. Italians living in New York at the time were particularly active at a political level, since most were part of the nationalist elite that escaped prosecution or detention by Austria, the Kingdom of Naples, or the Vatican to find freedom in the USA, which they considered a champion of liberalism.[4] Salvatore's business must definitively have taken off later, during the 1870s and 1880s, as the numbers of immigrants coming from the newborn Kingdom of Italy increased. However, figures do not compare with the tens of thousands of Italians –and potential clients– flooding into New York just two decades later at Lionello's time, so the difference in commercial success between the two banks can be easily explained. This chapter will try to illuminate the business uncle Salvatore started in America, which then allowed his nephew to step in the shoes of a prosperous family company and expand it even more.

Starting with Salvatore Cantoni's biography, a letter of his father Leon Vita to the military officials in Venice states his place and date of birth in Venice on March 21, 1842.[5] He was the second son of Leon Vita Cantoni and Rosanna Cesana, since the same letter maintains their older son Donato, born in 1834, had died still a young man. Various sources place his arrival in New York in the early 1860s, though the reason that brought him to the United States in his early twenties are unclear, since the family tree does not show any previous relatives residing there, at least from the Cantoni side. Among family materials, there is however a rich correspondence dating to the Summer of 1862, when Salvatore had just turned twenty.[6] It appears that he had departed from Venice for Geneva to apprentice at the financial business of the Rothschilds, but as early as July, he passed Strasbourg and finally arrived in Paris shortly before the national festival of July 14. He was seeking decent professional opportunities and at some point, before the end of 1862, he must have resolved to try his fortune in the United States. His first banking activity, of which he was the direct proprietor, may have started as early as 1862,[7] although some memorabilia indicate 1865 as the foundation year of the Cantoni Bank in New York, such as a business calendar of 1907 issued by Lionello Perera & Co.[8] Apparently, Salvatore's personal abilities and his insight on relying on the growing Italian American community made him quickly successful in the New York banking sector. The headquarters of his venture was at 49 Wall Street and his enterprise was granted access to the New York stock exchange in 1879.[9] Despite the rapid growth of Italian American private banks at the turn of the century, still in the 1920s, the bank taken over by Lionello Perera was the only Italian American business that had access to the city's stock exchange, which of course was a source of particular pride and reliance for its customers.[10] Exact data on Salvatore's banking activity is very scarce, though it is possible to get an idea of the scale of his business thanks to participation in a governmental ten-years bond subscription programme of 1894, as reported in several US financial newspapers of the time. Salvatore Cantoni & Co. directly placed a total amount of $25,000 with an individual bond price of $117, placing the bank at a good average share level in the list of subscribers nationwide, so it had the capacity of a million-dollar venture.[11] The business was probably flourishing already a decade earlier, in 1884, when

Salvatore purchased a one-block house in the expensive Fort Greene district of central Brooklyn, at 56 South Portland Avenue, which is also about the time he met Elsa Forster there as a supposedly unmarried millionaire.[12] In fact, most of the articles referring to Uncle Salvatore appeared in Brooklyn newspapers after that year, such as an elegant reception held by his wife Clarissa Douglas Olsen on May 27, 1893,[13] or the notable wedding of his daughter Olive Douglas to Mr. de Beixedon on October 12 that same year.[14] By then, he was considered a reputable Wall Street banker, whose wedding and those of his first two daughters had certainly contributed to gain him access to the city's elite. With regard to his own wedding, Salvatore might have married for a first time shortly after arriving in New York, though no children are reported. He married Clarissa around 1868, who became the mother of his three daughters and the final recipient of his estate on his death in 1896.[15] Apart from hosting fashionable events for high society, Lionello's uncle was personally involved in philanthropic activities, as was expected from a successful and distinguished businessman. Already in 1889, he set forth together with several kinsmen –Louis Contencin, Giovanni Lordi and Dr. A. Abruzzo amongst them– to plan the foundation of a building especially devoted to the welfare of Italian immigrants in New York.[16] On January 25, 1891, Salvatore Cantoni finally inaugurated the Italian Home at 179 Second Avenue, of which he was President.[17] It was a hospital devoted to Italians and entirely paid for by a league of Italian American entrepreneurs, amongst them a famous piano-maker and Carlo Barsotti, editor of the magazine *Il Progresso Italo-Americano*.[18] It was a four-storey building with twenty-seven beds for women on the third floor and an equal number for men on the top floor, while the second floor harboured rooms for sick Italian sailors and some for the management of the institution. On the first floor, the building had a large reception hall with a capacity of 250 people, where the inauguration of the hospital took place. The portraits of George Washington, the revolutionary commander Giuseppe Garibaldi, his companion and liberal thinker Giuseppe Mazzini, and of course the King and Queen of Italy hung also there, four unmistakable protagonists of the newborn Kingdom of Italy. It was considered a fine and modern healthcare centre with a distinct touch of Italian patriotism that underlined how this was an achievement of the Italian American community of New York.

Not much more is known about Salvatore's banking and philanthropic activity, but another mention appears about his political convictions that might account for the choice of portraits of both Garibaldi and Mazzini inside the new hospital. The presence of the former might shed some light for his reasons for emigrating in 1862 at the age of twenty. In a report of 1888, re-published in 1918 in the pages of the Italian American magazine *Il Carroccio*, Salvatore Cantoni appears among the honorary directors of a Federal

Committee of Italian Societies in the Americas, together with personalities of wide renown like the entrepreneur and telephone inventor Antonio Meucci, the Freemasons Master Adriano Lemmi and the freedom fighter Alessandro Oldrini, who fought with Garibaldi in the Parisian resistance of 1870.[19] Further members were the Secretary of State, James G. Blaine, and the President of the District of Columbia, Senator West. This highlighted the importance of the committee in the eyes of government bodies of the US Republic. The Italian revolutionary Giuseppe Garibaldi was beloved by American liberals, and he had been hosted in New York by Meucci in 1850, since he had to escape Italy after the failure of the Roman Republic.[20] Garibaldi passed away on June 2, 1882, and already on the 14th that month the committee was summoned to approve the financing of the General's marble bust to be placed in the US Senate. Salvatore was among the ten men who participated in the decision and a few years later, on August 23, 1888, the opening ceremony took place in Washington with all Senators standing during a commemorative speech made by Senator William E. Evarts, who had been a friend of Garibaldi. Salvatore Cantoni's role in such a politically charged occasion opens a window on the groups of Italians that emigrated to America before 1861, when the Kingdom of Italy was eventually established. Indeed, the numbers of Italian emigrants in the first part of the nineteenth century show that many were patriots seeking asylum in the liberal Republic of the United States to escape the dungeons of the various reactionary powers governing the peninsula.[21] Garibaldi's own arrival a decade earlier in New York was very much anticipated by Italian Americans and many official ceremonies were planned, which then had to be cancelled due to the official protest of several European kingdoms that considered the Italian freedom fighter a dangerous and unlawful rebel.[22] The good relationship of Italian liberals with America ran much deeper, with the United States informally offering economic and military support to the independence wars in Italy, while many former US troopers, such as William Theodore De Rohan, fought on the side of General Garibaldi.[23] Italians in America showed their gratitude by giving support in the fight to preserve the Union launched by President Abraham Lincoln on the eve of the Civil War. Many Italian nationals also enthusiastically joined the Garibaldi Guard in New York set up by reformer and editor Gian Francesco Secchi de Casali with the exiled commander Alessandro Repetti in 1861.[24] Hence, early Italian Americans earned a name for their patriotism, which explains the high honour conceded by the US Senate to the heroic memory of Garibaldi. The fact that Salvatore Cantoni found himself at the top of the celebration committee discloses his personal standing inside the Italian American community of the 1880s, which had probably developed due to his professional success during the previous two decades as a banker in New York. It further signalled his affinity with the ideals of the Risorgimento, the liberation ideology seeking unity for the Italian peninsula that had inspired especially the bourgeois elite, rather than the lower classes, in the first half of the nineteenth century.[25] Indeed, his association with these ideals and company clearly hints at his personal political views, siding very early in his life with the spirit of Italian independence.

Salvatore Cantoni was evidently an Italian liberal and patriot, thus, he might have supported or even facilitated freedom fighters on a financial level. It is of course a matter of conjecture, but considering the ideologically charged nature of the majority of Italian Americans in the nineteenth century, it would be highly unlikely that a prominent member of the nationwide committee such as Lionello's uncle did not stand with the liberators of his country. To the contrary, an official register of activities of Italian diplomatic affairs in the Americas discloses that Salvatore Cantoni was awarded a decoration in 1889, and the Kingdom further considered to grant him an even higher honour in 1894.[26] All these traces, news, and materials suggest he rather was an enthusiastic supporter of Italy imbued with Risorgimento ideology, probably having this worldview already in his youth in Venice under Austrian rule. In this regard, it is remarkable that he emigrated in 1860, right after the end of the second Italian independence war, which liberated the region of Milan but couldn't free Venice from the Hapsburg Empire. It was not unusual that young northern Italians who fought the Austrians or avoided military service with the Hapsburg Empire fled their fatherland to avoid being incarcerated.[27] In this regard, the aforementioned family correspondence between Salvatore and his father Leon Vita in the Summer of 1862 appears revealing. Writing from Paris on July 16, the young man enthusiastically commented about the patriotism he experienced during the national festival commemorating the French Revolution.[28] After this passage, almost out of the blue, he apologised to his father for having abandoned his hometown in a hurry but urged him not to conceal the motives of his sudden departure. To the contrary, Salvatore proudly invited his father to tell everyone the truth, that he escaped Venice to avoid becoming a soldier for the Austrian Empire: "… trovai la fonte dell'oro. No! è meglio dica che fuggii da Venezia per non andare soldato, come è vero infatti."[29] As Salvatore was twenty years old, at the time, he was due to enter the Hapsburg military service, so he rather fled because of his fervent patriotism and thus became a deserter. In August of 1862, Leon Vita tried to appeal to the Austrian authority to obtain a military leave for Salvatore, stating that his family was originally from Parma, thus, they counted as foreigners to the Hapsburg Empire, and that his other son Samuele had died.[30] Evidently, none of this impressed the Austrian army and Salvatore was left with the only option to emigrate to the United States as an Italian refugee. In addition to this revealing correspondence and to the official decorations earned from the Kingdom of Italy, there is also a visual proof of such a strong inclination towards the Italian independent movement. A photograph of Salvatore Cantoni, republished by Lionello Perera on the pages of the Italian American magazine *Columbus*, probably in 1924, shows the founder of the Cantoni bank, in his thirties or early forties, with a distinct long and curly moustache, a long goat's beard, and hair vigorously combed backwards (Fig. 5.1). All these features are clearly reminiscent of Vittorio Emanuele II of the House Savoia, who united the peninsula together with Garibaldi to become the first King of Italy in 1861, remaining as its ruler until 1878. Anyone in the USA coming from Italy at the time would have recognised the striking similarity.

When Lionello arrived in New York in April 1894 he became his uncle's apprentice both at a professional level, diving headfirst into the banking sector, and in his social contacts and political views, becoming somewhat of a confidant. So far, evidence suggests that in the 1890s, Salvatore Cantoni was considered an eminent personality in the New York finance sector and, at the same time, a reference point for the growing Italian American community. It must be noted that the two things were connected, because the Cantoni Bank gained its strength and wealth from the city's Italian constituency. Hence it would serve as a role model for Lionello's own business in the coming decades, one he would constantly and publicly rely on.[31] Even Salvatore's passionate commitment to the Risorgimento would live on as a genuine patriotism that Lionello cherished and translated into a proactive role towards the Kingdom of Italy especially at times of crises, for example, in the form of charity on the occasion of natural disasters[32] or during World War I.[33] Ignoring the shameful scandal with Mrs. Forster, Salvatore Cantoni immediately employed his nephew in the banking activity, probably even requiring him to accomplish delicate tasks, such as the purchase of the mentioned government bonds in 1894, which obviously needed direct contact with customers to resell individual shares. Lionello was even introduced at once to his uncle's closest business partners and friends. Amongst them was Charles Chauncey Allen (1835-1906), living in 12 East 64th Street, a banker of Jewish origins from Philadelphia[34] who was married to Louise Sondheim (1853-1930), who herself came from one of New York's most prominent Jewish families.[35] As bachelors, the two men had lived in adjoining rooms at the old Delmonico Hotel, then at 25 Broadway and Chambers Street, run by a family of Italian origin and founders of the famous New York restaurant. In the written recollections of Carolyn Allen Perera, the couple's youngest daughter born on November 16, 1883, she mentions the immediate affection and respect that Salvatore's young nephew earned from her family.[36] Lionello became a close friend of her older brothers and often visited the Allen's home or joined them on vacation. However, Carolyn is slightly unclear in her memoirs about the time she was introduced to Lionello, since she remembers being nine years old and he eighteen, but she probably was ten or eleven when he arrived at twenty-two in

New York. It is unlikely that Lionello had already been in America prior to his definitive emigration from Venice, since there is no evidence of such a journey and, in later accounts, he himself would always set 1894 as the year of his arrival. It may be simple inaccuracy or, perhaps, the approximation of a child who was rather uninterested in adults at that age. In Carolyn's recollections, the moment of Lionello's official presentation to the Allens remained but a faint memory. Most curiously, it appears that Lionello immediately developed strong ties to the Allens, much more than to the Cantonis in New York, and there might be a twofold explanation. On the one side, Salvatore's two oldest daughters were already married so they would not be in the household anymore, while on the other hand, there must have been strong feelings about the case of Elsa Forster and Lionello clearly was called to side with his uncle. Even worse, Salvatore's sons-in-law probably saw the young Italian as an intruder, an unwanted newcomer that might one day take over the lucrative family business.

As a matter of fact, the confidence and affection Salvatore Cantoni demonstrated towards his nephew through the introduction to the Allens was a clear sign that he would likely choose his nephew, a blood relative, for succession in the banking activity. Although these might seem mere conjectures, proof of such strained relations suddenly surfaced upon Salvatore's death. The already tense situation truly exploded when uncle Salvatore unexpectedly died while driving a four-in-hand carriage. Carolyn Allen Perera reports in her memoires he had a heart attack in Prospect Park, Brooklyn, on June 21, 1896, his wife next to him, though he alone perished. In the local papers, instead, the death by heart disease is reported to have occurred near the Cantoni summer house in Bayshore, Long Island, and friends of the couple tried to drive him home as soon as possible.[37] Later articles claimed his widow inherited the full estate, thus probably also the shares in the banking business and the seat on Wall Street.[38] In any case, a succession was due at the top of the Cantoni Bank and the two sons-in-law decided to oust Lionello at once to gain control of the business. Given the previous coverage of the Forster scandal, it is strange the succession quarrel among the Cantoni heirs was not mentioned in the newspapers, so there is only Carolyn Allen Perera's account to rely on. However, her recollections perfectly fit the scenario of a typical standoff between two American aristocrats, both feeling empowered by their ancestry, and a young Italian immigrant with nothing to lose. Regarding the husband of Olive Douglas Cantoni, Mr. de Beixedon, he worked in the real estate sector and his elitist character has been sufficiently examined in the previous chapter. He showed no hesitation in the Forster affair, when he was just the fiancé of Salvatore's second daughter, intervening directly in the private life of his future father-in-law, so it is plausible he would move to immediately dismiss Lionello. Salvatore's other son-in-law, the husband of his oldest daughter Natalie Holliday Cantoni, was also a prominent member of the New York aristocracy with influent connections and a professional expertise in legal affairs. Natalie, born on August 6, 1869, had married the reputed Louis Edwin Bomeisler at her parents' home at 56 South Portland Avenue on June 11, 1890.[39] Mr. Bomeisler was a renowned attorney and later even a counsellor to Thomas Alva Edison, advising the entrepreneur on various issues such as patent rights, financial operations, licenses, and royalties for his early filming enterprise. This is demonstrated by direct correspondence between the two in the years 1900 and 1901.[40] In the eyes of Mr. de Beixedon and Mr. Bomeisler, young Lionello Perera posed no real threat. They probably considered him an orphan child, a young Italian immigrant without any sort of backup. At first sight, Lionello did not stand a chance in these circumstances, though his contenders unexpectedly found themselves interpreting the role of Goliath. In fact, Salvatore's sons-in-law had not foreseen the swift and vehement reaction of the bank's core clientele, which comprised small merchants and businessmen of Italian origin. When the news came that Salvatore's nephew had been sacked without notice, the headquarters at 49 Wall Street were stormed by customers protesting and demanding the immediate return of their trusted kinsman.[41] If Mr. De Beixedon and Mr. Bomeisler had been so reckless in ousting the former proprietor's diligent nephew, who was an Italian like them and even a close relative of the bank's founder, customers feared they could be offered the same treatment one day. In her memoirs, Carolyn distinctly uses the term 'bank run', which held a specific meaning to anyone of that generation, because banking panics during the nineteenth century were extremely frequent due to the frailty of the US financial system, which lasted until the Great Depression.[42] Hence, when customers showed up in masses to protest and threatened to withdraw their money, the two sons-in-law became aware that they suddenly stood on the edge of a cliff. The clientele demanded to see the only *persona grata* they could count on. The two Americans had no other option but to summon Lionello Perera and offer him to manage the bank under their direct supervision. Usually described as a gentle and understanding character, Lionello categorically refused to work for them, as he evidently did not trust them. Considering the frequency of banking panics, the Cantoni company would probably have failed in a matter of days. Salvatore's sons-in-law were aware they risked paying off debts for the rest of their lives. Hence, they were forced to sell their shares in the bank at once and decided to offer Lionello the opportunity to purchase the company. Honouring the memory of his uncle, the young Italian was probably keen on keeping the family business, but he had other options too. He could have easily opened his own bank transferring all the customers, since they had shown personal loyalty. He could thus have walked away and leave the sons-in-law to pick up the pieces. Furthermore, he lacked the money to attempt a take-over bid. However, there was a good reason that led him to search for the necessary funds to buy the bank. Banca Cantoni had privileged access to the New York stock exchange, a truly invaluable asset for any banking activity. According to Carolyn's account, Lionello spoke to Charles Chauncey Allen about the situation and asked, if he could help. The old-time friend of Uncle Salvatore had recently retired from the stock exchange and trusted the young Italian completely. Thus, he decided to personally invest $7,500, while also convincing another bank to lend the same amount to cover the capital needed to purchase the majority share of the Cantoni Bank.[43] Lionello successfully made his purchase and renamed the business Lionello Perera & Co., officially starting in 1896 and proudly claiming it was the successor of Salvatore Cantoni & Co., thus stepping in the shoes of business established in 1865.

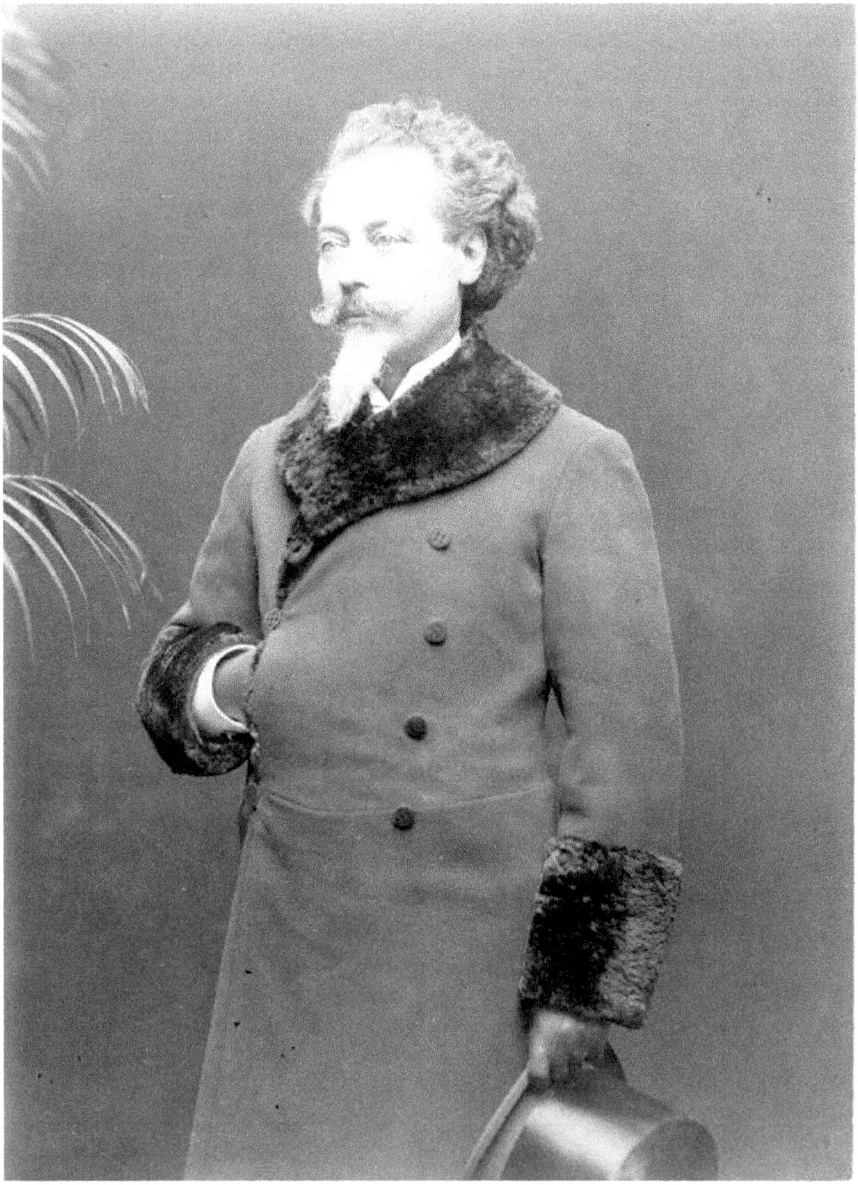

Figure 5.1: Photograph of Salvatore Cantoni (ca. 1880-90)
Probably taken in New York and dating to the 1880s or 1890s. This photographic portrait was republished through Lionello Perera on the pages of the Italian American magazine *Columbus*, probably in 1924, shortly after a bank run hit Lionello Perera's company. (Courtesy of the Perera Family Archive)

Chapter 6

The Largest Savings Bank of New York

Once the difficult issue of the succession was dealt with, presumably in the Summer of 1896, Lionello Perera became head of a bank that was already the major reference point of the Italian American community in New York, though in the following three decades he would turn it into the city's largest savings bank. This, at least, is what advertisements and articles in local magazines were claiming based on data of the State Banking Department.[1] This chapter is set to analyse the specific social and economic context his bank thrived on, as well as the precise development of his business over the years. Furthermore, particular attention will be paid to the kind of subliminal messages surfacing from the bank's communication strategy in the city and the peculiar architectural style chosen for its branches across Manhattan. As compared to the Salvatore Cantoni Bank, primary sources and official records of Lionello's professional activity are abundant, except in the first two decades when he was not yet registered as a State licensed business. Information is available, on the one hand, in financial magazines and newspapers, and on the other hand, in official documents by State authorities such as lawsuits and budgetary audits. Insight further emerges from advertisements and articles in widespread Italian American magazines of the time, such as *Il Progresso Italo-Americano, Il Carroccio* and *Columbus.* The first official appearance of Lionello Perera & Co. was in the *Bankers' Magazine* published by Bradford Rhodes & Co., which registered them as the successors to the Cantoni Bank in the July-December volume of 1896, thus confirming the starting date of his private activity.[2] It is necessary to highlight the kind of financial business Lionello was running, which did not substantially change over the years from the time of his uncle Salvatore. Until the Great Depression, the US banking sector had customs that made it competitive, deregulated and thus exposed to sudden panics as opposed to banks elsewhere, especially in Europe. It must be noted that under Federal law at the time nationwide branches were prohibited, while most States even prohibited or limited local branches, which soon led to an enormous number of banks within the United States, numbering more than 29,000 in 1920 alone.[3] The presence of banks was particularly numerous in big cities and there was generally no legal difference between commercial entities devoted mostly to low-interest loans, bonds, and savings, and proper investment companies, which operated also in high-risk brokerage. After a major panic in 1907, regulatory authorities introduced a series of measures in eight States, like the adoption of deposit insurance.

However, the situation remained substantially unchanged until Black Tuesday 1929. The US banking system suffered from overall structural frailty, over-competitiveness, endemic panics, and a potentially dangerous deregulation that allowed mixing of saving deposits and high-risk investments.[4] It was not until the Glass-Steagall Act in 1933, which was part of President Franklin D. Roosvelt's programme of regulatory reforms in the aftermath of the stock market crash, that the separation of investment ventures and commercial banking came into effect, further protecting the public from fraud by means of Federal deposit insurance.[5] The peculiar conditions of the banking sector in the years of the Cantoni Bank and of its successor, from 1865 to the early 1930s, made it a very difficult field to navigate without a high degree of strategic and managerial skills. For account holders, this system was equally difficult. Many customers felt it was generally opaque, often considering banks as untrustworthy, given that most runs started over the shared belief that savings were not safe anymore, thus initiating mass withdrawals.[6] This complicated field further included a high number of competitors and business hazards, thus highlighting the significance of a banker's personal standing to reassure clients of the financial solidity of a specific company. In New York, this was especially true, since banks were usually quite small in scale and with a single branch. The need for personal trust explains also why Italian immigrants would entrust their savings to a kinsman, rather than to an American national.

Considering this situation, at the time of the succession in 1896, Lionello Perera was aware he had to stick to the traditional image and consolidated activities of the former Cantoni Bank, especially to preserve customer confidence. Despite having access to the stock market, he preferred the business to remain a reliable commercial bank and expanded all those services his predecessor was already respected for. The activities of the Perera Bank thus covered money exchange, money transfer, savings, loans, safe deposits, and long-term investments such as gold, State or private utility companies, US or Italian governmental bonds. It is notable that the Cantoni Bank proudly claimed to be the first money exchange agency in New York and the Perera Bank indeed carried on this tradition.[7] This is confirmed by various sources, such as the bank's own window showing a 'money exchange' sign photographed at 69 Wall Street in 1907 (Fig. 6.1).[8] Ten years later, the papers reported a forger of Spanish or French origin that tried to cash French counterfeit notes to various banks in Wall Street on August 14, 1917.[9] His attempt started at the Perera Bank, but the teller recognised the forgery and kept the man waiting in order to contact the Secret Service, which immediately sent two agents to arrest the man. Furthermore, Lionello himself became a nationwide specialist on forgery and foreign currency, which was reason enough for J. Edgar Hoover to ask him for advice on a counterfeiting ring.[10] The Perera Bank conducted money exchange in gold, offering ingots as investment or accepting coins to weigh out.[11] Working in the sector of money exchange could easily cause legal disputes from time to time, especially with regard to the rates and overhead applied, and even concerning the origin of the exchanged foreign money. At least on two occasions from 1918 to 1923, the Perera Bank found itself in the position of defendant against customers who contested its conduct. In 1918 the Appellate Division of the Supreme Court of the State of New York decided on the case of Franklin Q. Brown and other appellants against Lionello Perera, in which the judgement was affirmed with cost in favour of the Italian banker.[12] In 1923 that same judiciary division discussed Enrique Solano y Rafecas against Lionello Perera, again with the latter winning the case.[13] The first trial was deemed of particular interest and became a case study in the law of bills and notes, because it involved the principle of negotiability with regard to foreign money.[14] What had happened in the years 1913-14 was that a Mr. Thomas Piptone, the manager for the foreign exchange department of a New York bank, Redmond & Co., was regularly in contact with the Perera Bank to have money in foreign currency exchanged into US dollars at the best possible rate. However, on ten occasions and for a total sum close to $30,000, Piptone did not enter the transactions in the bookkeeping records, since he had the checks paid out to an associate and basically stole the original money. The plaintiffs accused Lionello Perera of accepting stolen goods and demanded these be returned, but the judges found that foreign bills and notes were not merchandise, but currency as much as dollars, thus negotiable and transferable.

These were not the only legal challenges to the Perera Bank, since State scrutiny of private banks owned by non-nationals was particularly severe and often threatened their very legitimacy. Not by chance, Lionello Perera applied for US citizenship already in 1899[15], perhaps also to avoid possible legal problems for his company since, technically speaking, he did not actually succeed to Salvatore Cantoni's company. Instead, he purchased the bank from the estate of an American citizen, who his uncle was. It is unclear when Lionello was eventually granted citizen status, because the first time he applied for a US passport was in 1922. By that time, he was already married with children, while for the previous three decades it appears he retained his Italian citizenship. In any case, the uneasy succession of his late uncle did in the end, cause him legal troubles. All exemptions and privileges of the Cantoni Bank were automatically transferred to the new company, but on May 6, 1913, the Assembly of the State of New York found this was illegitimate, thus a misdemeanour.[16] According to banking law, section 112, and penal law, section 302, any company constituted after 1892 doing business in the banking sector without being subject to the supervision of the State Superintendent of Banks was prohibited in any way to refer to itself as a bank.

Lionello Perera & Co. had kept independence from direct State supervision by assuming the good will and name of the Banca Cantoni, as can be seen in the calendar pictures taken in 1907, which show both its branches, one in Wall Street and the other in East Harlem (Fig. 6.1). In the opinion of Attorney General Thomas Carmody, Lionello Perera & Co. had no right in maintaining this status and should thus be prohibited the use of the term 'bank', as well as its Italian translation 'banca', unless it was subject to the jurisdiction of the Banking Department.[17] Lionello's business certainly suffered an unexpected blow and was perhaps forced to remove all references to the term 'bank' from his offices, bill-heads, letter-heads, blank notes, certificates, and all written or printed paper. Subsequently he filed for authorisation to transact the business of a private banker within the State, in accordance with the banking law that was in effect at the time of his purchase in 1896. Lionello Perera & Co. probably continued its business unlicensed and eventually received authorisation after almost one and a half years, on October 26, 1914.[18] This example demonstrates that prior to World War I US authorities were quite suspicious of banking activities run by foreigners, believing they were not proper and safe depositories. However, in the 1920s, they noticed that a few individual private bankers acquired a reputation for honesty and integrity. In this regard, Lionello Perera & Co. was cited as the city's most reputable company, performing a useful administrative buffer between the State and the immigrant community.[19]

Being finally subject to State law, the company had to audit and publish its annual budget, offering a glimpse into the bank's turnover. The 'state of condition' for the years 1916 to 1919 show the overall size of Lionello Perera & Co., as well as the individual relevance of its various activities.[20] First and foremost, this temporal period highlights the remarkable increase of the business during World War I, with resources more than tripling, from roughly $800,000 in 1916 to almost 3 million dollars in 1919. In the same period, the inflation rate soared by twenty percent, but this cannot account alone for the 300 percent growth of the Perera Bank.[21] A detailed analysis of the mentioned annual budget is thus necessary to understand the main reason for such an extraordinary economic success. The Documents of the Senate of the State of New York for 1917 present the first five quarterly statements of Lionello Perera & Co., after it was licensed in the year 1914, thus allowing a good comparative view of the business' gradual increase.[22] Furthermore, a newspaper clipping preserved by Lionello in his memorabilia shows a 'report of the condition' on February 21, 1919, which has the same nominal entries and, therefore, can easily be compared with the previous official statements.[23] On the side of resources, what clearly emerges is a steep rise in three items: first, stocks and bonds; second, loans and discounts secured as collaterals; and third, trusts from companies, banks, and bankers. The first mentioned entry comprised public securities starting from $31,392 in December 1915 and peaking at

$660,793 in February 1919, as well as private securities almost doubling from $273,257 to $511,894 in the same period. The trend of loans and discounts was similar, commencing at $98,114 in late 1915 and expanding to $773,074 in early 1919. The growth was constant at first, while the exponential rise happened particularly between the end of 1916 and the beginning of 1919. Eventually, trusts rose in this period from $244,797 to $562,262, though the increase was proportionate over all four years. What remained stable were both the amount of foreign currency in the bank's possession and the real estate owned –namely, its two branches in Wall Street and East Harlem. This means that the rapid expansion of the business was not caused by its traditional activity of money exchange, nor in any sort of property, such as opening new branches across the city to favour the affluence of account holders. The reason for this steep rise can be found comparing resources with the development of liabilities, which shows how deposits rose considerably in the first two years reported by the statements, from $531,413 in December 1915 to $940,174 in November 1916. In the following two years, deposits grew at truly exponential rates to reach millions by February 1919: $2,311,013 to be exact, divided mainly amongst demand certificate of deposits and demand deposits withdrawable only on the presentation of passbooks. At this point, looking at resources and liabilities in parallel, it is presumed that the increase of investments in stocks and bonds was because of growing deposits at Lionello Perera & Co. The bank was evidently able to attract new account holders and small investors in times of global war by offering what to its customers appeared reliable options of public and private securities. The stunning growth of public securities between November 1916 and February 1919 –from $108,277 to $660,193– is particularly telling, when compared to the less than proportional increase of private securities over the entire period 1915 to 1919. The latter rose from $273,257 in November 1916 to $407,004 a year later, and then again to $511,894 after two more years. The figures demonstrate that customers evidently felt Lionello's bank was trusted to keep savings safe in such a difficult historical period. It further showed that the Perera Bank heavily invested in public securities, which is indeed confirmed by the company's participation with various millions of Italian Lire in five campaigns of the US Liberty Loan in New York City, which were used to finance the American intervention in Europe on the side of the Western Allies.[24] For the year 1917, at the time of the third campaign, Lionello Perera alone contributed with $205,000 of the overall two million US dollars received in the city.[25] This remarkable feat caused Milton Wright, Secretary of the Liberty Loan Committee, to offer the Venetian banker the chairmanship of the Italian subcommittee for the following campaign in 1918, collecting almost two and a half million dollar in American currency. This appointment, as stated by Wright in his letter, was a clear recognition of the high esteem

Lionello had personally earned from US authorities. By then, he was considered a reputable and prominent representative of Italian Americans in New York City, whose influence on his kinsmen came as the natural consequence of his trustworthy business conduct. A true stronghold for the Italian community, Banca Perera alone was able to place 10 to 15% of Liberty Loan locally, while sales of Italian Government bonds at a 5% interest rate went even better, with a total of 30 million Italian Lire in the years 1917 and 1918, the equivalent of $3,600,000.[26] After World War I, the Perera Bank invested even more in the Kingdom of Italy, reselling public and private securities to Italian Americans in New York, such as those of the Italian Submarine Cables & Co. in 1923.[27] Lionello himself publicly advocated American investments in Italian bonds after his personal visit to the country, stating in early Fall 1922 that business conditions were improving.[28] Unfortunately, he could not have anticipated that the Fascists were planning a coup on October 28 of that same year, which was staged with the infamous March on Rome.

So far, figures have shown that during the eight years ranging from 1914 – upon obtaining a state license– to 1922, Lionello Perera & Co. became one of New York's principle commercial banks, because it had been able to attract the savings of the city's Italian American clientele. At Christmas 1920, *The New York Times* reported that the bank shared this success with its employees, paying out bonuses of 25 to 50% of annual salaries.[29] In 1924, as reported by the magazine *Columbus*, the official audit of the New York banking system calculated that the Perera Bank had grown into the biggest savings bank of the entire state, accounting for $10,769,043 in resources out of a total of $41,540,121 for the entire sector. Ultimately, in the mid-1920s his company handled over a quarter of all deposits in the city and the wider State. Good management and reliability where certainly the key ingredients for this huge expansion, but Lionello Perera built his success also by a persistent and convincing advertisement campaign on all existing Italian American platforms. Page number eight of the *Evening Telegram* on March 11, 1917 (Fig. 6.2), which really served as the front page of its Italian edition, offers an eloquent example of the bank's relevance inside the New York community, and of the considerable sums invested in advertising.[30] Of the many commercials in the newspaper, Banca Perera was allotted the biggest and most prominent position of all in the lower-left corner, while the announcements of other Italian bankers, like Sessa Bank of Brooklyn or Banco di Napoli, were five to eight times smaller. In other widespread Italian American magazines, like *Il Carroccio* and *Columbus*, Lionello Perera & Co. purchased large slots of advertisement usually on the front pages of each edition, with the editors making flattering mention and sometimes even devoting entire articles to the bank in the inner sections.[31] It appears Lionello's company might have been at some point among the shareholders of *Il Carroccio*, though no direct evidence can be found to substantiate this claim.[32] In any case, it is notable that in all announcements, there is no mention of the company's access to the New York stock exchange, instead, they insisted particularly on two features that apparently made a much bigger impression on Italian immigrants. First and foremost, Banca Perera highlighted it was the oldest among the many Italian banks of the city, appropriating the history of Salvatore Cantoni's company, which was founded in 1865. Secondly, the advertisement often stated "banchieri autorizzati dal dipartimento bancario", stressing the fact that the company was licensed as well as controlled by State authorities.[33] This sounds ironic given the fact that Lionello was forced to conform to banking law very late, in 1914, but evidently, most Italian bankers in the city still ran non-authorised ventures.[34] With regard to its public image, the bank always tried to stress both its long tradition and Italian heritage, if one considers the aesthetics and location of the company's branches in Manhattan. When looking at the shop windows of 1907, it becomes evident that the business was for Italians, given that every sign was bilingual. Furthermore, the company was formally running its business under two names, as there was a sign stating "Lionello Perera & Co." as well as a metal badge with "Banca Cantoni" on it. This double identification can also be found on checks and letterhead, probably continuing until the bank was licensed in 1914.[35] Catering even more to the Italian community, Lionello Perera was among the first bankers to open a branch in the stronghold of East Harlem, in 1904, which held the highest density of immigrants together with Little Italy.[36] Already the 1910 census shows tens of thousands of Italians were located in these two areas, with many more scattered around the city and, by the early 1920s, the total number exceeded 800,000.[37] Most immigrants of this period were peasants of the poorer southern regions, but many were merchants and craftsmen.[38] All of them sought a safe place where to keep their savings and, possibly, send them back to relatives who had stayed in Italy. Skyrocketing business and the developing Italian community during the war allowed Banca Perera to improve the appearance of its two branches. The headquarters had moved from Banca Cantoni's original location at 49 Wall Street to number 69 already at the beginning of the century, but the increasing clientele and soaring revenues led offices to be moved into much larger premises at 63 Wall Street in Spring 1918.[39] The bank took the entire ground floor of the fashionable Sampson Building, which had a magnificent Art Deco portal with dark marble contours, clearly signalling the company's increased status (Fig. 6.3).[40] The headquarters were in the city's financial heart and close to Italian hotspots of lower Manhattan, such as the delicatessen shop Zucca, then on lower Broadway and already well-known retailers for refined Bertolli olive oil and Chianti wine imported from Tuscany. The building does not exist anymore, as it was later torn down and substituted in the development frenzy that characterised Wall Street. After the change of headquarters, Lionello planned a full refurbishment of his Harlem branch to give it a more polished aspect at the intersection of First Avenue and 116th Street, at 2261 First Avenue. In 1921, the magazine *Il Carroccio* featured the project drawn by Italian architects De Rose and Cavalieri, who planned to remake the two facades of the corner building in Renaissance style for an estimated cost of $150,000.[41] Banca Perera in Harlem was thus transformed from a friendly neighbourhood business to a distinguished Italian institution adorned with marble on the outer walls and with distinctive round arches above the first-floor windows (Fig. 6.4). The true novelty, however, was in the basement, where Lionello had safe deposit vaults installed for customers to keep their valuables in, which made this branch the first Manhattan bank to offer such a service.[42] This innovative feature went under the name of Harlem Safe Deposit & Co., officially founded in 1921, with costs for furniture and fixtures nearing $80,000.[43] Hence, by the early 1920s, the company was placed in two strategic places for Italian Americans in Manhattan, while the sign in bold letters on the buildings simply and elegantly stated: "Lionello Perera & Co. Bankers". It is telling, as well as consistent with his gentle and sympathetic character, that in the case of his East Harlem branch Lionello opted for an accessible architecture, which reminded one of a solid and fine refurbished house of the neighbourhood. This choice clearly distinguished his business from most banks of the same period that still can be found across Manhattan, which instead chose an architecture of typical classicist style, making them look like solemn and intimidating ancient temples.[44] Hence, Banca Perera was clearly different from other American banks and it stood out even among other Italian companies in the eyes of the immigrant community.

While Lionello counted among very few Italian bankers in New York at the end of the nineteenth century, during the 1920s, several new entities were established to cater to the needs of the enormous mass of Italian immigrants that had arrived over the last two decades. The oldest competitor was the Italian Savings Bank, Cassa di Risparmio Italiana, founded in 1896 by Giuseppe Francolini, an immigrant from the small southern Italian town of Viggiano in Basilicata. Similarly to Banca Perera, Francolini's company at 64 Spring Street experienced an extraordinary increase in savings during World War I.[45] The bank's development was the success of a series of Italian managers from the southern region Basilicata, who opened a branch in Harlem and, at the same time, added American personalities to the board of trustees.[46] It appears, thus, Lionello chose not by accident a southern Italian manager for his Harlem branch, Angelo Antonio Pinto from Saponara di Grumento, again in the Basilicata region, who could be considered more attuned with the then local clientele.[47] Italian finance was also represented by public owned companies such as Banca Commerciale, Banca di Sconto, Credito Italiano and Banco di Napoli.[48] Over the years also a considerable number of private bankers started doing business in town, amongst them Banca Tocci, Sessa, Verrilli, Prisco, Ferrari, Guarini, and Avalona.[49] These private banks were often tailored to specific local communities, either appealing to immigrants from the southern regions, or serving Italians living in specific areas of New York, like the Banca Sessa which operated in Brooklyn. After World War I, a number of newer companies appeared in New York –such as those led by Giannini, Sbarbaro, Berardini, Verrini, and Liccione, who adopted quite aggressive strategies of acquisition and chain banking to develop their business at the expenses of competitors and conquer a big segment of Italian savings.[50] Even some American companies opened their business to Italians, such as the Chase National Bank that had a dedicated department presided over by Salvatore Bonomidi, and the Madison State Bank which had Domenico Candela as a Vice President.[51] All these bankers and entrepreneurs moved a massive amount of money from America to Italy, both in the form of savings and bond investments, hence they were particularly interested in lobbying for friendly relationships between Italy and the United States, in order to keep the circulation of capital flowing.[52] Given the strength and wealth of Italian American bankers in New York, right from the start, the Fascist government courted these institutes, in order to let big investments flow towards Italy. Furthermore, Benito Mussolini aimed at reaching an agreement for the settlement of Italy's war debt with the United States, which in fact was reduced by almost four-fifths in 1925.[53] However, already before the inception of the Fascist regime, the Italian government had sought to get favourable treatment from America on long term loans with the help of these reputed bankers, as well as to indirectly steer the Italian American community and, through them, make internal pressure on US politicians.[54] For their part, these entrepreneurs proudly represented Italians in America and they were eager to help their fatherland, as they had in fact done during World War I. In the case of Lionello Perera, it must be said though he earned his appreciation from Italy and his status inside the immigrant community long before the advent of Mussolini, as will be extensively dealt with in the forthcoming chapters. Furthermore, the evidence collected on his banking career does not support the hypothesis of an endorsement of the Fascist government, nor does it mention any personal involvement. No public remarks by Lionello or his partners can be found favouring the new regime in Italy, a fact that rather hints at the probability he privately disapproved of the Fascists. To the contrary, Lionello had overtly supported Italy in previous years, summoning his fellow countrymen for donations during World War I by means of official letters published in widely read Italian American magazines.[55] This is important, because Lionello's public exposure in the pre-Fascist period is in stark contrast with his utter silence after the March on Rome, although he still held an important position inside the Italian American community. As a respected personality, after the mid-1920s, he still participated in activities that fostered the community's sense of belonging, though in a decidedly minor role as compared to the times of the Liberty Loan campaign. Regarding his company, evidence shows it was on the frontline of advertising Italian bonds until roughly 1924, while afterwards the bank's effort was concentrated on the extremely competitive US environment. In any case, during the 1920s it is undeniable that the Fascist government exploited the Italian Americans' genuine sense of patriotism to let hundreds of millions of Lire flow into Italy for its industrial development and –willingly or not– also to consolidate the Fascist regime.[56] In this fluid situation, it was impossible for any individual Italian banker in New York to withdraw support for Italy, because it would have seemed inexplicable in the eyes of its clientele. A bank withdrawing support for the homeland risked its Italian customers becoming disaffected. Furthermore, the US government initially gave its support to the new regime, mainly for anti-communist purposes or at least until the Fascists started an aggressive military campaign to colonise Ethiopia in the 1930s.[57] The intention here is not to understate or downplay the role, influence, and money of the Italian American community in supporting Italy during the inception of fascism, as well as in shaping the latter's initial relationship with the USA. The point here is to show the complexity of the situation, which saw numerous Italian entrepreneurs in New York and even more immigrants reacting to the rapidly evolving economic and political events in their homeland –at times tentatively and at times with due awareness.

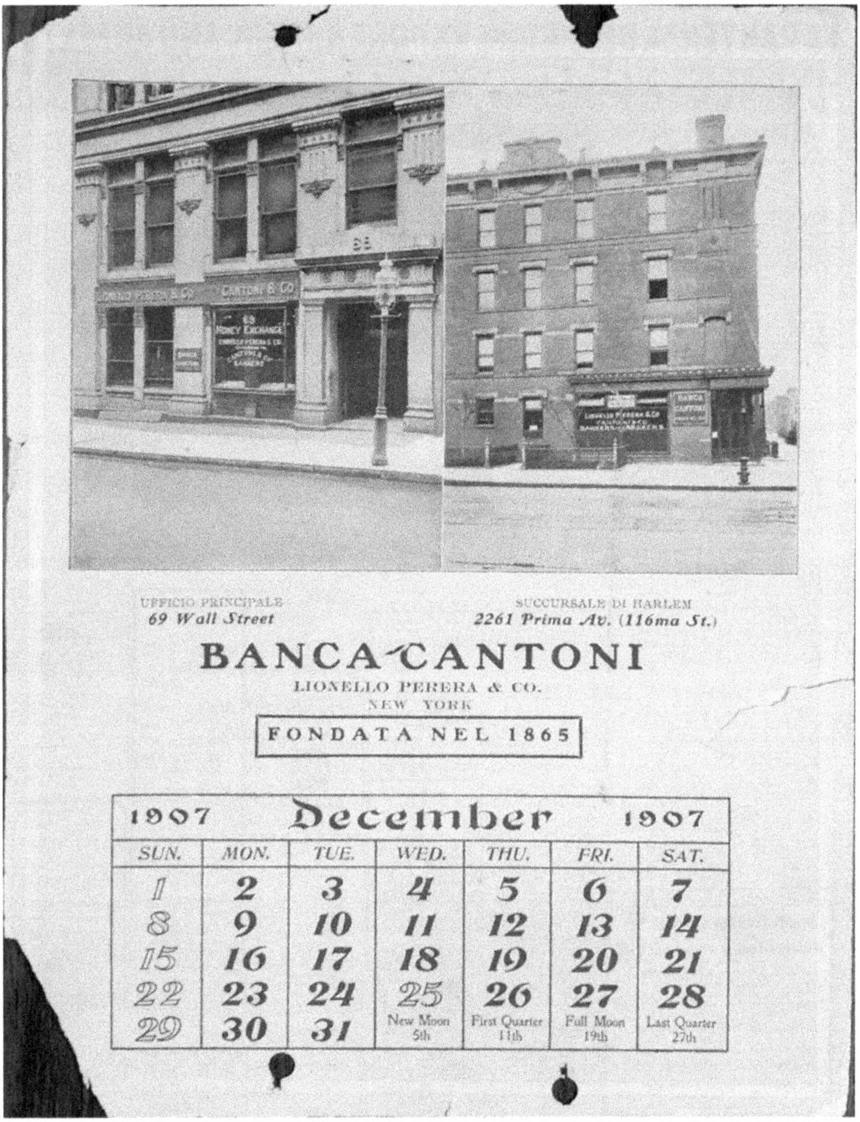

Figure 6.1: Calendar picture of Lionello Perera & Co. (1907)

December page from the calendar of Lionello Perera & Co., also called Banca Cantoni at the time, showing its Wall Street (left) and East Harlem (right) branches in 1907. (Courtesy of the Perera Family Archive)

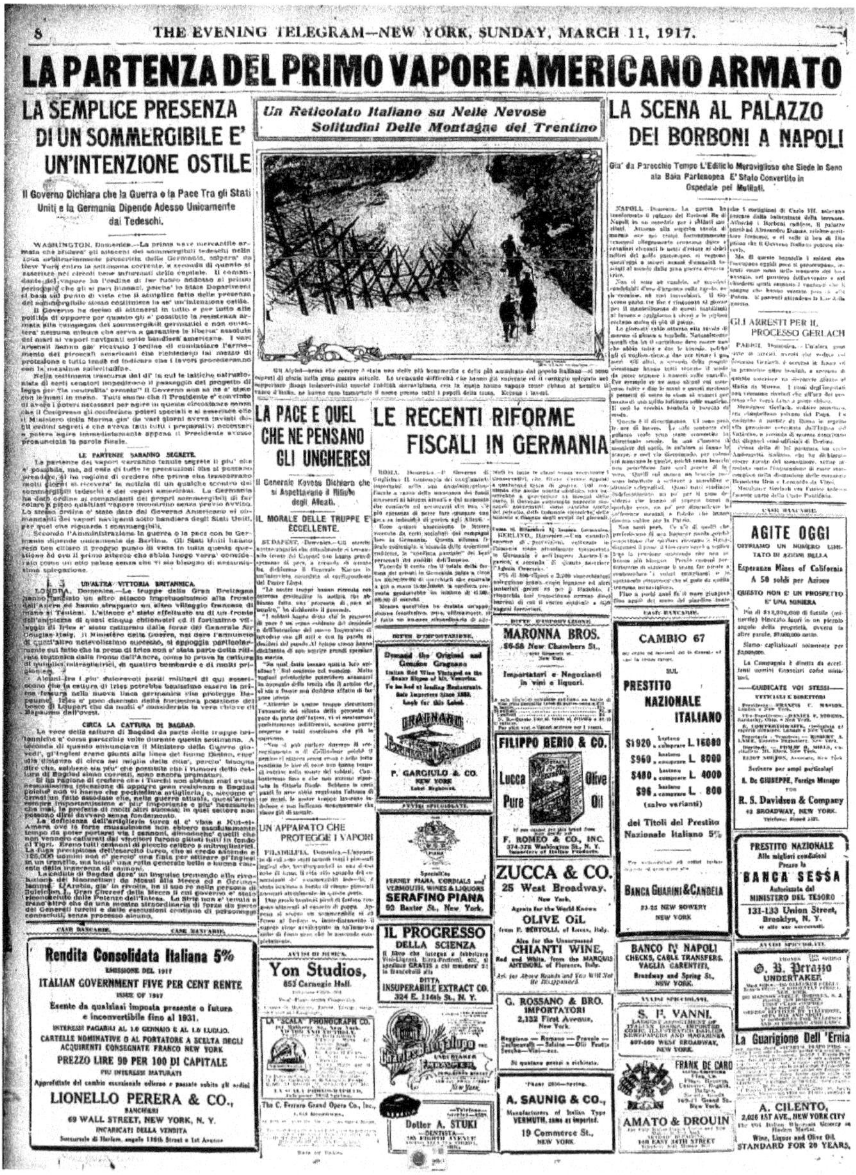
8 THE EVENING TELEGRAM—NEW YORK, SUNDAY, MARCH 11, 1917.

LA PARTENZA DEL PRIMO VAPORE AMERICANO ARMATO

LA SEMPLICE PRESENZA DI UN SOMMERGIBILE E' UN'INTENZIONE OSTILE

Il Governo Dichiara che la Guerra o la Pace Tra gli Stati Uniti e la Germania Dipende Adesso Unicamente dai Tedeschi.

Un Reticolato Italiano su Nelle Nevose Solitudini Delle Montagne del Trentino

LA SCENA AL PALAZZO DEI BORBONI A NAPOLI

LA PACE E QUEL CHE NE PENSANO GLI UNGHERESI

LE RECENTI RIFORME FISCALI IN GERMANIA

GLI ARRESTI PER IL PROCESSO GERLACH

UN APPARATO CHE PROTEGGE I VAPORI

AGITE OGGI

MARONNA BROS.

CAMBIO 67

PRESTITO NAZIONALE ITALIANO

FILIPPO BERIO & CO.

ZUCCA & CO.

IL PROGRESSO DELLA SCIENZA

Yon Studios,

BANCO DI NAPOLI

BANCA SESSA

Rendita Consolidata Italiana 5%

ITALIAN GOVERNMENT FIVE PER CENT RENTE

PREZZO LIRE 90 PER 100 DI CAPITALE

LIONELLO PERERA & CO.,

69 WALL STREET, NEW YORK, N. Y.

A. SAUNIG & CO.,

AMATO & DROUIN

A. CILENTO,

Figure 6.2: Front page of the Italian edition of the Evening Telegram (1917)

Page number eight of the *Evening Telegram* dated March 11, 1917, which served as the front page of its Italian edition showing an advertisement of considerable size paid for by Lionello Perera & Co. in the lower-left corner. (Courtesy of the Perera Family Archive)

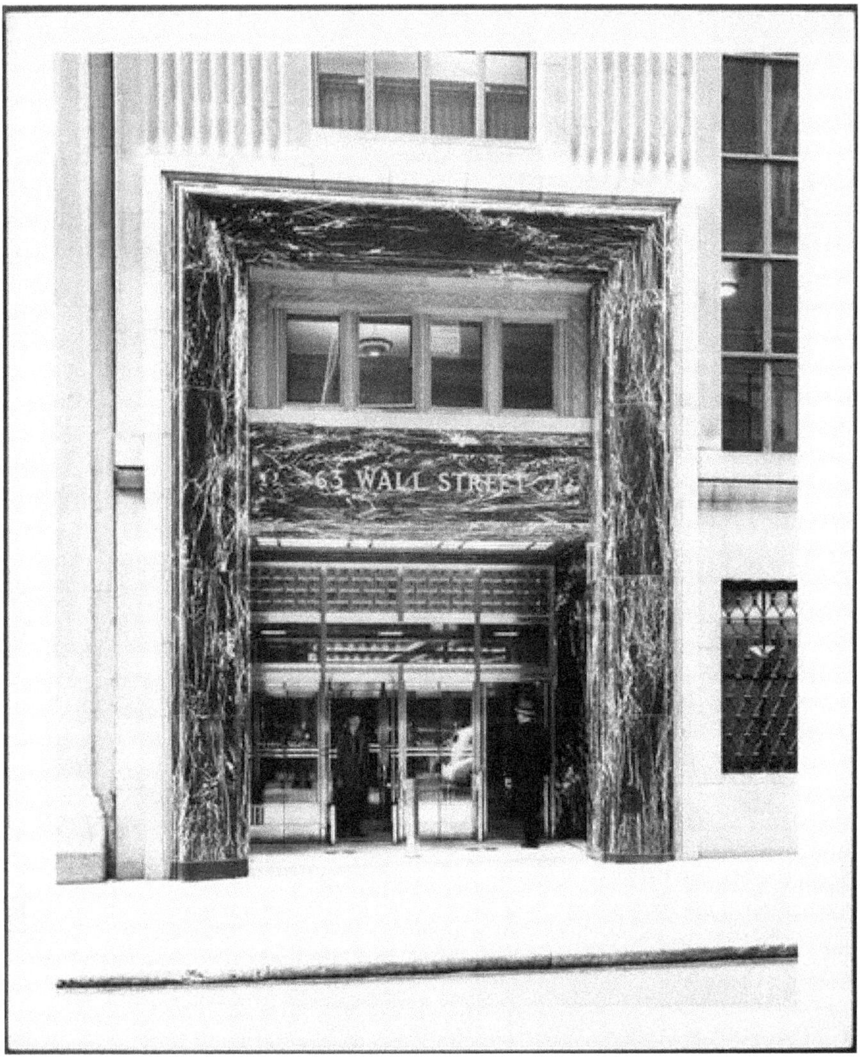

Figure 6.3: Sampson Building entrance at 63 Wall Street (ca. 1920)

Photograph of the Sampson Building entrance in Art Deco style built with Italian marble for the headquarters of Lionello Perera & Co. at 63 Wall Street, New York, probably in the early 1920s. (Courtesy of the Perera Family Archive)

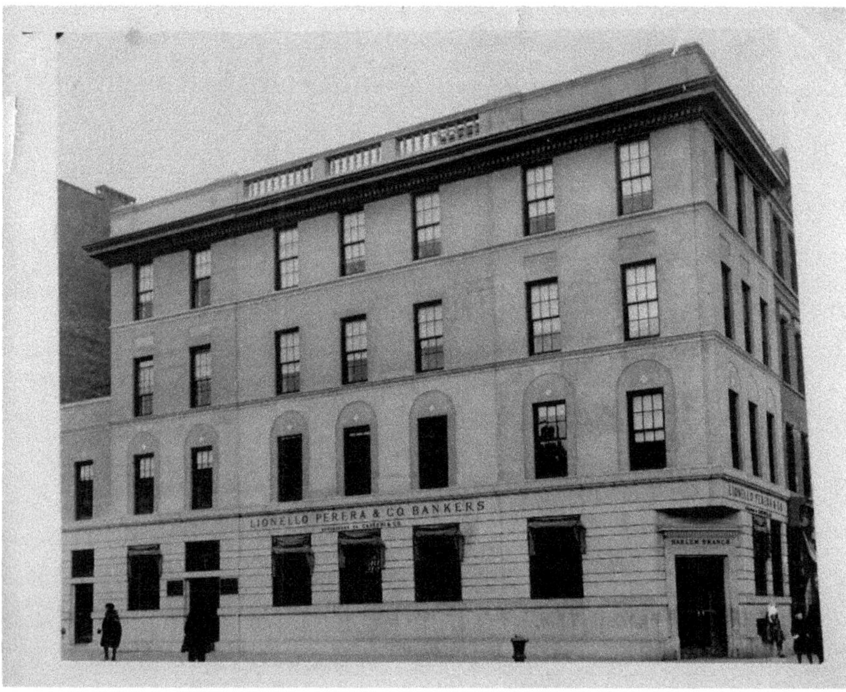

Figure 6.4: Harlem branch of Lionello Perera & Co. (1921)

Photograph of the Harlem branch of Lionello Perera & Co. after refurbishment works in Italian Neo-Renaissance style by Italian architects De Rose and Cavalieri. The building still exists at the intersection of First Avenue and 116th Street, at 2261 First Avenue. (Courtesy of the Perera Family Archive)

Chapter 7

Turbulences, Mergers, and Bank of America

A fierce battle for the hearts, minds, and money of Italian immigrants was raging across New York City between the two world wars, as many bankers acted as loyal Italians to win over their many kinsmen for their savings. It was a difficult situation to navigate, but Lionello Perera & Co. had the advantage of being the oldest and most reliable private bank for Italian Americans in New York and the entire State. Tradition matters for Italians, so there was a good chance that things would develop smoothly over the coming years, but suddenly this certainty was shattered. In the early morning hours of February 21, 1924, the East Harlem branch was visited by a long line of customers asking to withdraw all their savings. The outflow of capital started as a trickle and became a torrent. Italians standing at the door of the bank soon were hundreds in a panicking mob. A bank run had unexpectedly hit Lionello's company and, at first, it seemed unstoppable. This shocking event would have profound consequences for the future of the Perera Bank. Given the frenzy around bank runs, police were sent to quell the crowd and several journalists followed close on their heels. A number of newspaper articles can be compared with family recollections about that distant day, in February 1924, that threatened to ruin what Lionello had patiently built over almost three decades.

According to various accounts, from the early morning hours customers lined up at the Perera Bank in East Harlem to ask about the solvency of the company, while many more withdrew their deposits altogether.[1] The tellers tried to accommodate every demand, but long before noon, the branch director Mr. Pinto, either Angelo or his brother Frank, noticed withdrawal requests were unusually high.[2] Meanwhile, a large crowd had gathered in front of the building at the junction of 1st Avenue and 116th Street asking for the return of their savings. The manager set out to confront his clients, mostly Italians from the district, and enquired as to why they were showing up on that particular day and, above all, why they were doubting the bank's solidity. He did not get satisfactory answers, until one small business owner in the neighbourhood confessed, he had received an unsettling phone call the night before.[3] An unknown person, pretending to be 'a friend', advised to withdraw all savings from the Perera Bank, insinuating that the company was failing.[4] A few other customers confirmed the story, having also received the same information in an anonymous phone call. The rumour rapidly spread among the Italian clientele of Lionello Perera and, out of the blue, the bank was in the eye of the storm. Given the growing number of depositors rushing to the branch, it was necessary to call out the police reserves from the East 128th Street station to maintain order.[5] At this point, Pinto decided to stop withdrawals at the bank and informed Lionello of the situation straight away. To the manager's surprise, at the news of the panic developing in East Harlem the founder of the bank responded with a countermand. In fact, he urged Pinto to immediately reopen the teller and hand out money to everyone who asked for it, in order to restore the depositors' confidence in the bank's solvency.[6] Lionello's counterintuitive suggestion came from a deep understanding of his customers, who were hardworking Italian immigrants clearly afraid of losing all their savings. He then set forth to reach East Harlem by car from his headquarters at 63 Wall Street bringing as much cash as possible stuffed in several suitcases. He even called his wife Carolyn to reach the branch with some more apparent cash in suitcases stuffed with newspapers.[7] Arriving at 2261 First Avenue, Lionello stepped on the entrance stairs and addressed the hundreds of depositors at the door, trying to calm them and reassuring them there was no reason to worry for the bank's solvency.[8] He soon gave up, though, because of the excitement of the crowd. Words could not mitigate their fear, only the sight of money could do miracles. The banker instructed his employees to pile high in the teller windows all the bundles of notes he had brought from Wall Street.[9] Furthermore, Lionello declared to the papers that $1,500,000 in cash was on hand to meet all demands and that the bank would return savings to everyone who requested a full refund.[10] He also added that rumours were completely unfounded and that an official investigation was underway to discover who had spread the falsehood.[11] In the afternoon, depositors were still queuing to withdraw their money, but many felt reassured by the presence of the bank's founder, as well as by his prompt and reasonable reaction. By the end of the day, a counter-line had formed in front of the building, of customers returning their savings to the Perera Bank.[12] On the first day of the banking panic, approximately $350,000 had been withdrawn, while $100,000 had promptly been re-deposited.[13] In the coming days, many depositors came back to deposit almost the full amount that had previously been withdrawn and, on February 26, 1924, the run on the bank had subsided.

Thanks to the preparedness and response of its founder, Lionello Perera & Co. had survived a dangerous run. The event constituted a major news topic over the next few days in New York, with some reassuring articles probably prompted by Lionello himself to restore confidence in his company (Fig. 7.1). *The New York Times* recalled the widespread banking panic of 1907, when sieges like the one experienced in East Harlem were common.[14] However, the journalist Anne Seward stressed the fact that thanks to the Federal reserve law, which enhanced systemic liquidity, bank failures were very rare by then and thus should not be the cause of serious worry. As recent economic surveys have shown, panics in the United States were instead not at all rare in the 1920s, but rather on the rise again, because American banking business substantially differed from that of European countries.[15] The article published in *The New York Times* was an understatement probably aimed at reassuring depositors at a time when the finance market was increasingly perceived as unstable. A pamphlet in favour of the Perera Bank was also published on the pages of the Italian American magazine *Columbus*.[16] Written by the editor Vincenzo Campora in first person, the Banca Perera was presented as a solid and reliable company, which had been hit by malicious rumours. Lionello himself was depicted as a prominent and trustworthy figure, a true founding father of the Italian community in New York, while his uncle Salvatore Cantoni was called a pioneer. Campora's message was aimed directly at Italian Americans to correct false perceptions about Lionello Perera & Co.'s solvency, which in fact was in good shape. Of course, the company could not have paid out every depositor at once, because liabilities were for the most part invested in public and private securities, bonds, and shares. Nevertheless, the bank had enough liquidity at the time and the rumour was undoubtedly orchestrated maliciously, most likely by a business rival. As has been argued in the previous chapter, during the 1920s banking activities that catered to the needs of Italian nationals soared exponentially with many new businesses competing for the savings of the immigrant community. Several depositors leaving the Perera East Harlem branch, on February 21, immediately tried to open an account at the private bank of Raffaele Prisco located downtown at 73 Mulberry Street, in the heart of Little Italy. Just one day before the bank run, it had been announced that Police Commissioner Richard E. Enright was to sit on the Prisco Bank board of directors and that the company would soon be organised as a state bank.[17] The size of Raffaele Prisco's company, reorganised under State banking law in 1914, was however hardly comparable to the Perera Bank. Still in 1918, while Lionello opened his new premises in the elegant building at 63-65 Wall Street, the Prisco Bank had liabilities at best of just $143,643 with business not doing much better in the forthcoming years.[18] A much bigger competitor in 1924 was the Italian Savings Bank, which might have profited from the sudden failure of Lionello Perera & Co. The company originally founded by Giuseppe Francolini, deceased in 1920, was planning the inauguration of its new headquarters in lower Manhattan, on Lafayette Street at the corner with Spring Street. On September 28, 1925, the twelve-storey building with an imposing entrance, was inaugurated in grand style. On that same day, Italians rushed to open new accounts and deposited a total of $200,000.[19]

It is impossible, of course, to find the smoking gun in the case of the Perera Bank run, but the important point in this event is how easily a banking panic could be unleashed in the 1920s, either on purpose or by chance. Lionello's efficient reaction also hints at the fact he was accustomed to bank runs. Having personally experienced the turmoil of 1907, he seemed prepared to face a run if it hit his own company. Eventually, the episode set off an alarm and definitively influenced subsequent decisions on how to further develop the Perera business in this strongly competitive, as well as uncertain environment. A brief insight to the mechanics of banking panics is due, given that such events characterised banking in the United States for an entire century, roughly between 1825 and the Great Depression.[20] The US banking system prior to the 1930s can be seen as a result of private or government reactions to unexpected crises, which were in fact rooted in the very laws that regulated financial activities across the Federation.[21] First, the definition of a 'banking panic' must be stated, as economists maintain it is of higher level than the term 'bank run', and not synonymous. For a banking turmoil to be recognised as a panic it requires a significant number of banks be involved. If only one bank is affected, the event is defined as a run, which evidently does not spread over to the entire system.[22] It is relevant to distinguish these two terms, because the history of banking panics comprises an important series of disruptions that affected one or more States. In this period, a very high number of single companies also failed. Past surveys showed that seven major banking panics occurred at a quite accelerating pace –in the years 1857, 1873, 1884, 1890, 1893, 1896, and 1907. Hence, economists such as Charles Calomiris and Gary Gorton maintain that panics were actually short-lived moments of confusion generated by insolvency or a loss, thus resulted in few bank failures as compared to the Great Depression.[23] More recent economic studies add another twenty minor panics in single cities or local communities with very disruptive effects.[24] In the case of New York City alone, for example, Andrew Jalil identifies two other severe panics after the major one of 1907.[25] The latter was caused by trust companies that had misappropriated funds and overpriced stocks, with consequences then spreading to the entire country. A year later and then again in 1914, at the outbreak of World War I, the city was hit by two more crises. There is agreement amongst economists about the general circumstance that no major panic occurred in the 1920s, but opinions on the financial situation of the decade preceding the stock market crash differ widely. For instance, Charles Calomiris and Joseph Mason initially thought that shocks in these years were due to loan losses in agricultural banks, thus geographically isolated and relatively transparent.[26] However, later research into banking panics showed they were much more widespread and usually occurred in overbanked States, that is, those with too many individual banks and very few chain banking organisations.[27] Jalil's new panic series offers a wider picture of single bank runs and failures that contained the clear symptoms of general instability over the entire decade and which eventually burst on Black Tuesday, 1929.[28] Regardless of which interpretation is more accurate in describing the financial situation of the 1920s, these studies help in understanding the mindset of a banker like Lionello Perera who had outlived one major and two minor banking panics in New York alone. Bankers working in the US financial sector at the beginning of the twentieth century lived in constant fear. It was not a question of *if*, but rather *when* a systemic panic would occur in their business lifetime, perhaps even directly involving their company in a bank run. This might explain the remarkable preparedness Lionello showed on the occasion of the troubles that struck his East Harlem branch in February 1924. Furthermore, this general atmosphere accounts for the choices he made in the immediate aftermath of the bank run and are consistent with the opinions of economists studying the financial market of that decade. Given that crises were part of the everyday experience for American bankers, over the years, companies searched for solutions to the problem, such as group, chain and branch banking, either within one State or in more than one State.[29] Although the structural frailty of the banking system was driven by the relatively small size of companies, the US government was especially suspicious of large banks until after the Great Depression.[30] The reason perhaps lay in the belief that big financial corporations might influence the industrial development of the Federation to the detriment of political power, and similarly, many governors disliked the idea of a banking monopoly in their own State.[31] US law prohibited nationwide branch banking, and most States even barred or limited branches within one single State. Hence, companies were extremely numerous and unable to coordinate their behaviour to prevent panics.[32] In the 1920s, however, government control was more relaxed, and bankers chose consolidation and mergers to overcome the faults of the financial system, thus lowering the risk of individual failure. This means that companies tried to grow bigger either by acquiring other banks or by founding multi-branch groups together with partner banks. For the same reason, there was also a growing mixture of commercial activity and investment banks. Statistics for this decade show that the number of US banks investing in securities grew from 277 in 1922 to almost 600 in 1929, while mergers and acquisitions went up both from roughly 180 to well over 570 each year.[33] Clearly, bankers tried to defend their businesses by buying smaller companies or by forming alliances with same-size banks to reduce the impact of local crises.

In the case of Lionello Perera, the bank run of February 21, 1924, came as a wake-up call that convinced him to initiate a complex process of subsequent acquisitions and mergers to strengthen his business. Between 1926 and 1928, it is impossible to say whether he acted on a deliberate plan from the beginning, or if he reacted piecemeal to emerging opportunities. In either case, it becomes apparent that he relied on his established contacts among Italian American bankers, particularly Attilio (or Albert) H. Giannini, the brother of the ambitious California-based banker Amadeo Peter Giannini. The latter was a much-talked-about rising star in the American financial community of the West Coast, who firmly believed in the strength of branch banking and dreamed of establishing a first-ever nationwide bank.[34] What is known today of Giannini's life and business was mostly derived from his personal archives at Bank of America, being disclosed with restraints and thus considered as generally biased in favour of the Giannini narrative.[35] There are, however, a number of historical records, such as the Hearings of the US House Committee on Banking and Currency after the stock market crash, as well as recent critical analyses that allow a deeper understanding of his character and business attitude.[36] Amadeo Peter Giannini was born in California on May 6, 1870, to immigrants from Genoa and, as a child, lost his father. He entered the commercial sector at fourteen as a salesman for his Italian stepfather Lorenzo Scatena, supplying fruit and vegetables for ships transiting at the port of San Francisco.[37] Rather than going to university, he learned the business on the ground, recognising the value of keeping close contact with immigrants, assisting them through the ups and downs of business life, cherishing their aspirations. Despite differences in their upbringing, Amadeo and Lionello had much in common, like a general mistrust towards the kind of American banking that left little depositors on the fringes.[38] Overall their business attitude was comparable, especially since they had grown strong on an Italian clientele, though their kinsmen on opposing coasts of the continent had their differences. While the Perera Bank catered to the needs of small Italian businessmen squeezed in the metropolis, Giannini's venture specialised in loan services to immigrant peasants dispersed in the agricultural sector of California.[39] Furthermore, the many Italians on the Atlantic Coast were on average of lower-income and constantly connected with their homeland, especially through wire transfer of their savings. On the contrary, the fewer immigrants that had arrived on the Pacific Coast were determined to stay, thus opening a good number of businesses and other holdings.[40] After having worked in various companies, in 1904, Giannini founded his own small corner branch in San Francisco, optimistically calling it Bank of Italy.[41] He started with a small number of farmers, mostly of Italian descent, and over the years, became the prime lender in Californian agriculture.[42] The story –or rather the myth– goes that, after the disastrous earthquake of 1907, Giannini saved most of the deposits from the remains of his bank and was able to reopen business in the port of San Francisco straight away, lending money especially to the poorest.[43] He was a maverick and anti-elitist in his loan policy, and equally so in his eye-catching advertising campaigns, which appealed to the average

Italian American reader rather than to high-end investors.[44] In 1909 Giannini opened his second branch in San José and then started acquiring offices all over California, either by the purchase of existing banks or by building new branches.[45] His interest in branch banking predated his involvement in the financial sector, since he had experienced the benefit of a branch structure already in commerce, at his stepfather's company Scatena & Co.[46] During the 1910s, Giannini's branch ideology led him to attempt state-wide coverage, which earned him strenuous opposition from independent banks and rival branch systems. Competitors in California soon charged the Bank of Italy of seeking a financial monopoly and accused Giannini of using intimidation to acquire banks, though these allegations remained unproven and were of course categorically denied by Giannini himself.[47]

Expanding in California was not Giannini's final goal, since in 1917 he announced to the New York-based magazine *Il Carroccio* that he intended to branch out in Manhattan by means of a subsidiary company, which had the same trustees as the Bank of Italy.[48] Right after World War I, the Giannini brothers launched their acquisition campaign in New York, first of all through the foundation of the Bancitaly Corporation in 1919.[49] This corporation allowed Amadeo to secure a foothold in the East as early as 1921 by purchasing the majority shares of the old East River National Bank, founded in 1865.[50] At the time, it was a relatively small institution with resources of about $3,500,000 and Attilio was named president.[51] The Gianninis were determined to enter the Manhattan finance sector in a leading position, which certainly made them clash with many bankers who had earned a stable position in the city, especially among Italian Americans. However, their relationship to Lionello Perera, who was the biggest Italian banker in town at the time, must have been one of friendly rivalry and reciprocal respect, perhaps even of tentative collaboration. In fact, on June 20, 1921, Lionello and Attilio were special guests at the Biltmore Hotel on the occasion of a luncheon given by the Italy America Society in honour of Richard Washburn Child, the newly nominated US Ambassador to Italy.[52] At the table with them were other prominent members of the Italian American community, such as the High Commissioner for Italy in the United States, Francesco Quattrone, and the recently elected President of the New York City Board of Aldermen, Fiorello La Guardia. On this occasion, perhaps, the two bankers were already discussing the benefits of chain banking and the opportunity to organise a federal association of Italian banks in North America. In any case, the prospect of a nationwide alliance was certainly premature, because the Perera Bank needed to consolidate its rapid expansion in deposits, while Amadeo Giannini was busy fighting California State lawmakers that tried to coerce him into stopping his explosive growth, obtained by means of branch and chain banking.[53] Despite the Gianninis competitive attitude, it is unlikely they were behind the Perera Bank run of 1924, especially because Amadeo's banking ideology contrasted with the idea of putting little Italian depositors at risk. If Lionello had failed, the savings of many Italian Americans would have been lost, so the Gianninis could hardly have profited from it. On the contrary, Lionello's prompt reaction in the bank run had shown the two California-born brothers that in New York there was no way around the Venetian banker to get at the deposits of the Italian community. In addition, Amadeo Giannini needed the strongest Italian American bank in New York, such as Lionello Perera & Co., to have a loyal associate that could assist him in uniting the two Coasts. Discussions on a nationwide collaboration probably intensified after February 1924, with Attilio surely trying to convince Lionello that a consortium of banks and branches would have consolidated his own business too. Having survived a perilous bank run, Lionello Perera was probably keen to listen to this kind of proposal and, in fact, he was preparing for the consolidation of his company. In 1925, however, Amadeo Giannini was not ready to embark on a nationwide association of banks yet. Back in California he was stuck in preliminary procedures, attempting to obtain permission to merge his subsidiary companies, the Liberty Bank and the Bank of America of Los Angeles, with the Bank of Italy, a plan that generated a heated debate during the California gubernatorial race in 1926.[54]

The goal to establish the first nationwide banking association had probably been decided as early as 1924 or 1925, but the delicate situation and the many rivals against such an achievement required caution. Lionello Perera and the Giannini brothers needed to play it by ear and see how events evolved, step by step, in order to seize opportunities as they appeared. What followed was a head-swirling spate of financial operations and new banking ventures. For the readership's ease, in the next pages of this chapter all company names are set in quotation marks at their first appearance, since they match the exact historical trademark filed in US bank registers. Furthermore, a comprehensive diagram provides a convenient visual pattern describing the development of the Perera and Giannini businesses respectively (Fig. 7.2). Looking at the various events involving Lionello's company, between 1926 and 1928, it becomes clear he relied on a premeditated strategy, likely coordinated with Amadeo and Attilio. Retracing this development is quite tricky though, as it is not clear what exactly was agreed upon between the cooperating companies. The frequent intermingle of trustees and associates among banks, as well as official announcements made to the press all give a vague idea concerning the nature of the operations carried out, leaving doubts about whether they were genuine mergers or straightforward acquisitions. This was probably part of the game to keep the relationship among shareholders as smooth as possible and proceed swiftly towards the final consolidation. Even the special House Committee on Branch and Chain Banking in the early 1930s had to dig deep into various company records to understand how Amadeo Giannini arrived so quickly at the foundation of Bank of America National Association, in 1928, with the cooperation of Lionello Perera and a few other Italian bankers of New York.[55] On Lionello's part, his first move was the transformation of his company into the "Commercial Exchange Bank of New York", established on August 31, 1926.[56] He was still head of the bank and had all his trusted associates, such as his nephews Mario and Guido Perera, as well as Angelo and Frank Pinto. This step may be explained by the fact that the previous company was a private bank under the name of Lionello Perera, but it needed to become a trust in order to take part in a national banking association.[57] *The New York Times* noted that "Bancitaly Corporation", owned by the Giannini brothers, had officially expressed their interest in the new company.[58] At the time of its consolidation in 1926, the Commercial Exchange Bank owned resources of $18,000,000, and a few months later, it led to the acquisition of the second-largest Italian private bank of the city, "Sessa Bank of Brooklyn" with resources of $5,000,000.[59] The papers underlined the operation was a merger, and not a consolidation, probably because Lionello did not want to antagonise his long-time competitor Anthony Sessa.[60] Instead, he hoped he would join in the bigger cause of the forthcoming national association with the Gianninis. In any case, on January 3, 1927, Sessa Bank was incorporated into the Commercial Exchange Bank and the latter filed for participation into the Bancitaly Corporation presided by Attilio Giannini. While Lionello was putting together the biggest Italian American bankers of the city, the Gianninis were acquiring all sorts of commercial banks in New York. Among these were smaller ventures such as the "Commercial National Bank of New York" in 1924, then in 1925 the "Old Colony Stat Bank" and the "National Bank of Bay Ridge", eventually the "Richmond Borough National Bank" in 1926. More important were the acquisition by the Bancitaly Corporation of the "Bowery Savings Bank" in 1925 and the "Discount National Bank" in 1926, thus developing into the "Bowery East River National Bank" with resources of about $100,000,000.[61] From 1926 onwards, the Gianninis started buying shares of Lionello's bank, finally converting it into the "Federal Commercial Exchange National Bank in New York" on March 1, 1928.[62] Thanks to the merger with Lionello, Amadeo and Attilio were physically allowed into Wall Street for the first time, gaining also access to the New York stock market.[63] Given the company had grown much bigger and richer, Lionello set forth to build an entire new building at 70 Wall Street, again furnished with classy Italian marble, to host both the Commercial Exchange National Bank and the Bancitaly Corporation on twelve floors.[64] He must have been very proud of finally having his own spot built in Wall Street. It seemed to be the peak of his banking activity after three decades in the business.

The new venue was not yet finished when everything changed in the blink of an eye. The building at 70 Wall Street was never to be used by Lionello and the Gianninis, because in the winter months of 1928, Amadeo seized the opportunity to accelerate on his aim to consolidate a nationwide banking company. What happened was that he eventually got hold of the majority shares of "Bank of America" in New York, with the informal permission of J. Pierpont Morgan, thus controlling the direct successor to the "First Bank of the United States" founded in 1791.[65] In February, Bancitaly had persuaded Ralph Jones and associates to sell their 35,000 shares at $510 each, which gave Giannini control over the total of 65,000 outstanding shares of the entire stock.[66] The takeover bid was vehemently opposed by the remaining shareholders who joined President Edward C. Delafield and together, they attempted to avert being replaced by Amadeo.[67] The latter thus needed to quickly merge Bank of America with his other Italian associates in New York to consolidate its majority of shares. In March the board of the Bowery and East River National Bank, with roughly $106,000,000 resources, and also the trustees of the Federal Commercial Exchange Bank, with its $45,000,000 of resources, opted for the definitive consolidation into Bank of America, which instead owned $167,000,000 of resources, becoming altogether a National Association.[68] Lionello's company held a special meeting with its shareholders at 44 Wall Street, the Bank of America's headquarters, of course, to confirm this decision.[69] On April 1, 1928, the constitution of the new "Bank of America National Association" was eventually announced, being the first bank to operate on the entire continent. To satisfy the minority shareholders, Delafield was confirmed as President, while Lionello Perera was given the position of Vice President in recognition of his standing among Italian American bankers. Amadeo Giannini had scored a tremendous victory by purchasing Bank of America, because its name and position in Wall Street were fundamental to take on the role of a national banking institution.[70] The name Bank of Italy simply would not have appealed to American depositors. Amadeo further needed the presence of Lionello, a loyal Italian and experienced Wall Street banker, to control the company and keep balance among the shareholders. As a matter of fact, the extraordinary aspect of this merger was that Italian American bankers lay behind the foundation of the first-ever national bank in the United States. Then Amadeo dissolved Bancitaly and founded "Transamerica Corporation" to consolidate all his shares in various banking businesses across the country.[71] In the aftermath of the stock market crash Bank of America was not significantly affected, but the numerous mergers and acquisitions of the 1920s came under scrutiny at the House Committee on Banking and Currency that investigated the reasons of Black Tuesday. Between May 6 and 8, 1930, Henry B. Steagall of Alabama summoned Amadeo Giannini to the committee hearings on group, chain and branch banking. The hearings offered the opportunity to understand the financial strategy adopted by Bancitaly and its successor Transamerica Corporation, although no concrete evidence of fraud or mischief was found.[72] Soon after, though, the Great Depression started to affect the assets of Giannini's company structure, especially in California where he had left the business in control of Elisha Walker, who won over shareholders and ousted Amadeo in the fall of 1931.[73] Part of Walker's strategy was to capitalise on selling out pieces of Transamerica Corporation, commencing with the New York branch despite the strenuous opposition of Amadeo. The unity of Bank of America was doomed, despite the will of the Gianninis and Lionello, who could not avoid a hostile takeover by Charles Mitchell, the head of the then-largest bank in America, the "National City Bank". The consolidation was staged as a merger on November 1, 1931, through which the "Federal National City Bank of New York" was founded, the direct ancestor of today's "Citigroup".[74] Mitchell needed fresh money and stable assets to fill in the gaps he had caused by tampering with City Bank's stocks, which eventually had caused the market crash in 1929. Indeed, in 1932 Ferdinand Pecora, chief counsel to the US Senate's Committee on Banking and Currency, called Mitchell as his first witness on the hearings setting off a true media campaign against the irresponsible 'banksters' of Wall Street.[75] Senator Carter Glass of Virginia commented that Mitchell, more than any fifty men, was responsible for the stock crash.[76] It took several more years for Amadeo Giannini to win over control of his former corporation and put Bank of America back on track to become one of the biggest companies of the country.[77] After the hostile takeover bid, Lionello Perera decided to retire for good, as he evidently did not want to serve under Mitchell and his acolytes. First, however, he made provisions for all his children and grandchildren. No physical traces remain of his company in Wall Street, because all buildings were redeveloped after just a few years. The East Harlem building, instead, still exists and, until today, it is a branch of the Citigroup that took it over in 1931. It stands as a silent memory of those long-lost days, when the war between bankers was raging across New York City.

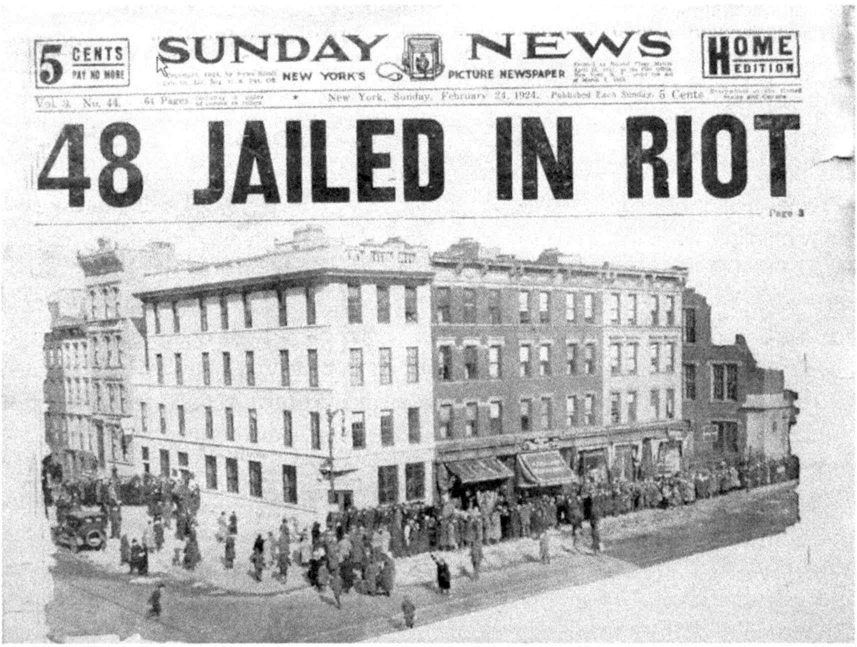
5 CENTS PAY NO MORE

SUNDAY NEWS

NEW YORK'S PICTURE NEWSPAPER

HOME EDITION

Vol. 3. No. 44. 64 Pages New York, Sunday, February 24, 1924. Published Each Sunday. 5 Cents

48 JAILED IN RIOT

Page 3

Figure 7.1: Front page of the Sunday News with bank run picture (1924)
Newspaper clipping from the front page of the *Sunday News*, dated February 24, 1924, showing a picture of the bank run that occurred to the Harlem branch of Lionello Perera & Co. The headline shown is though for a different story on page three. (Courtesy of the Perera Family Archive)

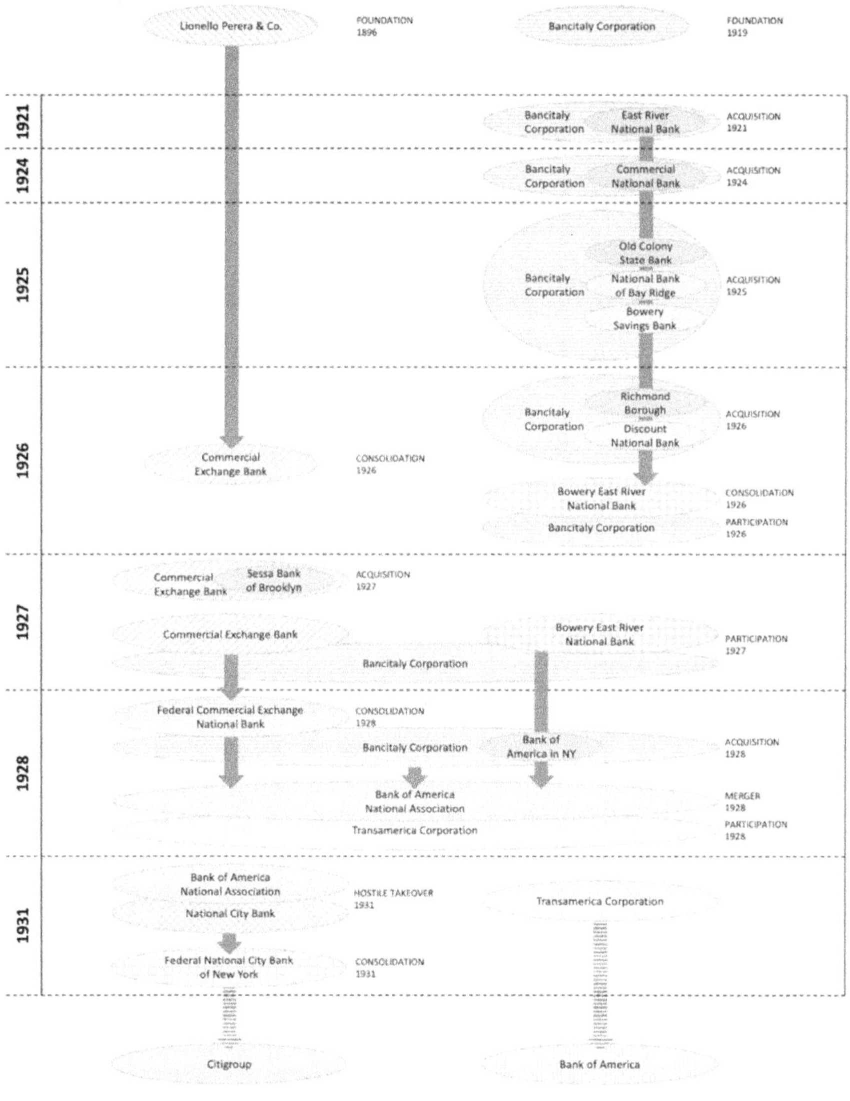

Figure 7.2: Financial operations towards Bank of America (1921-31)

Diagram showing the subsequent financial operations of merger and acquisition by Lionello Perera & Co. (left side) and the Giannini brothers' Bancitaly Corporation (right side) that occurred in the State of New York since 1919 and finally led to the foundation of Bank of America National Association in 1928, as well as further to the hostile takeover by the forerunner of Citigroup. (Designed by the author upon the analysis of company records and newspaper articles)

Part III: A Discreet Patron and Benefactor

Chapter 8

Of Drawings, Caricatures, and Portraits

Lionello Perera's good fortune in business, as well as his cultural upbringing and social status made him a passionate patron of the arts. At a first glance, the rich materials from family recollections and newspapers suggest his interest lay mainly in the field of classical music, particularly in Italian opera. He was a talented mandolin player and shared a passion for music with his wife Carolyn Allen Perera, a violin player. Hence, as a couple, music was a common denominator and played an integral part in their family life and social contacts, which singled them out in New York as well-known patrons.[1] Lionello's lure of visual arts remained personal, an individual passion he cultivated into a true expertise, particularly with regard to eighteenth-century genre painting, as well as to nineteenth-century European Naturalism.[2] He thus became a major collector of scenes by Venetian painter Pietro Longhi, a very specific choice that probably reminded him of the glorious past of his hometown. These exquisite paintings highlighted his refined taste for collecting and were publicly displayed at important American museums, such as at the Metropolitan Museum of Art in 1938.[3] The particular choice of Venetian Settecento matched him with other big American collectors like J. Pierpont Morgan.[4] In the first decades of the twentieth century, most collectors and newly founded institutions in the United States were trying to surpass one another by finding new trends and niches for their collections. Lionello's understanding of art and his taste thus reflect the formative stage of the American bourgeoisie, when museums and private collectors set out to buy Old Masters and Academic Art to be displayed in dedicated buildings. Lionello's case is special in that he commissioned a unique Art Deco home in the heart of Manhattan in order to house his collection. This new home, which he built in 1929, at the height of his banking career, was carefully designed to become a Modernist mansion in every detail, from the facade to the interiors, thus displaying an avant-garde cultural attitude. With regard to contemporary artists, Lionello concentrated mostly on artists of Italian descent, such as Giovanni Viafora and Arturo Noci, or those who could provide portraits, copies of famous masterpieces, and other kinds of paintings on commission. His attitude towards living artists was based both on personal commissions or buying finished artworks, further eagerly participating in societies of artists and art lovers, such as the Salmagundi Club founded in 1871.[5] Family recollections indeed mention Lionello's passion for art and direct involvement with specialist associations. He is remembered for buying paintings from members of the Salmagundi Club, to support their careers, or he would accept artworks as collateral for bank loans. The contacts he developed cast an interesting perspective on an artist milieu striving to find a clientele among the New York elite in the early twentieth century. Besides buying paintings, perhaps the most specialised artistic passion of the Italian banker was drawings and caricatures, which he collected in great numbers throughout his lifetime. They were portraits and cartoons of people he had met, either drawn by artists he encountered or by himself. Lionello loved to draw caricatures at public events or private dinners, often to be exchanged with the artist present at the occasion, or simply with his friends and tablemates. The drawings of Lionello Perera capture faces of New York socialites and businesspeople. He thus poignantly pictured the diverse humanity he encountered, often with sharp humour. Lionello's passion for portraiture and caricature was very specific and deserves to be analysed thoroughly, since his personal taste and individual interests developed over the years into recognisable collecting habits and active patronage.

The first known contact he made with an artist was in the late 1890s over the commission of two portraits of his beloved parents, Cesare Lopes Perera and Emilia Cantoni. The paintings of his deceased father and mother were based on photographs (Fig. 3.1), thus, he needed a reliable painter with a solid pedigree. John Alfred Mohlte, a specialities painter of Swedish origin active in New York, seemed the right person to have his parents' photographs turned into oil paintings. The artist's signature, "J. Alfred Mohlte", appears on the upper left corner with a shortened date indicating 1898 or 1899. According to the best canons of academic tradition, Cesare and Emilia are rendered in a realistic way, their recognisable faces emerging from a yellowish background, while the garments are rather standardised. Emilia's rendering is more accurate, with her eyes vividly looking towards the spectator (Pl. 1.a), while Cesare's appearance has some oddities, like an unusually long left moustache, and a very short right eyebrow (Pl. 1.b), which relate to the overexposure of the original photograph Mohlte used to copy the portrait from. Evidently, the painter was a recognised professional, but rather accustomed to serial portraiture to make a living. Little is known about the painter, but it appears he was born in 1865 in Mollösund, a coastal village in the town of Orust.[6] He took his first formal training as a painter in Gothenburg and then emigrated to the United States as a painter on commission for portraits, genre scenes, and other sorts of pictures. He later travelled to Paris for further training, where he is recorded in 1896 as an American painter at the Académie Julian, studying under famous teachers like Paul Laurens and Jean-Joseph Benjamin-Constant.[7] In the last quarter of the nineteenth century this private academy in the French capital had become a major point of attraction for the international community, because it allowed the enrolment of foreign students and provided training that was sympathetic with changing styles in French art.[8] Founded in 1868, the academy initially intended to prepare students for entrance at the prestigious École des Beaux-Arts, but later developed into its principle rival and also became the first to grant women access to higher education in the arts.[9] The Académie Julian was liberal, encouraging students to pursue an individual style and nurturing some of the most significant post-Impressionist painters, like Henri Matisse.[10] From the 1890s onwards, it became a major establishment for American artists seeking further education in Paris, offering both improvement of technical skills and access to a wider artistic network.[11] Upon his return to the States, Mohlte settled in New York and over the decades participated in the local art scene. His name appears in several issues of the specialised magazine *American Art News*, as well as other art bulletins, either because he took part in group exhibitions or as a painter offering his skills on commission. Indeed, the first reference that can be found dates back to 1905, when Mohlte had just finished a commission for a Mr. Daniel M. Clemson in Pittsburgh, as well as a double portrait of Mr. and Mrs. Vail Brokaw in his atelier.[12] It is understood that he painted easel pictures and portraits for the New York elite for revenue, while he made other works for art shows such as two "ideal heads" displayed at the Lenox Art Academy in December 1906.[13] This first annual exhibition was very much in the style of a Parisian independent salon, with a jury selecting artworks for display among many hundreds submitted by local artists. The magazine *Brush and Pencil* reported that sales amounted to $2,000, while the attendance was several thousand visitors and a new exhibition was planned for 1907 with Mohlte on the selection panel.[14] The Swedish-born painter was clearly associated with the Lenox Art Academy over the next few years, but strived to find more opportunities in New York.[15] He worked exhibiting and selling at the Powell Art Galleries that offered good retail prices.[16] In the early 1910s, he was present at Snedecor Galleries, where he showed his oil paintings comprising landscapes, hunting and religious scenes, as well as portraits.[17] Relying on his ability to paint traditional themes, Mohlte went on to make copies of famous paintings. In 1922 he made a copy of the portrait of Shakespearian actor Edwin Booth by John Singer Sargent in the Players Club of New York, which was donated to the Shakespeare Gallery in Stratford upon Avon.[18] Still, in 1936, past the age of seventy, he participated in an exhibition on "Dance in Art" at the Gallery for Living Artists of the Brooklyn Museum.[19]

The few sources on John Adolph Mohlte show the career of a rather traditional artist, imbued with Academism, and bound to a client-artist relationship reminiscent of pre-Modern Art. The contact to Lionello Perera was certainly occasional and ended with the production of the two commissioned portraits in relatively small size. On his part, Lionello probably fulfilled the desire to pay tribute to his parents, as he felt he owed them and

Salvatore Cantoni for his success as a young banker in New York. In the mindset of the time, having a portrait painted added much more value to a person than a simple photograph. It showed an understanding of the bourgeoise portrait as a behavioural code and means of representation, which clearly signalled a higher social status, one that progressively replaced aristocracy during the long nineteenth century.[20] Hence, this commission demonstrates Lionello's attitude towards the act of painting, which led to his interest in portraiture, as well as caricature. Drawing other people's faces, having portraits of his own and his beloved ones, collecting and exchanging caricatures and cartoons would indeed become his greatest passion over the decades. Such a fascination of caricatures and cartoons in the nineteenth century was related to the extraordinary development of the periodical press and the use of wood engraving for printing images.[21] All over Europe, as well as in the United States, cartoonists and caricaturists were employed to comment on political, economic and social issues, thus attracting new readerships through the use of visual means, ridicule, exaggeration, and the re-inscription of the already known.[22] In fact, the use of caricatures as editorial cartoons was aimed at confirming common beliefs or fuelling specific preconceptions through over-simplifications of extremely complex and nuanced positions, events or characters.[23] Although biased, caricatures made their entrance in art schools between 1891 and 1914, with students holding annual exhibitions all over the East Coast –from New York to Boston and Philadelphia– that made fun of artworks displayed at major salons and shows.[24] The Salmagundi Club itself, of which Lionello was a member, started as a centre for sketch classes and later developed into an association of art lovers and artists devoted both to painting and illustration.[25] As far as American newspapers are concerned, the 1890s are regarded as the golden age of editorial caricatures, as well as of cartoons used for leisure and distraction.[26] The character of *Yellow Kid*, for instance, was at the heart of a battle between New York publishers Joseph Pulitzer and William Randolph Hearst who both used the comic strip to boost their sales.[27] Hence, by the time Lionello arrived in the United States, such caricatures and cartoons appeared in newspapers and magazines of all sorts, conveying attractive images on the printed page. While the Italian banker may have been fuelled by the spread of this visual language in America, by the time there also was a tendency to make caricatures as an amateur game of the bourgeoisie. This draws a direct parallel to the fashion of silhouette making in the German middle classes during the eighteenth century, a practice that was later imported to the German regions of Pennsylvania.[28] In the Anglo-American tradition, it is well documented that caricature making was a social game eagerly played at rendezvous of the well-offs –even involving artists such as John Singer Sargent and writer Henry James– when hosts and guests would each prepare informal drawings, made in fun and with humorous references to one another.[29] It is further found that a close friend of Lionello Perera, the tenor star Enrico Caruso, was in the habit of drawing caricatures and exchanging them both as a gift and a sign of familiarity. Indeed, the Parisian art dealer Goupil once 'inflicted' the drawings of the Neapolitan singer onto the American art historian Bernard Berenson during a soirée.[30] Caruso arrived in the United States upon his engagement by the Metropolitan Opera in 1903, arranged thanks to the intercession of the Italian Savings Bank manager Pasquale Simonelli, and thus came into contact with the many Italians in New York.[31] Enrico must have befriended Lionello at some point in the 1910s, because the tenor drew a caricature of the Italian banker in slim shape, evening dress and a moustache with pointed tips, as was in use at the time (Fig. 8.1). It is unclear, when Lionello Perera got into the habit of drawing and whether he took classes at the Salmagundi Club, but the years of his friendship with Enrico Caruso may have been the starting point of this activity. What remains of the Italian banker's many caricatures is perhaps just a small part of those he made or collected over the years, amounting today to hundreds. However, they are sufficient to judge his skills as well as the company of people he spent his time with. The pictures he drew himself shall be discussed first, because they are a visual expression of his character, thus offering a glimpse of his worldview and beliefs. Furthermore, if taken altogether, they are a relevant and humorous visual reminder of the New York elite at the beginning of the twentieth century, highlighting their appearance, mannerisms, whims, and habits. Through these caricatures, Lionello emerges as a keen and ironic observer of the humanity that filled the city's restaurants, theatres, social events, and business meetings. Drawing people he met demonstrates he was able to distance himself from high society, as well as from his own public persona. Indeed, it takes a man that was never too serious about his own achievements to display such an amount of irony and even self-mockery. These caricatures show how deeply he thought of human nature, and they also reflect what he valued in life. Despite his considerable success and prominent role in the Italian American community, he never put himself in the limelight. He evidently was a discrete man, firm and reliable, but also joyful and generous, as well as of satirical and reflective temperament.

On a technical level, it must be said the caricatures show Lionello Perera was talented in drawing, although he probably received little formal training, if any. As an amateur, he had a sense of human proportions and intentional distortion, making him capable of rendering the depicted person's likeliness, while at the same time emphasising distinctive traits and peculiar features. Concerning the materials, Lionello drew on everything that was at hand, such as hotel letterheads, envelopes, restaurant menus, concert programmes, business cards, headed scratchpads, calendar pages, and sometimes even napkins. This stresses the fact that he drew his subjects live, out of an impulse to capture aspects that lit up in his mind as particular, funny, or simply worth noticing. It is, as if he urgently needed to put down his impressions about the people he met, commenting on them by drawing. In most cases, they are quick sketches that render the subjects by their main contours, while a few are heavily worked on and present a careful finish complete with shadows, colours, and garments. Such details can be found for instance in the portrait of a young, pensive man wearing round glasses and a white shirt, with the inscription "Brandon, Vt", where his nephew Mario Perera had a summer cottage on September 12, 1931 (Pl. 2.a). Some drawings are proper cartoons with a small caption or phrase, such as a badly shaved man sipping from a straw saying: "Lemonade not good!" (Pl. 2.b). Another has an Italian man called Ulderico Bellini colourfully rendered, playing cards, and uttering with Tuscan inflection: "Eh! Huattro picche un sce l'aveva miha!!!" (Ha! You ain't got a four of spades!!!) (Pl. 2.c). There is also the drawing of a girl, Nancy Dyson, dressed up for a walk, holding an umbrella and a bunch of flowers, who lovingly pleads: "Can't I come to luncheon, too?" (Pl. 2.d). Unfortunately, most of the caricatures have no date nor are the subjects easy to identify, unless Lionello wrote a name, or the person portrayed is a recognisable celebrity among his close connections. Nevertheless, it is possible to make out different categories of people that captured his attention. There are numerous male portraits, which appear to be socialites in cocktail dress, military officials, gentlemen smoking cigars, perhaps also businessmen, artists, and intellectuals. A wide array of beards and moustaches allows one to guess the depicted men's age or the time the drawing was made (Pl. 3). The trend goes in fact from thick moustaches of the early twentieth century to slimmer whiskers of the interwar period. Thanks to some occasional captions or the likeness of famous people it is possible to recognise many star musicians of the time, which gives an idea of Lionello's and Carolyn's involvement in the musical world of New York (Pl. 4). There are distinctive caricatures of Italian conductors Giulio Setti and Arturo Toscanini, pianists Joseph Lhevinne and Józef Hofmann (Pl. 5). In the collection of the Library of Congress, among memorabilia of the musicians, there are also Lionello's portraits of composers and pianists Leopold Godowsky and Ignacy Jan Paderewski.[32] Again among the Perera drawings there is also the writer E. Philips Oppenheim, North Carolina University president Harry Woodburn Chase, Italian aviators Guido Scelsi and Raul Lampugnani. It is also possible to recognise the young politician Fiorello La Guardia, as well as the banker Amadeo Peter Giannini and perhaps even his brother Attilio. Some of the caricatures were published in newspapers, such as the portrait of Italian inventor and entrepreneur Guglielmo Marconi. Of particular interest are the female portraits among Lionello's caricatures, showing some younger and many elderly ladies of the New York elite dressed up for a night out with their hairdos and jewels (Pl. 5). In this regard, there is a robust woman seen from the back, her hair tied up, which means Lionello drew her unaware of being depicted, perhaps while attending a concert sitting a few rows in front of the Italian banker. There are also two girls playing music, one at the piano, the other one with a violin bow in the right hand. Evidently, all these women were drawn at special occasions, while the male portraits might stem both from business meetings and social events. Taken altogether they render an animated picture of the high life in New York in the first half of the twentieth century and set Lionello Perera as an acute observer of these buzzing socialites.

Among the many portraits, there are two of his cousin Gino Lorenzo Perera, which introduces us to the banker's vivid relationship with visual artists. In fact, Gino lived in Boston and was known as a landscape painter, as well as a sculptor.[33] The son of Cesare's older brother Alessandro, he was born in 1870 in Alexandria of Egypt and emigrated to the United States in 1891, shortly before Lionello. At the time, Gino was playing in a group of mandolinists that successfully performed across North America, particularly in Minneapolis.[34] Perhaps in fear that this success might end abruptly, he then became an artist around 1899 after marrying the slightly older Caroline Thacher, the daughter of a family of original settlers in Yarmouth, Massachusetts. The couple went to live in Boston, but in 1901 they moved to Brussels for a year, probably to seek contacts in the progressive art circles of the Belgian Art Nouveau.[35] Back in the States, Gino started painting landscapes that were reminiscent of both Divisionism and the Decorative Arts (Pl. 6).[36] He had several on display during the first decades of the twentieth century and then reached a recognised position as a catalyst of art activities in Massachusetts.[37] Indeed, Gino became the president of the Cobley Club organising exhibitions and prizes, as well as supporting artists like Greek-born Vasileos Kapousouz, who sculpted his bust in wood, a work that is now in the collection of the Museum of Fine Arts in Boston.[38] It is unclear, whether Lionello ever owned any artworks by his cousin, but the two little drawings he did of Gino –elegantly dressed, probably at the age of fifty or slightly older– prove they had a good relationship. In that same period, around the 1930s, at least three women artists drew a portrait of Lionello of very fine quality, though nothing is known about them. It is likely they were ladies that had received formal training but did not pursue an artistic career or could not join the male-dominated art world of the time. The first drawing is a quick sketch signed by Jessica J. Lange on February 4, 1930, while in August 1932, perhaps on vacation, one Mrs. Camilla Mary made a set of three professional-looking silhouettes, which included Lionello's wife Carolyn. One last portrait is of Lionello, reading a book with his hat on, which was made by a certain Maria Luisa Ferrero on July 23, 1936, at the Alpino mountain resort. A year later, on July 7, 1937, Lionello paid a visit to or just encountered Alessandro Milesi in Venice, who left him his business card and the beautiful sketch of a woman wearing a turban. Born in 1856, Milesi was indeed a well-known Venetian painter who was part of a wider group of artists trying to renovate genre painting and portraits, further exhibiting several times at the Biennale. It is unclear, whether Lionello looked up the eighty years old painter for a particular commission or to buy a finished painting, but it confirms his special liking of the figurative arts, especially genre painting and Naturalism.

There are also two more portraits of the Italian banker, drawn nine-years apart from each other, that deserve particular attention. Recognisably signed by Arturo Noci (1874-1953), they were both made in the United States, the first in Stamford on August 24, 1924 (Pl. 7), while the second one is dated 1933 and was probably produced in New York, because of its resemblance with an oil portrait of Lionello Perera by the same artist painted that same year (Pl. 8). A well-known Roman painter, who had participated in the artistic Secession of the Italian capital, Noci was introduced to the international art audience through the Venice Biennale, as he regularly participated in its exhibitions from 1901 to 1922.[39] Together with other artists of the Italian capital, his international reputation also allowed him to directly invite the French sculptor Auguste Rodin to Rome in 1912 for a much-awaited solo show.[40] In addition to such important contacts among the artist milieu, Noci's success in the early twentieth century among international collectors came about due to his remarkable ability as a portraitist. Inspired by the kind of pastel portraits made by renowned British painter James McNeil Whistler, whose reputation was expanding in Italy at the turn of the century after his Parisian period, Arturo Noci set forth to become Rome's most sought-after portraitist.[41] Over the years, he painted many dignitaries such as the Prince Viktor Gagarin and the Countess Gianotti, both in 1907, as well as many female portraits for the high-bourgeoise such as the American Miss Beatrice Thaw, in 1908, and Signora Lannino presented at the Venice Biennale in 1910. This makes Noci the most relevant artist who portrayed Lionello in his lifetime, hence it is necessary to dig deeper into the relationship between them, to clarify the circumstances of the portrait commissioned in 1933. The drawing of 1924 might give some clues about the first meeting between the banker and the painter, who had emigrated to the United States in late 1923, officially just for a brief period to paint portraits for some prominent members of the New York elite.[42] The drawing is just a quick sketch of the banker's head and the fact that it mentions a specific day means it was probably made on a particular occasion. Like many families of the New York elite, the Pereras rented a home in Stamford during the summer holidays to enjoy the Long Island Sound beaches.[43] Arturo Noci might have been a guest of the Pereras, who usually welcomed Italian musicians and artists, though he could also have met them as a guest of some other family during vacation and thus exchanged his little drawing with Lionello, as was customary for the latter when he met an artist. Precisely because this exchange happened, it is highly likely that this was the first encounter between the two, but it is unclear who might have prompted it. There is a link between the two Italians that can explain how this encounter came about, since the earliest portrait painted in America by Noci is the one of Mrs. William Guggenheim, finished in February that same year. The photograph of the now lost portrait shows a self-assured, blond lady in a fashionable evening dress with thick necklace of pearls and gleaming with beauty in her fur coat, open to reveal her left shoulder.[44] The portrait is painted in a clear Classicist style, which diverges from Noci's previous Divisionist style, probably because American patrons were not yet ready for such a Modernist turn. Known by her maiden name as Aimee Lilian Steinberger, then Stoneborough, she was the wife of William Guggenheim (1868-1941), the youngest son of patriarch Meyer Guggenheim. In 1920, she was a Honorary Vice President of the Italian Welfare League, which was presided by Lionello's wife Carolyn Allen Perera to assist immigrants in need, their children and Italian convalescents.[45] On his part, William Guggenheim was particularly active in the American Defense Society as chairman of the executive committee during World War I, a pressure group that tried to push the US government to intervene on Italy's side promoting propaganda against the war crimes of the Germans.[46] Founded in response to the sinking of the Lusitania in 1915, the society developed into an early nationalist organisation supported by former President Theodore Roosevelt and seeking the adequate defence of the United States from external aggressors, internal opponents, and even immigrant communities, especially Germans.[47] In 1921, William and Lionello were then elected to the board of trustees of the Italy America Society, a prestigious gathering of businessmen, politicians and diplomats that fostered commercial and political connections between the two countries.[48] Hence, the Guggenheims and the Pereras were evidently on good terms, as they had a shared commitment to Italy and both belonged to New York's Jewish elite. It is highly likely, then, that Lionello met the Italian artist through William, especially because the latter had been awarded a decoration in Rome in 1920 for his service to Italy, just months after Noci was given a civic award on comparable circumstances in the Italian capital.[49] The connection with William Guggenheim and his wife might explain the first drawing by Noci quickly sketched in Stamford in 1924. The artist had apparently gained access to New York's high society and decided to settle there for good as an esteemed portraitist, further keeping good contacts with his immigrant community. It is reported he even hosted meetings of the Italy America Society at his studio in 1927.[50] It is obvious, then, that there must have been plenty of occasions on which Noci met the Italian banker in New York during the 1920s and in the following decade.

Differing from the sketch of 1924, the second drawing the Roman artist made of Lionello in 1933 is instead a thorough study of the banker's upper body seated on an armchair with the right fist under the chin. The execution of this piece is much more detailed and careful, as it was likely made in preparation of the large oil portrait that Noci painted that same year. However, the position of the arms and hands in the painting is slightly different as compared to the drawing, the latter displaying a rather pensive character. In the painting, instead, Lionello is holding the armrests as if to reach out and cheer his imaginary visitor (Pl. 9). The portrait admirably shows the generous and gentle temper of the Venetian banker, his ebullient blue eyes shining, and his elegance underlined with a silk tissue in the breast pocket. The position of the body resembles that of an earlier portrait made in 1929 by Noci, the one of baritone Giuseppe De Luca, a famous Italian opera singer who was then active in New York.[51] Lionello probably knew of that portrait, since De Luca was registered among his guests at the Perera Upper East Side home in 1930, or maybe Noci opted for this final position of the body to give the banker a more open appearance. It is indeed very curious that a man like Lionello, who always proved quite discreet about his own persona, suddenly commissioned a portrait of himself. The fact that he knew the artist for a long time, as testified by the two drawings, further adds to the mystery, thus the question arises why it took him so many years to decide to have a portrait painted. It must be noted that the painting was not made at the height of his banking career, as one would expect, in an act of self-celebration. Lionello Perera was the Vice President of Bank of America between 1928 and 1931, but the portrait was painted after his retirement in 1933, so it was not meant to directly celebrate his business success. There is a clue that might account for the decision to have this portrait painted. In fact, the banker's nephew Guido Perera and his wife Mae Major were portrayed by Noci that same year, and even their daughter Genevieve. Some of these paintings are still in the family belongings, others are unfortunately lost, but photographs of all of them survived at the archive of Arturo Noci in Rome. Guido was the oldest son of Lionello's sister Clary Perera and he had probably been summoned by his uncle to New York to assist him in the banking business in the immediate aftermath of World War I, as he had done with his other nephew Mario, Rosa Perera's son, who had bravely fought against the Austrian Empire.[52] Surely Lionello involved his two nephews in order to perpetuate his company among his closest family members, as Salvatore Cantoni had done with him. Also, he needed Italian relatives to help him with his immigrant clientele. Mario and Guido were very fond of their uncle, as well as grateful for the opportunity he had given them, and continued to work in the finance sector even after Lionello's retirement. Mario stayed as a foreign exchange manager at City Bank Farmers Trust, while Guido founded Perera Company at 10 Broadway, involving also his uncle's son Lionel.[53] Among the memorabilia in Arturo Noci's archive there is a big caricature of Guido drawn in 1934 on the occasion of a festive dinner among Italian friends held at the estate of Lionello's nephew.[54] The drawing is made in the style of a so-called 'papiro', the poster Italians receive on graduation day made by their university mates, with the caricature positioned at the poster's centre and several handwritten phrases placed around it, including the menu of the dinner. Such work is proof enough that Guido Perera and Arturo Noci were good friends, having probably met years before through uncle Lionello. Furthermore, besides some more portraits, through Guido several other paintings by Arturo Noci remain in the Perera's extended family estate, such as still lives (Pl. 10) and landscapes (Pl. 11) that were probably bought as finished artworks. Hence, it presumably was Guido who commissioned all portraits of the Perera family in 1933. In fact, since Guido asked to also have a portrait of his wife and daughter, certainly Lionello would have done the same at least for his wife, if he had commissioned his own portrait. However, there is no trace of a portrait of Carolyn Allen Perera in the artist's archive, thus one can assume Lionello did not ask for the painting, rather that it was Guido paying tribute to his uncle. Although he may not have commissioned it directly, the portrait by Arturo Noci in 1933 came at the right moment in Lionello's life and was to take centre-stage in the images he and Carolyn had chosen for their new Manhattan home. Hanging above the fireplace, gazing at the guests in the reception room, Noci's painting delivered a sense of cordiality and sophistication (Pl. 12). The artist had truly pictured the banker as a gentle and refined Italian patron, devoted to the art of portraiture, as much as he was passionate about drawings and caricatures.

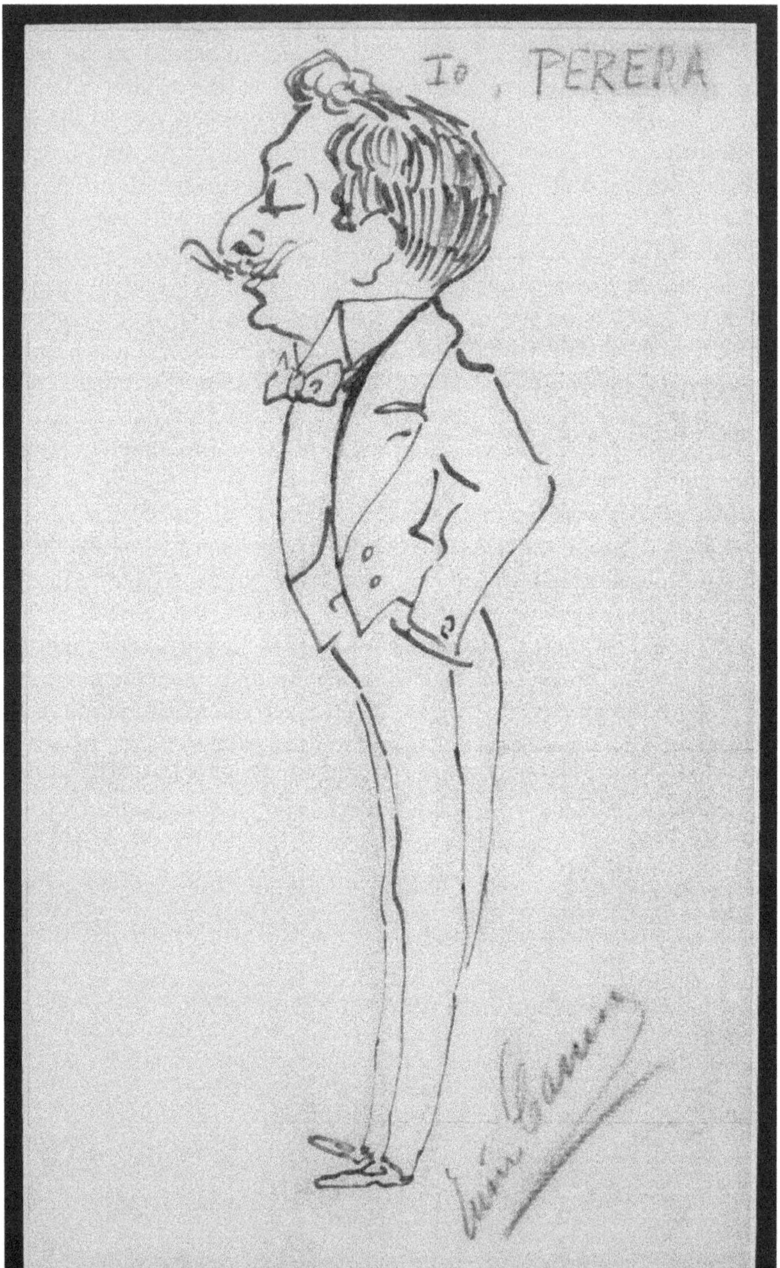

Figure 8.1: Caricature of Lionello Perera by Enrico Caruso (1910?)

Caricature of Lionello Perera with the inscription "Io, Perera" drawn and signed by star tenor Enrico Caruso, probably in the early 1910s. (Courtesy of the Perera Family Archive)

Chapter 9

Musicians and Paintings in a Modernist Shrine

Hundreds of signatures, some with amusing musical flourishes, fill the pages of the Perera guest book, which Lionello and his wife Carolyn kept since moving into their new home at 49 East 80th Street in 1930, just a few yards from the Metropolitan Museum of Art.[1] Already on March 16, for the inauguration of the house, the book records the presence of celebrities of the musical world, as well as prominent members of both the Jewish elite and the Italian American community. Among guests were star conductor Arturo Toscanini, the composer Ildebrando Pizzetti, and violinist Adolfo Betti. A month later, on April 6, Lionello and Carolyn invited another famous conductor, Giulio Setti, together with pianist Zygmunt Stojowski and several singers of the Metropolitan Opera, such as baritone Giuseppe De Luca and tenor Giovanni Martinelli. Leafing through the guest book one finds the names of the international music jet set that performed in New York's main theatres and concert halls, thus turning their home into one of the most refined private dwellings of the city. Amongst the many signatures, there are those of renowned musicians such as composer Ottorino Respighi, violinists Yehudi Menuhin and Adolf Busch, violists Emanuel Vardi and Lillian Fuchs, NBC concertmasters Max Hollander and John Corigliano (Fig. 9.2). Basically, over a whole decade, the Pereras hosted recitals and concerts of chamber music with every important musician in town, which resulted in newspapers frequently mentioning their refined events. Already the very first 'musicale' at 49 East 80th Street was mentioned by *The New York Times* on March 17, 1930, when Pizzetti had an original sonata performed by cellist Alfred Wallenstein.[2] At the time, the Italian composer had just premiered his *Fra Gherardo* at the Metropolitan Opera and was touring the United States for the first time under the auspices of a board of guarantors, which included Carolyn Allen Perera.[3] Most interestingly, that same night the Perolé String Quartet made its first public debut playing Pizzetti's *Quartet in A*. Led by violinist Joseph Coleman and violist Lillian Fuchs, both became famous performers in America, being one of the very few ensembles in the interwar period that had a female musician amongst its leaders. At the inception, the Perera Upper East Side home became a preferred venue for the quartet's rehearsals and Carolyn also provided precious instruments to its musicians, like a Baroque viola of the

Venetian luthier Matteo Goffriller.[4] Lionello's wife further involved other friends in the foundation of this quartet, thus acting as its true patron. Indeed, she then acted similarly towards many musicians that entered her home, with some even lodged at the Pereras for some time. Carolyn further arranged meetings of young musicians under her wing with established artists who were her friends, in order to foster the career of those she thought talented, as well as to create unprecedented musical experiences. For example, she introduced composer Bela Bartok to violinist Yehudi Menuhin, who was staying at their home, and this encounter led to a long-lasting collaboration that started with an original sonata performed at the Pereras' before premiering at Carnegie Hall.[5] Many more famous musicians benefitted from Lionello and Carolyn's patronage and became close friends of the couple, as testified by very affectionate letters they received over the years.[6] Among them are Rudolf Serkin, the Busch family, Isaac Stern, Erika Morini, Ania Dorfman, Emmanuel Feuermann, Vladimir Horowitz, Gian Carlo Menotti, and countless others.[7] During the 1930s, the support of the Pereras was directed primarily towards either musicians of Italian descent or Eastern Europeans of Jewish origin, all of whom were escaping Europe's troubled countries. Carolyn in particular was very active in music education, promoting young musicians, and finally earned a citation from the Violin Teachers Guild of New York on April 19, 1933, "for her aid and encouragement in the advancement of string playing in the musical education of our youth".[8] Even after Lionello's death in 1942, Carolyn continued to be involved in the city's musical life and her activism is recorded in the rich material left in the archives of New York Public Library.[9] She was on the board of trustees of Marlboro School of Music, founded in 1951, and later created the Carolyn A. Perera Fund at the Manhattan School of Music.[10] Furthermore, her private correspondence gives testimony of the friendship and affection she had earned from many famous musicians, especially Menuhin, Stern, and Horowitz.[11] Israeli composer Paul Ben-Haim, who had fled Germany after the Nazis came to power, dedicated a violin concert to Carolyn in 1960.[12] She was also instrumental in the foundation of the Toscanini Memorial Archives, organising an exhibition of the Maestro's memorabilia with his son Walter at the Public Library of Cincinnati and in Hamilton County.[13] Thanks to the influence of the Italian conductor, who gave her a biography of Giuseppe Verdi for relief from her bad arthritis, she also became an eager collector of Verdiana, comprising letters and rare editions of the celebrated nineteenth-century composer.[14] In her final years, Carolyn became involved through her daughter Nina in bringing classical music nearer to children, founding the programme *Young Audiences* to include concerts in the context of school education.

Such passion and activism, which had developed over the years of their happy marriage, finally peaked in the big reception room that Lionello had planned for Carolyn in their Upper East Side home, built in 1929. Indeed, music was a common interest that tied them closely as a couple, although Lionello probably preferred opera due to his Italian upbringing. On her part, Carolyn was evidently keen on symphonic music as she was a trained violinist and had also performed publicly in her youth. Even their engagement was characterised by a curious musical twist, as recalled by Carolyn in her memoirs.[15] They had known each other for many years and with time, their friendship grew into fondness, as she turned from a child into a young woman. In the fall of 1903, Lionello bought her parents tickets for the opera, just to have them out for the night and seize the opportunity to see Carolyn by herself for a surprising, but long-awaited proposal. The first thing next day, he called the Allens to disclose his love and asked for an official engagement. Much to the delight of Charles Chauncey Allen and Louise Sondheim, their daughter married the young Italian on October 17, 1904 (Fig. 9.3), and together they set forth to have five children. Charles (Allen) was born in 1905, Nina two years later in 1907, then came Lionel (Cantoni) in 1909 and George (Alfred) in 1911, finally Lydia in 1917 (Fig. 9.4). It must be noted that, at the time, the wedding between Lionello and Carolyn would have been considered an intermarriage between an Italian American and a Jewish American. At the turn of the century though, there were historical and sociological patterns that made intermarriages among these two ethnic groups quite likely. In fact, Italians and Jews were present in the United States as early as the mid-nineteenth century, but numbers soared between the years 1880 and 1930 with both groups settling mainly in New York, as well as in adjacent neighbourhoods inside the city.[16] Besides the presence of large populations in the same small geographic area, Italians and Jews displayed a similar sociological pattern characterised by strong family ties and being relatively secluded from the American political elite of that time.[17] However, what rather facilitated intermarriage was educational or professional homogeneity, which acted as an important endogenous variable of class identity, even more than religion or ethnicity.[18] Hence, before World War I only about ten percent of first-generation Italians did marry-out, because the large majority of immigrants came from the poorer regions of southern Italy.[19] In the case of Lionello and Carolyn, there were several factors that predisposed them towards marrying. The young Italian was a dear family friend who had earned the Allens affection and esteem over the years, as well as being an associate of Charles in the banking business. Carolyn recalls that Lionello really was like a son to her parents and his Judaism surely evened out possible religious differences with his Italian origin.[20] As Mrs. Lionello Perera, Carolyn would soon enter a complete new ethnic dimension of her life experience, being immediately involved in the cultural and social landscape of Italian Americans. She also became a frequent traveller, since the couple returned every year to spend their vacation in Italy and visit Lionello's sisters, thus interpreting the proverbial role of the so-called 'zii d'America', the uncle and aunt from the United States who brought watches and radios to their relatives.[21] Lionello's involvement in the Italian Red Cross, as well as in the various campaigns for the Liberty Loan during the war, probably prompted Carolyn's participation in the problems and care of Italian immigrants in New York. However, music certainly was an important bridge for her into the milieu of Italian Americans, if not the most relevant. Opera meant very much to Lionello, as it did for almost all Italian Americans at the time, because of the admiration and respect that Italian opera stars and musicians had worldwide. In fact, music was the one thing that made Italian immigrants look good, or at least better, in the eyes of Americans. This was clearly the case of the monument for Giuseppe Verdi, erected at Broadway and 72nd Street after the composer's death in 1901. The sculpture was commissioned with the intention to enhance public acceptance of Italian immigrants, to improve their perceived reputation as cultured people with a unified national identity.[22] The celebrity status of many Italian musicians, singers, and composers was useful to fight discrimination against immigrants across America, but it hardly sufficed to erase deeply rooted stereotypes. Even in the case of star tenor Enrico Caruso, the specialised press always used a double standard in its reactions, on one side praising his marvellous voice, while on the other one criticising his vulgar simplicity. Despite his singing talent, he simply was not the kind of Italian that appealed to the US elite and critics tended to diminish his acting abilities, as well as to contest his choice of repertoire, as they deemed it insufficiently sophisticated.[23] Nevertheless, Italian Americans were proud of their rich musical legacy and often used it as a catalyst for general appreciation in early twentieth-century America. Thus, throughout his life, Lionello was on good terms with many Italian singers performing at the Metropolitan Opera House, which is well documented in family materials. His friends included Caruso himself, who died prematurely in 1921, and his successor Giovanni Martinelli, who came from the wider Venice region.[24] Apart from the caricature of Lionello drawn by Caruso, short newspaper entries prove that in the early twentieth century they often attended events together, such as a series of curious fruit auctions organised for charity purposes to help Italian Americans in New York.[25] They were further honoured for their respective achievements by the King of Italy the same year, in 1920, the tenor being nominated 'Grand'Uffiziale', while the banker was made 'Commendatore'.[26] To Lionello, music surely was a private passion, one he cultivated by entering the Bohemians Club in 1921, New York's renowned association for amateur musicians.[27] However, opera music meant much more to him, since it publicly symbolised his support of Italian Americans taken as a true act of patriotism.

First records of the Pereras participating in music events in the city date back as far as the 1910s, usually as donors or special guests of charity concerts and receptions, particularly during the war period for the allied countries and their populations. One of the earliest appearances of their names in specialised magazines was in 1915 in *Musical America* with Carolyn as a performer. Indeed, she accompanied on the violin the famous pianist Zygmunt Stojowski on the occasion of a concert given on August 21 at Crags Moor Inn on top of Shawangunk Mountain, Ulster County, for the benefit of the Polish Relief Fund and the Floating Hospital of Bensonhurst.[28] It appears that Lionello and Carolyn further supported the New York music world with occasional donations, particularly in connection with Italian opera singers or with events prompted by the banker's involvement in welfare activities. As the head delegate to the Italian Red Cross, Lionello participated in the organisation of recitals and entire operas that helped raise money for various beneficial aims or war relief. In March 1916, he was among the Italian patrons of two special performances of Verdi's *La Traviata* staged by the Sulli Grand Opera Company at the Amsterdam Opera House for the benefit of Italian reservists' families.[29] Later that same year, the Pereras participated in the Italian Bazaar organised at Grand Central Palace, as representatives of the Italian Red Cross.[30] Their booth was visited by many distinguished musicians, including the tenors Enrico Caruso and Giovanni Martinelli, as well as the mezzo-soprano Nanà Genovese and the conductor Giorgio Polacco. Madame Genovese held a recital of her *cheval de bataille*, with arias from Georges Bizet's *Carmen*, to an applauding audience of twenty thousand people.[31] A few years later, in April 1919, the Italian Red Cross in the United States, still represented by Lionello, offered a medal to the mezzo-soprano in recognition of her service in raising money for portable hospitals through unpaid concerts she had given during the war period.[32] At this time, the banker's involvement in the Liberty Loan campaign and in the Red Cross was instrumental in his connection with the musical society of New York. The Pereras regularly appeared as distinguished guests at concerts and receptions connected with Italian opera and musicians, as well as alongside decorated Italian soldiers who had fought in the World War against the Austrian Empire. One such occasion was the meeting held on West End Avenue at the home of Delia Valeri, a noted singing teacher, to honour the birthday of George Washington.[33]

After this round of donations and participations in music events of the 1910s, in the following decade the Pereras finally joined the circle of New York's most prominent patrons. On the occasion of Arturo Toscanini's return to the United States with Milan's Teatro La Scala orchestra, in the summer of 1920, Lionello was approached by the organisers of the tour to be on the supporting committee and offer a financial contribution.[34] After his abrupt departure from the Metropolitan Opera in 1915, Arturo Toscanini had returned to Italy to participate in the country's war efforts and later devoted his talent to the reconstruction of the orchestra at the famous Milan opera house. Hence, the comeback tour of the Maestro was poised to be a major musical event in New York, with sold-out concerts at Carnegie Hall.[35] Carolyn recalls Lionello was probably brought in by Juliette de Coppet Stengel, the daughter-in-law and manager of the famous opera singer and then Juilliard teacher Marcella Sembrich, who was on good terms with the Maestro.[36] Two letters in the Toscanini Memorial Archive, however, state that Lionello was contacted by an Italian National, Ugo Ara, the first time on July 21, 1920, asking him for a contribution to bring the Maestro back to America, while the second letter, six days later, acknowledged the receipt of two thousand dollars.[37] The banker acted very quickly and this large sum allowed him to have the Italian star conductor give a benefit concert at Mecca Temple for the Italian Welfare League. It also turned out to be the opportunity to be personally acquainted with the conductor at a dinner after the performance, which started a long friendship. The Pereras invited Toscanini and his orchestra to dinner at an Italian restaurant, which the Milanese musicians greatly appreciated, since so far, they had been disappointed by American food.[38] This special attention towards the orchestra led Arturo Toscanini to introduce Lionello and Carolyn to his wife Carla De Martini at the Hotel Astor the next day. Ever since that encounter they became good friends, sharing family events, visiting each other on vacation, and travelling together between Europe and the United States for the coming two decades. This special relationship between them is shown in rich correspondence in the Toscanini Memorial Archive, as well as in letters, postcards, and photographs in the Perera memorabilia (Fig. 9.5). The intimate tone used in the letters and the wide scope of this correspondence show their friendship was one of deep affection. In the 1930s, Arturo and Carla are featured as frequent guests in the Upper East Side home of the Pereras, also bringing many colleagues of the Maestro's NBC Radio Symphony Orchestra. The two families frequently shared support for their reciprocal charitable activities, like when Toscanini offered an NBC charity concert of Beethoven symphonies at Carnegie Hall for the benefit of the Italian Welfare League on February 6, 1938.[39] On their part, that same year, Lionello and Carolyn started donating to Casa Verdi in Milan, a retirement home for musicians that was close to the heart of the Maestro.[40] A letter from Arturo to Carolyn written on April 3, 1952, thanking for her yearly donation to Casa Verdi, well presents the affectionate tone of this great friendship.[41] In the opening remark, the Maestro addressed the banker's then widow "My dearest Carolina", using the Italian form of her name, while in the closing note he wished her a "happy reunion with our dear Lionello's sisters" back in Italy, whom Toscanini appears to have met years before. As a matter of fact, the two families spent much free time and many holidays together.

Travelling together, they followed the conductor's concerts and operas across Europe before the outbreak of World War II, including Bayreuth in 1930 or 1931, then Salzburg in 1936 or 1938 and finally Lucerne in 1939.[42] While on vacation in northern Italy, they frequently exchanged visits, either at the Toscanini estate on Lago Maggiore or at their Milan apartment in Via Durini, or again at the Alpino mountain resort where the Pereras stayed in the summer of 1936.[43] With Toscanini's increasing difficulties due to the Fascist regime in Italy, given also his wife's Judaism, the Pereras became his trusted friends in America. Carolyn was consulted by the Maestro about his grandchildren, while Lionello helped to find them a home in Riverdale to leave Italy for good.[44] In 1939 they were even entrusted with a quite dangerous task, when Carla asked Carolyn at the Festival in Lucerne to carry four paintings of the Maestro's collection out of Italy to New York. Toscanini was a serious collector with almost two hundred paintings purchased during his lifetime, particularly of Italian Modern artists such as Pompeo Mariani, Gaetano Previati and Giovanni Segantini from the Milan area, as well as prominent *fin de siècle* painters like Telemaco Signorini and Antonio Mancini.[45] This passion came about through his direct contacts with many living artists, making him a connoisseur whose interests and expertise spanned through various art forms.[46] The episode of the artworks smuggling is adventurously recalled in Carolyn's memoirs, since it was of course illegal, more so as the Toscaninis were closely watched by the Fascists.[47] With Lionello's consent, Carolyn conducted this bold action by picking up "the box of candies" at a Milan art dealer after evading a Fascist agent in the room. They were two eighteenth-century paintings believed to be Guardis, though it is unclear whether by Francesco or other relatives, given they were a family of Venetian landscape painters comprising three generations of painters from the Baroque period to the inception of Neoclassical art. Then there were two more recent works of Giovanni Boldini and Francesco Paolo Michetti, both of whom were Modernist Italian painters of the late nineteenth century. The Pereras packed the four unframed canvases in their suitcases and safely embarked in Genoa, after diverting the attention of the military police at the port. Once again, Carolyn and Lionello earned Toscanini's gratitude and the paintings were thus displayed for the benefit of the American Red Cross, returning to Italy only after the end of the war.

Interestingly, Toscanini's paintings were in parallel with Lionello's own attitude and taste as an art collector. In fact, the two Guardis among the saved paintings surely were views of Venice, which were something of a must-have for a refined art lover of Italian origin, either originals or as replicas. The banker himself owned a view of St. Mark's Square, though it was a late nineteenth-century copy by Giovanni Grubacs[48] of Francesco Guardi's famous *The Doge of Venice Carried by Gondoliers after His Election on Piazza San*

Marco, the original one painted around 1770.[49] Lionello further purchased several more recent views and genre scenes of Venice, particularly in Naturalist style, which surely held meaning to him given his Venetian heritage. At the time, however, such a collecting trend towards Italian masters, older and newer ones, was typical of the American high bourgeoise, as it reflected the choices of prominent private collectors whose artworks were shown in museums and galleries across the country. Indeed, scholars argue that most art lovers in the United States felt culturally unsure at the beginning of the twentieth century, thus, buying European art helped them conform to a cosmopolitan taste and conferred them with a sophisticated reputation.[50] Already at the beginning of the nineteenth century Joseph Allen Smith started an important collection in Philadelphia, comprising numerous Italian artworks, not just of the Renaissance but also many from the Baroque and Rococo periods with several landscapes by Salvator Rosa.[51] Between the late nineteenth and early twentieth century many more remarkable collectors appeared in America and their collecting taste varied considerably. To name but a few, William Preston Harrison became a specialist of French Modern Art, Thomas B. Clarke concentrated on American Modern Art, Wallace Nutting cherished Decorative Art, and Ada Small Moore devoted herself to Ancient and Oriental Art.[52] Perhaps one of the most comprehensive collections in the United States was the one of banker J. Pierpont Morgan, whose exhibits covered an extremely wide range of art periods and objects that were donated to the Metropolitan Museum of Art in New York, among which were numerous Italian paintings, including the Venetian Settecento painter Pietro Longhi.[53] As far as the comprehensiveness of European art is concerned, a comparable collection was that of entrepreneur Samuel H. Kress, which ended up at the National Gallery in Washington D.C. with a remarkable number of Italian masterpieces highlighting the different currents and schools that developed over time, thus extending also to various Venetian artists.[54] Despite individual differences in taste and preferences, these collectors provided the role model and artistic benchmark in America for anyone attempting to become a reputable art collector, especially in the interwar period when most of these private collections were turned into publicly accessible foundations or merged into established museums.[55] Far from owning a mere Guardi replica, the private collection of Lionello Perera comprised several European masterpieces such as a panel of the Flemish painter Pieter Bruegel the Younger and six genre scenes by Pietro Longhi, mixed together with various other works by living or recently deceased artists. Regarding Old Masters, he distinctly preferred genre painting, with scenes representing peasant life or popular topics, rather than the Renaissance or Classicist subjects. In his choices of newer artists, the Italian banker was more conservative if compared to Toscanini's taste. The Maestro was decidedly inclined towards a Modernist vein, as recognisable in his collection by works of painters like Telemaco Signorini, characterised by the *plein air* approach that was typical of the Macchiaioli Realism, and Giovanni Segantini, whose pictures disclose an arcane Symbolism. Lionello instead persisted with his strong interest in genre scenes, thus favouring painters close to Naturalism or with an Academic background. The banker's penchant for popular or rural subjects accounts for the presence in his collection of a painting by Eugène Feyen showing two young barefoot women, probably fisherman girls, sewing at the border of the sea in Brittany (Pl. 13).[56] The painting has no date and is signed on the lower corner "Eug.Feyen", as was usual with this French artist. Given the depicted topic, this piece likely belongs to the artist's late period, after 1860, when he concentrated on rural scenes, which according to Academic standards were not painted *en plein air* but constructed as easel paintings in his studio.[57] The same can be said of a painting by Antonio Ermolao Paoletti, a Venetian painter of the late nineteenth century who had trained at the local academy and later specialised in historical painting and genre scenes representing Venetian life.[58] It shows several peasant women on a bridge along a canal carrying baskets to the marketplace (Pl. 14). This interest in Naturalism must be seen as a principal feature of Lionello's collecting and it likely matched his general sympathy towards working-class people.

Unfortunately, there are no precise records among family materials that list the artworks the banker purchased or owned in his lifetime, but there is sufficient circumstantial evidence to get an idea of the quality and scope of his collection. As with antiquities, various sources make it possible to define the chronological construction of Lionello's collection. Perhaps the most important are provided by a series of black and white photographs taken in the Perera home at 49 East 80th Street. On a picture of the series one can distinctly recognise the portrait of Lionello Perera by Arturo Noci hanging over the fireplace in the sitting room, which was finished in 1933, hence the photographs were surely taken around the mid-1930s. Considering that Carolyn sold the house soon after the death of her husband, which occurred in 1942, these photographs document their home at the height of the couple's activity as patrons. The paintings were hung with individual lighting in two rooms, which also were the most visited ones by guests coming for concerts or receptions. Both set on the first floor, they were the library and the sitting room, though the latter should really be defined as the music room, since it was used for concerts with a grand piano set close to the big windows opening onto the street. In both rooms, the installation of each painting was intentional, as it was incorporated in the furniture and decorations, as well as being perfectly illuminated. Hence, the artworks were purchased before the construction of the home and the rooms were designed specifically to hold them, thus conferring a very sophisticated atmosphere to the building and its owners.

Starting with the description of the library, the room was also in use as Lionello's private studio. Here he met acquaintances around a central desk with many framed photographs on it showing the banker's beloved ones, as well as the portraits of celebrities that counted among his and Carolyn's closest friends, first and foremost being Arturo Toscanini. Since bookshelves covered every wall of the room, the library did not allow for many paintings to be displayed, though they were the most ancient and precious ones in the Perera collection. Pictures show one hanging behind the desk and over the fireplace (Pl. 15.a), the other set on an easel in the opposite corner (Pl. 15.b). Although the focusing of the latter photograph is not sharp enough to recognise the panel, on the stylish Art Nouveau easel was a Renaissance artwork of Tuscan origin. In family recollections it was a *Crucifixion* believed to be by Andrea del Castagno (1421-1475). Indeed, it is recorded that Lionello Perera bought this masterpiece as an original del Castagno, dating to the second half of the fifteenth century, from Alphonse Kahn Collection of Paris at an auction at the American Art Galleries in New York on January 7, 1927.[59] Only decades later, when the panel was donated to Bryn Mawr College in 1980, it was discovered this *Christ on the Cross* was instead by another Florentine painter, Cosimo Rosselli (1439-1507), and probably painted later than 1460 (Pl. 16).[60] Setting the Crucifixion on the background of an imaginary landscape, recent restoration shows that it was probably cut down from a larger panel and then framed in the seventeenth or eighteenth century with a wooden frame inscribed in golden letterings with an extract of Psalm 45 (44.3 in the Greek numbering) in Latin: "Speciosus forma es prae filiis hominum, diffusa est gratia in labiis tuis [, propterea benedixit te Deus in aeternum]."[61] The frame and its inscription, commenting on the nature and beauty of Christ, hints at the fact that the panel was later cut down to a smaller size, 21 per 15 3/4 inches, in order to be arranged as an altarpiece conveniently shaped for private use, rather than for display in a church or monastery.[62] It is unlikely that Lionello purchased this painting for any religious reason, given his Judaism. To the contrary, as it was sold as a genuine Andrea del Castagno, it rather stood in his private studio and library as a statement of refined collecting taste, thus participating in the fever for Tuscan Renaissance that characterised prominent museums and collectors in America. The fact that an easel was chosen for its display can be explained either with the relevance of the masterpiece, being the oldest in the banker's collection, or with the date of purchase, which was very close to the construction of the Perera house and perhaps did not allow for changes to the library setting.

Another difficult case regarding provenance and attribution is the *Self-Portrait* of Lorenzo Lotto (Pl. 17), which does not appear in the photographs of the interiors at 49 East 80th Street, but it is registered in the belongings of Lionello's daughter Nina, as was the Crucifixion. Auction records further disclose it was bought two years prior to the Cosimo Rosselli panel, on

November 27, 1925, again at the American Art Galleries from the Chiesa A. Collection in Milan.[63] At the sale in New York the painting was however titled *Portrait of a (Bearded) Gentleman* and attributed to the Venetian Renaissance portraitist Vincenzo Catena (1480-1531), who is counted among the most prominent apprentices of Giovanni Bellini (1430-1516). In advance of its last recorded sale in London on December 11, 1974, Sotheby's found the painting to be by Lorenzo Lotto (1480-1557), who was a much more famous and troubled painter active in the wider Venice region, and it finally entered in the Thyssen-Bornemisza collection in Madrid from the UK art market in 1977, given its collectors particular taste for portraits.[64] Right upon the purchase by the Spanish museum, art historian Federico Zeri suggested that the depicted man was the artist himself, given the likeliness with the known features of Lorenzo Lotto, as well as because of the peculiar gaze and three-quarter position of the model, who seems to look out of a mirror for self-depiction.[65] It must be said, that at the time of this acquisition by the Thyssen-Bornemisza there was a heated debate among the scholarly community with regard to the true aspect of the Venetian painter. An assumed portrait of Lotto was included as an engraving in Carlo Ridolfi's *Le Meraviglie dell'Arte*, a comprehensive biographical dictionary of famous painters from the Venice region first published in 1648, which showed an elegantly bearded man with an elongated face and prominent nose.[66] In the second half of the twentieth century, Italian scholars like Paolo Della Pergola, Francesco Cortesi Bosco, and Norberto Massi started to contend what the true look of the Venetian painter was.[67] Thus, several known altarpieces, frescoes, and portraits by the artist were scanned to detect possible self-portraits corresponding to the general features displayed by the original Ridolfi engraving. The aspect of Lotto varies from that of a slim and anguished young man, like in the *Self-Portrait* at the Doria Pamphilj gallery in Rome,[68] to that of a stout and fatigued adult, as can be found in the central Roman soldier of the *Crucifixion* for the Church of Santa Maria in Telusiano, Monte San Giusto, near Macerata.[69] All of them, however, keep the general features of a long and bearded face with a big nose, such as can be found in the painting owned by Lionello Perera. None of this was known at the time the Italian banker made his purchase at the American Art Galleries, hence the wrong attribution probably accounts for the absence of this now celebrated Lotto self-portrait from the photographs documenting the Perera home in the Upper East Side. Ironically, as far as art historical knowledge at Lionello's time is concerned, the *Bearded Gentleman*, which was believed to by Catena, could be defined as a nice purchase, though definitely a minor one if compared to the *Crucifixion*, which was supposed to be by del Castagno. Given its lesser value, Lionello's reason for buying the portrait must lie in the depicted gentleman's attire. Although the banker did not recognise the bearded man being the artist himself, his black mantlepiece and small hat were reminiscent of Venetian artisans, civil servants, and merchants of the Renaissance period. Hence, it is likely that Lionello Perera somehow saw it as an interesting historical reference to both his hometown and profession.

Finally, over the library's fireplace hung a painting by Bruegel the Younger, which is instead easy to identify in the photograph series. Indeed, it is the conventionally titled *Summer*, a rural scene showing peasants at work on the fields. It belonged to the series of *The Four Seasons*, which was produced in several copies in the highly lucrative studio the artist had inherited from his famous father, Pieter Bruegel the Elder. In fact, the drawing for this version was painted by Bruegel the Elder in 1568 as a variation to the famous painting *The Harvesters* (1565), which entered the collection of the Metropolitan Museum of Art in 1919 from the Rogers Fund.[70] The museum also holds the etching *Aestas* by Pieter van der Heyden of 1570, which reproduces the exact iconography of the *Summer* painting used as a basis by Bruegel the Younger in 1624 to make several series of *The Four Seasons*.[71] A complete set of the latter can be found in the collection of the National Museum of Art of Romania, in Bucharest, while another one sold for almost six and a half million pounds at Christie's in 2016.[72] In the Early modern period this series became widely sought after as it suggestively illustrated the passage of time and the cycle of nature. Not much is known about the purchase of the *Summer* painting by Lionello Perera, nor is it possible to find its current location as it was later sold by his heirs.[73] Nevertheless, it seems relevant that he would harbour that particular painting of Brueghel the Younger in his library. This choice clearly highlighted his ambition to be counted among New York's finest collectors, if put in connection with the famous *Harvesters* at the Metropolitan Museum of Art. The purchase of the Bruegel by Lionello cannot be seen as a mere coincidence, as he was aware of the activities of museums in town, being also listed as a donor to several of them.[74] Hence, it was certainly bought on purpose to gain prominence, singling him out for his keen eye, and directly connect his collection to that of the Metropolitan, which indeed was very close to the Pereras Upper East Side home. Any of his refined guests entering the library would have recognised the painting and, thus, understood the level of sophistication of the Italian banker. Having a private conversation with him at the library's desk with an autographed portrait of Maestro Toscanini on it and surrounded by these Renaissance masterpieces, one could only but feel privileged to be in the company of Lionello Perera.

Turning to the sitting room, this large reception room harboured six small canvases by Pietro Longhi. Some were hung around the grand piano, others between the fireplace and the northern corner wall, the remaining on the eastern side of the room. To recognise the paintings from the photographs, one can draw information from several exhibitions and sale records that featured Lionello Perera's name. Of great assistance are records held at Federico Zeri Foundation, which registers most Italian paintings that left the country over the last three centuries. In this archive, there are indeed six works by Pietro Longhi, all painted between the 1750s and 1760s, that were listed in the private collection of Lionello Perera in New York.[75] Although the collection is now dispersed, by matching the subject of the six panels present in the Zeri archive with the provisional titles found in other museum catalogues and auction records it is possible to identify the six Longhi paintings with precision.[76] Following the order of display in the music room, as seen in the photographs (Pl. 18-19), the six Longhi paintings of the Perera collection are listed here with the title they had at the time of purchase, while the title in square brackets is the one they have today in their respective museum collection. The northern corner wall to the left of the fireplace displayed *The Game of Cards [The Visit]* (ca. 1760), now at the Alte Pinakothek in Munich, Germany, which presents a refined party of Venetians playing cards when suddenly interrupted by a visitor (Pl. 19). Next to it hung *The Itinerant Charlatan [The Quack Doctor]* (1763-1770), today at the Los Angeles County Museum of Art, representing a dentist summoning people on the public square in front of a small puppet show (Pl. 20). The next painting was *A Gentleman and his Wife* (ca. 1760), now in a private collection in St. Moritz, Switzerland, which portraits two unidentified patricians tenderly sitting next to each other in their fashionable reception room (Pl. 21). Between the piano and the fireplace, photographs show another Longhi, which probably was *The Coffee Party [Portrait of the Artist Sketching an Elegant Company]* (ca. 1760), today at the Norton Simon Museum in California (Pl. 22).[77] The painting was later renamed, because it portrays Pietro Longhi himself armed with pencil and paper while discreetly observing a cheerful group of aristocrats having coffee served at the dining table. Unfortunately, the pictures taken in the 1930s don't show the eastern side of the music room, where surely the remaining two Longhi paintings were hung. In any case, according to archival records, they were *A Musical Party [The Spinet Concert]* (ca. 1760), showing a musician at the spinet accompanying a singer (Pl. 23), and *The Dancer* (1750-1760), presenting a typical genre scene of a woman performing in the street on a tambourine (Pl. 24).[78] The six works by Pietro Longhi owned by Lionello Perera must be considered a very refined collection, particularly in the light of the growing trend of displaying eighteenth-century Venetian painting. As a matter of fact, Settecento artists from Venice became fashionable among American collectors in the 1930s, with dealers and museums increasingly devoting exhibitions to this artistic period, such as New York's Van Diemen Galleries in 1929.[79] Several of the Longhi canvasses in the Perera collection were featured as loans at other museums, which conferred high prestige to Lionello as an art expert. In March 1936 the City Art Museum in St. Louis organised an *Exhibition of Eighteenth Century Venetian Painting* thanks to special loans from other museums and private collectors.[80] Lionello contributed his *Coffee Party* and *Game of Cards*, which hung next to *The Letter* from the Metropolitan Museum of Art and to others originally from the J. Pierpont Morgan donation.[81] Following the St. Louis exhibition, New York dealers Knoedler and Co. arranged for a display of Venetian paintings in April that same year, which included again some works from Lionello's collection, as well as from renowned collectors such as Samuel H. Kress. The Metropolitan Museum in New York finally had its own exhibition of Venetian Settecento, titled *Tiepolo and his Contemporaries* opening on March 15, 1938.[82] Being asked to lend *The Itinerant Charlatan*, Lionello Perera was featured as a prominent collector on an occasion that offered great artistic acknowledgment of eighteenth-century Venetian painting.

In the case of Lionello Perera, choosing artworks by Pietro Longhi did not follow a generic pattern or the overall American collecting habit of the time. It was more likely influenced by his own Venetian heritage, since he had certainly had the occasion to admire these Venetian genre scenes as a young man in his hometown. One of the first permanent displays of Longhi paintings in Venice was publicly installed at the Querini Stampalia Foundation, which opened in 1869.[83] Besides the museum collection, the legacy of Count Giovanni Querini Stampalia further allowed the opening of a public library in his former home, devoted to students and workers. Given that the palace lies in Campo Santa Maria Formosa, a short distance from the house of Lionello's grandfather Leon Vita Cantoni, it is highly likely he frequently used the library during his university studies, thus visiting the collection too. The banker's purchase of Longhi's genre scenes was not only a matter of taste but should be considered as a clear message to visitors of the Perera home, highlighting the Venetian heritage of its collector. Furthermore, the paintings were bought in bulk early on, in 1917, which reinforces the hypothesis that their purchase was a deliberate choice, as they should enter the iconographic programme Lionello had in mind for his self-representation. Provenance records show that all six Longhi paintings in the Perera collection arrived from Italy through Elia Volpi, one of the most prominent Florentine art dealers of the time who provided numerous private collections and museums in America with works of the Italian Renaissance and Baroque period.[84] More precisely, Volpi brought the six paintings to New York to auction them at the American Art Galleries, thus they were included in the sales catalogue of 1917, which presented many other Italian art treasures he had shipped to the United States.[85] Matching information from the bulletin of the St. Louis Art Museum in 1936 and archival material collected at the Zeri Foundation, it is possible to reconstruct the likely path of the six Longhi genre scenes in the Perera collection. It seems that most of them previously belonged to Count

Miari in Padua since the eighteenth century, but they were thought to have been originally commissioned by the Gambardi family of Florence as a set of twenty subjects of *Scenes of Venetian Life* and *Portrait Groups.*[86] Four paintings of this series arrived in America about the time of Lionello's purchase at the American Art Galleries and entered the collection of the Metropolitan Museum of Art by different means. *The Letter* (1746) and *The Visit* (1746) had been purchased by the museum already in 1914, while *The Temptation* (1746) was donated by J. Pierpont Morgan in 1917 and, finally, *The Meeting* was given by Samuel H. Kress in 1936.[87] At the American Art Galleries in 1917, Lionello purchased four paintings originally from the Gambardi set, thus joining the most prominent New York collectors. They were *The Card Players, The Coffee Party, The Itinerant Charlatan,* and *The Dancer.* The remaining two paintings owned by the Italian banker, which were the family portrait and the spinet concert, are of uncertain provenance instead, which hints at the fact that Volpi probably had many different Longhi canvasses in his possession at the same time. Lionello probably was not interested in buying all paintings from one specific series but purchased the chosen six as they were auctioned in New York. It was an occasional sale, rather than a question of philological collecting. However, his choice held a specific meaning in the context of the iconographic programme he would later devise for his new home in Manhattan. The paintings conveyed a message related to the virtues and passions of the building's owner, elegantly concealed in the genre scene, though at the same time rather obvious at a swift association of ideas. Considering Lionello's keen eye for caricature and illustrations, he bought each of the six canvasses for a particular reason that must be found in their specific content. He was by nature a sharp observer of humanity and saw in Pietro Longhi this same attitude, thus finding a deeper meaning in the six collected paintings that matched his own intentions. Almost as if they were painted cartoons, a closer look at the topic of each canvas may disclose the role it played in the overall display of artworks in the Perera sitting room. The family portrait of *A Gentleman and his Wife* clearly referred to Lionello and Carolyn's relationship and activity as patrons, thus associating them to the portrayed couple of Venetian noblemen. Most obviously, *The Spinet Concert* perfectly fitted the image of a room that was frequently visited by the music elite of New York. The characters depicted by Longhi in *The Game of Cards,* featuring a party of elegant card players stopping at the arrival of a visitor, drew a nice parallel to the attention the Pereras had for their guests, as well as to society games they eagerly played as underlined also by Lionello's own caricatures. Finally, *The Coffee Party* showed the Venetian artist Pietro Longhi sketching a refined group, which surely reminded everybody of Lionello's habit to draw caricatures of his companions at any given social event.

At this point it becomes evident that the banker's new home in Manhattan was built as a deliberate act, as it was part of a wider plan to promote his and Carolyn's role among principal patrons of the arts in New York. For this reason, the building had to be something never seen before, both in its architecture and decorative details. It was to be a Modernist shrine with a thoroughly studied iconographic programme, which would prove the couple's level of sophistication. During previous decades they were already appreciated as generous donors to music events, but to upgrade their status and be considered some of the most prominent patrons in town, their home needed to be planned accordingly. At the height of his business success as Vice President of Bank of America, in 1928, Lionello was able to fulfil this aspiration, as well as to encourage Carolyn's activity as a patron and catalyst of the New York musical world. Before embarking on the new home project in the Upper East Side, the Pereras had lived in various one-family homes across Manhattan. By means of real estate bulletins and newspapers it is possible to reconstruct their location over the decades. In 1910 they probably lived in a four-storey dwelling at 38 West 83rd Street, which Carolyn had bought from her sister Florine A. Lyons.[88] Their next home was most likely a six-storey tenement at 2,095 First Avenue near 107th Street, which Lionello purchased in 1920 from an Italian kinsmen, Antonio Sorge.[89] For their new home as eminent patrons they finally bought the house of the socially-prominent William Adams Brown family at 49 East 80th Street, but chose to demolish it and rebuild the home from scratch.[90] Plans by architect Harry Allan Jacobs were drawn to have a cutting-edge townhouse echoing the geometric style of Art Deco, which was by then transforming the appearance of Manhattan's skyscrapers. During the 1910s and 1920s, Jacobs had built many of the most prestigious private residences in town, though most of them in historical styles like Neo-Renaissance, Neo-Classical, or Tudor-Revival.[91] For the Pereras he turned to a decidedly Modernist style in decoration as well as in materials, in order to reflect the spirit of the new artificial and practical age.[92] Completed between 1929 and 1930, Lionello and Carolyn's house was unique in every aspect. It was the only Art Deco private residence in Manhattan, designed in detail from the exterior facade to the interiors for a total cost of more than $100,000.[93] The facade on 80th Street looked very severe in contrast to adjoining traditional limestone houses, but for the same reason, it was also considered extremely modern (Pl. 25). Without any unnecessary decoration, it was characterised by changing brick patterns, wide luminous window openings, and only one carved stone frieze to separate the ground floor from the upper ones. The entrance was a remarkable decorative gate made of Monel, a new metal alloy that became popular with the Chrysler Building.[94] The ground storey was entirely capped by a cast-stone band with zig-zag pattern, while the upper floors were in plain brick. The rear of the house opened on a garden with an apsis in the boundary wall (Pl. 26). It was a five-storey building with the kitchen and the sitting room in front, while the dining room and the library looked towards the garden. The ground and first two floors can be considered the public space that guests might have seen when invited, thus their interiors and fittings were designed in the most minute detail. Lighting sconces and chandeliers took the forms of shells, geometric shapes, and scrolls according to Art Deco style, though mixing with some classical elements like columns, wall panels, and the marble contours of the fireplaces. The third and fourth storey were less adorned since they held the bedrooms and were thus kept for family members alone. The Perera house in the Upper East Side truly was a Modernist shrine, a unique one-family building in Manhattan with the right aspect and sophistication for a couple of prominent New York patrons. For the entire 1930s, it functioned as a place for refined musical meetings and social gatherings, very much like the palaces of those Venetian patricians depicted by Pietro Longhi hanging in the marvellous sitting room of the Pereras. The building at 49 East 80th Street was thus one of the principle dwelling places of New York's musical world for a whole decade. On a lighter note, it also became the perfect setting for family events. Already in 1931, Lionello and Carolyn's oldest son Charles Allen Perera married Ruth Hoopes Brinton, while in 1933 the entire city took notice of a double wedding in the house on October 14, when son Lionel married Dorothy Fern Bittel, and daughter Nina married Charles Wood Collier. In 1944, two years after Lionello's death, Carolyn sold the house as it had become too big for her alone. Decades later, on March 31, 1970, a new queen of the city's music landscape purchased the home for roughly $420,000. That lady was the acclaimed singer and actress Barbra Streisand.[95]

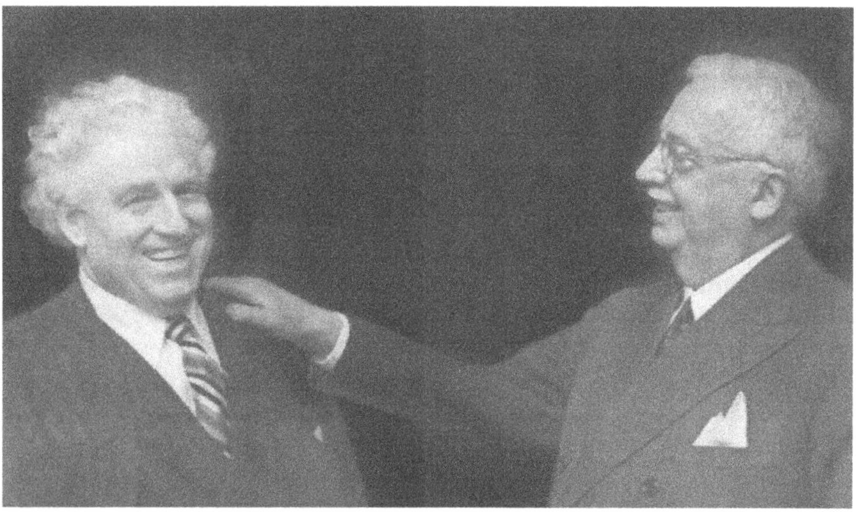

Figure 9.1: Lionello Perera and tenor Giovanni Martinelli (1930?)
Photograph of Lionello Perera (right) with star tenor Giovanni Martinelli (left) of the Metropolitan Opera, probably taken in the early 1930s. (Courtesy of the Perera Family Archive)

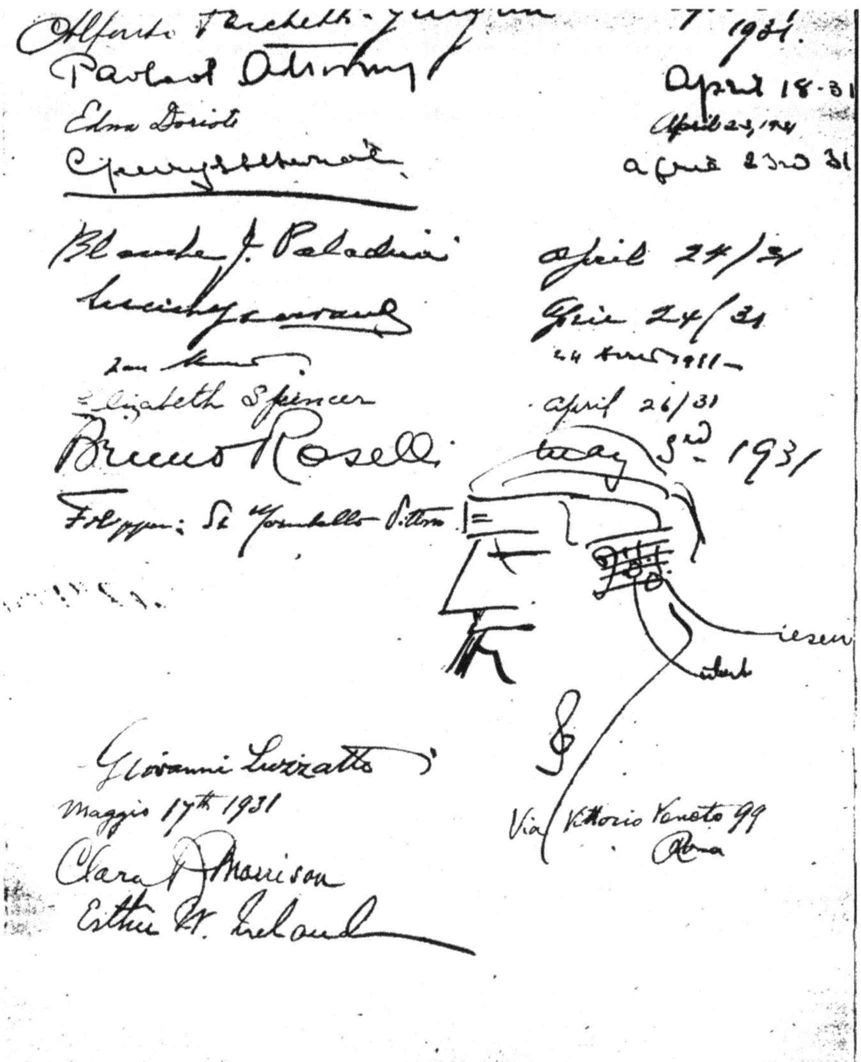

Figure 9.2: Extract from the Perera guest book (1931)

Page 27 with signatures and drawings commenced on April 19, 1931, taken from the Perera guest book, which was kept for events at their new home in the Upper East Side, at 49 East 80th Street, New York. (Courtesy of the Perera Family Archive)

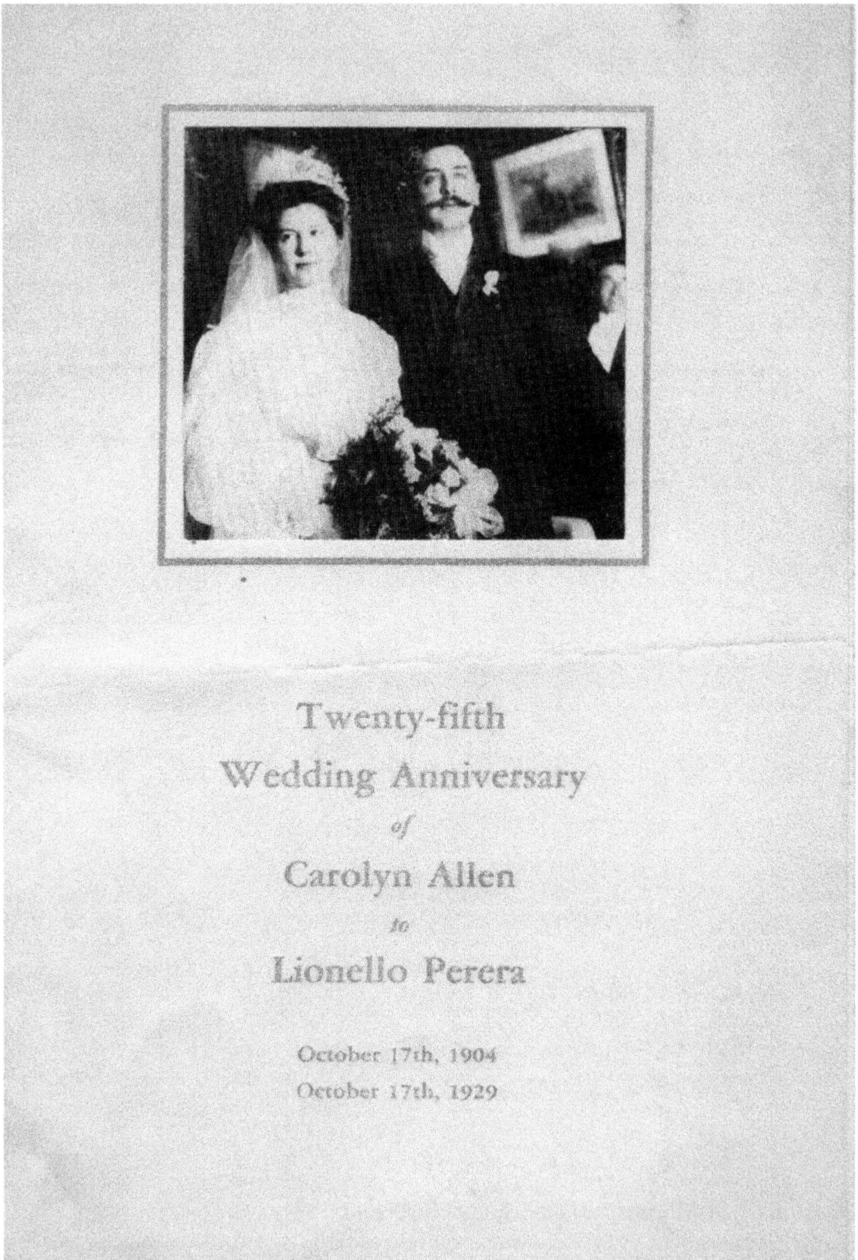

Figure 9.3: Lionello Perera and Carolyn Allen at their wedding (1904)
Photograph from the wedding of Lionello Perera and Carolyn Allen, celebrated on October 17, 1904, republished on their 25th anniversary in 1929. (Courtesy of the Perera Family Archive)

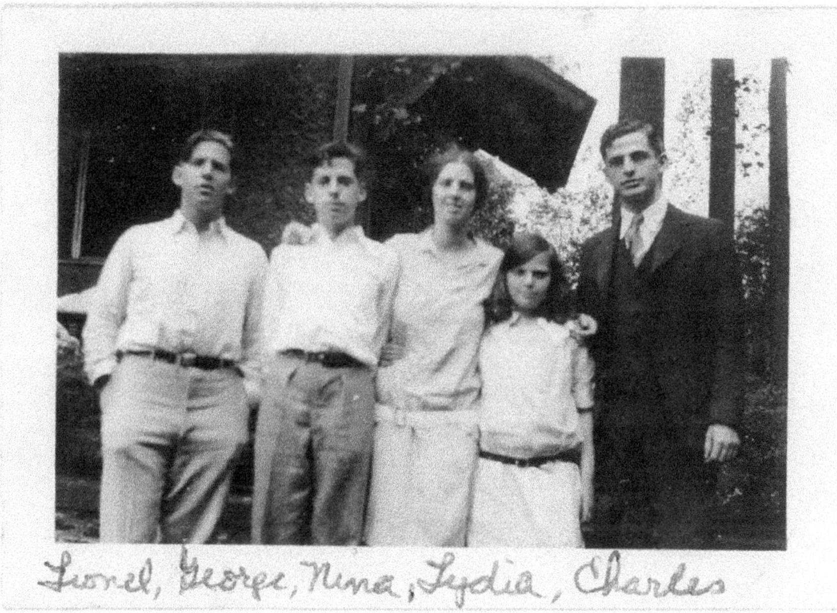

Figure 9.4: The children of Lionello Perera and Carolyn Allen Perera (1930?)

Photograph of Lionello Perera and Carolyn Allen Perera's five children, probably in the early 1930s, from left to right: Lionel Cantoni (born in 1909), George Alfred (born in 1911), Nina (born in 1907), Lydia (born in 1917), and Charles Allen (born in 1905). (Courtesy of the Perera Family Archive)

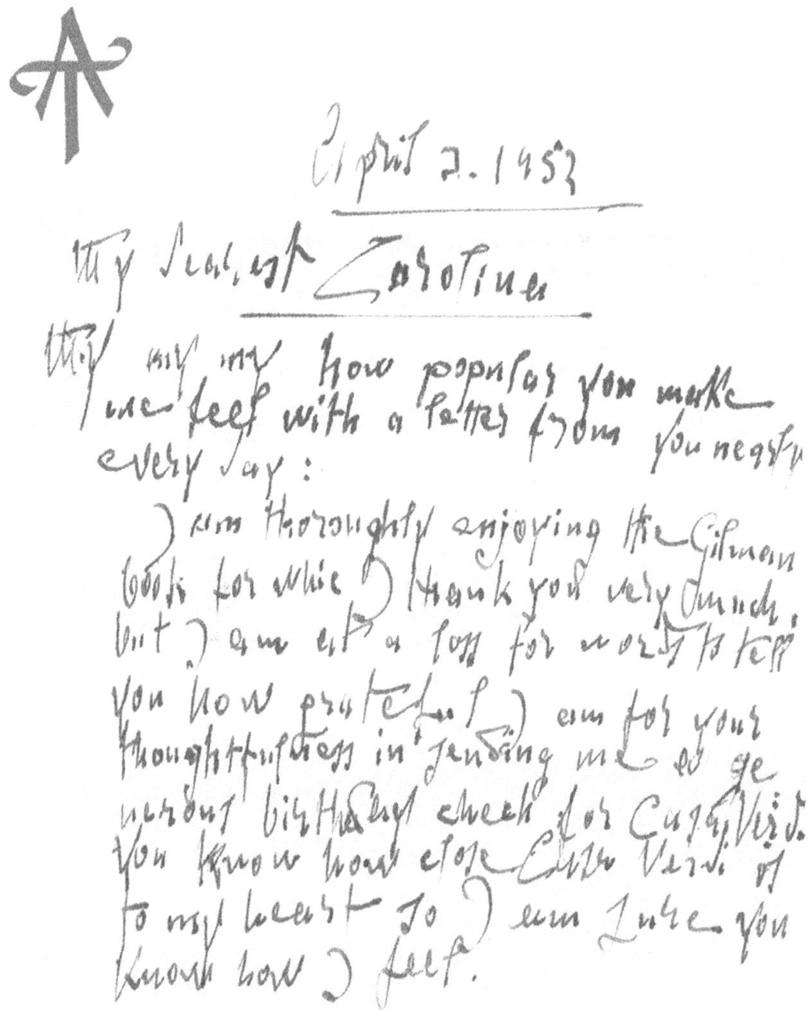

April 7. 1952

My dearest Caroline

My my my how popular you make me feel with a letter from you nearly every day:

I am thoroughly enjoying the Gilman book for which I thank you very much, but I am at a loss for words to tell you how grateful I am for your thoughtfulness in sending me so generous birthday check for Casa Verdi. You know how close Casa Verdi is to my heart so I am sure you know how I feel.

Figure 9.5: Letter from Arturo Toscanini to Carolyn Allen Perera (1952)

Recto and verso (next page) of a private letter sent by Arturo Toscanini to Carolyn Allen Perera on April 7, 1952, written on the Maestro's letterhead with his monogram "AT" on the upper left corner. (Courtesy of the Perera Family Archive)

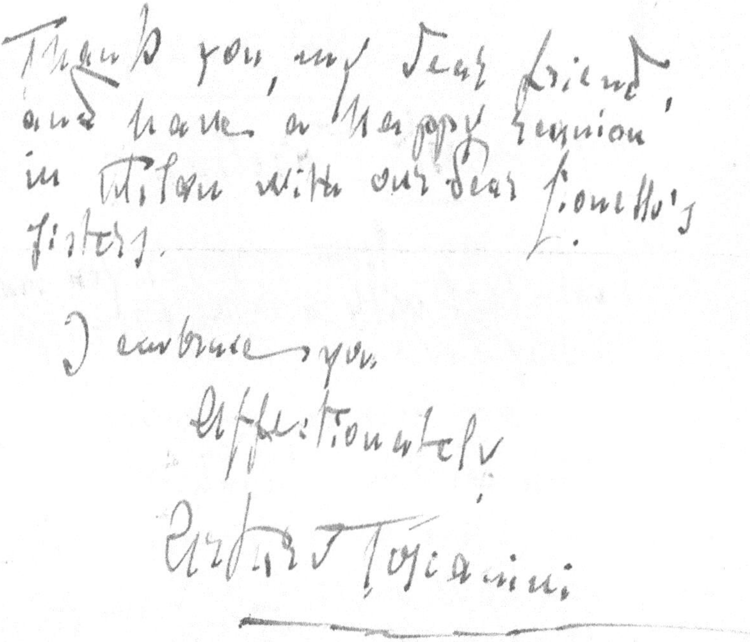
Thank you, my dear friend,
and have a happy reunion
in Milan with our dear Lionello's
sisters.

I embrace you.
Affectionately
Arturo Toscanini

Chapter 10

Nurturing the Italian Americans of New York

Of the six paintings by Pietro Longhi that Lionello Perera collected for the music room in his Modernist home, two remain to be discussed as far as their meaning is concerned in the home's overall iconographic programme. It has been argued that the first four panels, which are all set in a domestic and aristocratic environment, somehow refer to the artistic passions and social virtues of the banker and his wife. Guests invited to their house at 49 East 80th Street found their love for music and art reflected in the paintings, as well as their hospitality towards friends and their unity as a couple. The iconological intention behind the last two Longhi canvasses is a bit more difficult to guess, since they present genre scenes connected to popular activities set in eighteenth-century Venice. *The Itinerant Charlatan* shows a doctor standing atop of a platform to summon gullible folk, while *The Dancer* depicts a woman entertaining people in a rural setting. At first glance, these two paintings appear very distant from the refined atmosphere at the Pereras' Upper East Side home. At a closer look, however, both genre scenes highlight two specific features of Lionello and Carolyn's activity as patrons. The charlatan promising miraculous treatments cannot but jokingly refer to the banker's Italian heritage, since the presence of screaming vendors at street markets and fairs in the Italian strongholds of Manhattan was widespread. Furthermore, the quack doctor can be considered a true *topos* for Italian culture, which is often found in nineteenth-century literature and opera, such as with the proverbial character of Dulcamara in Gaetano Donizetti's celebrated *L'Elisir d'Amore*.[1] There is another element of this Longhi painting that directly relates to Italian identity in early twentieth-century New York. Facing the charlatan on the opposite side of the scene, as if to ridicule him, the Venetian painter positioned a little puppet theatre. Longhi painted a performance that requires the puppet-master to pull the characters over his hands, but in the context of the city's Italian districts it could be referred to another sort of marionette entertainment that gained momentum in the 1930s. In fact, throughout the decade Sicilian immigrants had established several puppet theatres across Manhattan, known as 'Opra dei Pupi', a traditional and much-beloved show centred on the stories of Charlemagne and his valiant knights fighting against the Ottomans.[2] Far from being spurious, at the time, such cultural references were obvious to Italian

Americans and probably even to Americans acquainted with Italian traditions, or even just with very basic stereotypes. Hence, *The Itinerant Charlatan* must be seen as Lionello's humorous comment on his Italian heritage, which he cherished throughout his lifetime and represented in America on different occasions, the likes of his uncle Salvatore Cantoni.

The earliest mention of the banker in this regards was in 1909 as Honorary President for the dedication of a monument in honour of Giovanni da Verrazzano, the Italian explorer who first entered the New York Harbour under the auspices of the King of France in 1524.[3] As had happened with the monument for the composer Giuseppe Verdi, the bust of Verrazzano was commissioned by a committee of prominent Italian Americans led by Carlo Barsotti, the editor of the magazine *Il Progresso Italo-Americano.*[4] This new monument was again part of an overall project to enhance the reputation of Italian Americans and foster their acceptance in New York. At the same time, honouring great Italians served also to fortify the national self-consciousness of recently arrived immigrants.[5] The dedication of the bust in Battery Park, held on October 6, 1909, was conveniently included in the wider programme for the Hudson-Fulton Celebration that commemorated the three-hundredth anniversary of the Hudson River discovery. Stirring historical pride, the overall festival aimed at establishing New York as a global hub for commerce and industry, thus it was a major success for Italian Americans to officially participate with a monument to the Italian navigator that actually had discovered the Isle of Manhattan eighty-five years before the Hudson-Fulton exploration.[6] Although the official programme of celebrations stated that Verrazzano "visited the New York Bay in 1524", the Italian inscription on the back of the pedestal highlighted that he was the first European who navigated the waters that would see the rise of one of the world's great cities.[7] In a way, the Verrazzano bust was an attempt by Italians to take credit for the discovery of New York and historically legitimise their presence in the city. Given Lionello's participation amongst honorary presidents at the unveiling of this monument, it is highly likely he had been involved already with the Verdi statue in 1906, proudly using Italian materials like Carrara marble and Montechiaro limestone. The banker might also have participated in the erection of the monument to Dante Alighieri in Dante Square, in 1921, which was the last public project accomplished by editor Barsotti to honour great Italians in New York.[8] In the 1910s, Lionello's civic activism for Italian Americans developed into primary roles, for instance, the inclusion in the board of trustees of the influential Italy America Society, joining prominent businessmen such as William Guggenheim.[9] Another major achievement was his appointment as the head of the Italian division of the Liberty Loan campaign during World War I and later even the Victory Loan, thus officially representing his country at a mass rally in New York's Hippodrome to raise

$430,000.[10] Such efforts definitely turned Lionello Perera into a true founding father of the Italian American East Coast community. In order to understand how the Italian banker interpreted his role of national representative, it is useful to analyse his call for the Fourth Liberty Loan campaign published in Italian in the October 1918 edition of the magazine *Il Carroccio*.[11] The two-page text was directed at his kinsmen to raise funds for US war relief and, of course, contained a dose of explicitly belligerent rhetoric that was typical at the time, although he did not sound deliberately acrimonious towards the German and Austrian aggressors. He rather pinpointed them with poetic phrases reminiscent of the language used in operatic tradition to describe villains, such as for example "acerbo nemico" (bitter enemy) and "fosco Sire d'Alemagna" (Germany's dark Lord). Purged from war references, the piece written by Lionello Perera is interesting especially because of the ultimate motivation he believed would convince Italian Americans to contribute to the Liberty Loan. In his opinion, supporting the effort of the United States was a moral duty as an immigrant community that had been welcomed in the country. Hence, the commitment to America is the key to understand Lionello's mindset. He was evidently convinced immigrants in New York and across the country needed to show gratitude to their new homeland for the acceptance they had received. This text discloses the banker's belief in how Italian immigrants should behave towards America, as well as signalling his personal standing among the Italian American community. He was in a position to preach to his kinsmen and act as their moral guide in the United States. Given Lionello's mindset, *The Charlatan* may thus have represented a very different kind of orator in the banker's intentions. In his eyes, it was not a simple quack doctor, but a man who stood up for his people and led them into the heart of a new nation.

The last Longhi painting in the banker's collection, *The Dancer*, is apparently more difficult to relate to a specific aspect of Lionello's biography and thus needs a careful inspection at an iconographic level. First, it must be noted that it represents a particular topic, that is dancing women, which the Venetian painter replicated several times over the decades, though in slightly different settings. Perhaps the earliest version of this theme is the famous *The Dancing Lesson* of 1741, donated by the prominent Contarini family to the Gallerie dell'Accademia in Venice, in 1838.[12] It shows a young aristocratic woman attempting first dance movements, holding her dress with the right hand, the head slightly inclined, the breast and the left foot put forward. As her mother attends the lesson sitting in an armchair, the daughter dances to the sound of a violin in an elegant private room with the instructor holding her left hand and indicating her feet. The exact position of the dancing woman with her breast and arms wide open is replicated in another painting, originally in the Giovanelli collection, which was probably painted between 1750 and 1755. This version was described as "scena galante", a chivalrous episode set on the proto-romantic backdrop of archaeological ruins.[13] The woman is well dressed, adorned with flowers in her hair and wearing a pearl necklace, while sensually dancing towards an older man in aristocratic attire placed in the lower right corner and enraptured by the dancer. All servant women around them seem very excited about the courting episode going on in front of their eyes. Maintaining the same dancer pose, but completely changing the context into a rural scene, a well-known version of this theme is the painting conventionally titled *La Furlana*. Painted in 1750 among various panels for the prominent Grimani family in Venice, since 1936, it was set on public display at the city's Ca' Rezzonico Museum and may have been visited by Lionello himself.[14] The country woman with her arms stretched open, the hands holding her gowns, and the left foot set forward, seems ready to engage in the dance with her partner to the sound of a tambourine. *La Furlana* refers to the name of a rural dance in ternary rhythm, which probably came from the Region of Friuli, close to Venice. This painting thus depicts a traditional dance of the popular classes that could be performed by one or more couples, but still giving iconographic prominence to the dancer woman who takes centre stage. Even in Lionello Perera's panel, which was commissioned by the Gambardi family of Florence around the 1750s, the woman presents this exact iconography, which evidently became archetypical for the Venetian painter to represent a dancing scene. This version makes a mixed-use of two characters and their poses as already seen in the above-mentioned paintings, which are a young folk dancer in the middle of the scene and an older man in aristocratic attire in the lower corner attending the dance. However, there is one difference, since the elderly nobleman does not look intrigued, but rather exhausted, sitting on a crate in heavily worn-out clothes. A maid stands by him pointing at the young dancer, as though he had not noticed her presence. Indeed, he seems almost unaware of what is going on around him, thus, the young lady tenderly calls for his attention towards the dancer, perhaps to get some relief from his condition. Furthermore, on the back of the scene, there are countrymen and women preparing a meal, which led art historians at the Frick collection in the mid-twentieth century to describe the scene as "The dance at the picnic", thus receiving the title that was used by Elia Volpi at the New York auction in 1917.[15] To viewers in the Italian-American community of New York, however, the scene might well have recalled a local street market, rather than a picnic. The entire episode would also have appeared as the young ladies trying to lift the spirit of the helpless, elderly man. It might seem a far-fetched interpretation of this genre scene, but if all six Longhi canvasses of the Perera collection functioned as illustrations of Lionello's character, almost as vignettes, then this last one must have referenced his tireless devotion to health support and welfare in favour of Italian Americans. Salvatore Cantoni was an example for him in this respect, having promoted the foundation of the Italian Home in 1891 as a hospital and patriotic centre. Hence, Lionello spent an integral part of his life aiding Italian immigrants and veterans in New York, as well as Italians affected by war and natural disasters back in his home country. He also made it his moral duty to lead support for the Italians in need by means of dedicated programmes and even self-established institutions.

One of the first newspaper articles about Lionello Perera's philanthropic activities in America was for financial aid to the southern Italian population hit by an earthquake in 1905.[16] He was able to collect a total amount of 50,000 Lire sent directly via his company to the Bank of Italy for the relief of Sicily and Calabria.[17] It is worth noting that he acted as representative of the Italian Red Cross and, in general, worked with institutions directly connected with Italian authorities in which he took an official position. It is uncertain when exactly Lionello began his appointment as official delegate of the Italian Red Cross in the United States, but it must have been at some point between his succession to Salvatore Cantoni in 1896 and the mentioned subscriptions for financial aid in 1905. Upon the banker's direct request, the Consul General of the Kingdom of Italy in New York issued a certificate, in May 1908, that appraised Lionello's impeccable conduct as a businessman, as well as his role as the delegate of the Red Cross, considering him a highly respected Italian national in America.[18] This document was likely needed for a much more important procedure back in his homeland. In fact, on January 24, 1909, he was officially designated as "Cavaliere", that is an Italian Knight.[19] Lionello's continuous effort for the benefit of the Italian Red Cross soon prompted an even higher decoration, again granted by the King of Italy on March 11, 1911, who made him an "Ufficiale", thus an Official of the Crown.[20] These swift and impressive public recognitions reflected the banker's tireless commitment for the well-being of Italian Americans, as well as of his kinsmen back in Italy. After the devastating Sicilian earthquake of Messina on December 28, 1908, he immediately organised the collection of material help and money for financial relief. His proactive approach was so quick and efficient that the American Red Cross, while slowly rolling out its own effort to coordinate aid packages for Italy, was caught by surprise. Wishing to centralise all monetary donations, in April 1909, the American organisation issued a statement containing much praise for the banker's swiftness, though at the same time trying to divert all wire-transfers of Italian donors through its own channels.[21] This example shows that Italian Americans did not rely on external help but organised aid to Italy directly through the efficient management of Lionello Perera and other bankers. Hence, it is understandable that he quickly earned the highest possible honours in his homeland, and the respect and gratitude of the immigrant community in New York. Henceforth the banker was regularly featured in various Italian American magazines, both as a successful businessman and a benevolent leader, revered to as "Cav. Uff. Lionello Perera".[22]

Offering relief to Italy was not the only function of the Italian Red Cross in the United States. Lionello's biggest task as a delegate was instead to organise healthcare services in America for the increasing population of Italian immigrants in New York City. In doing so, he was trying to help his kinsmen in their new homeland, as he knew America did not offer sufficient support for a swift and effective integration of Italians. Organisations and policies put in place by US charities and local government often fell short in efficiently assisting Italians. The failure of the New England Kitchen movement to help immigrants from Italy in the late nineteenth century is telling in this regard. Inspired by bourgeois rationality, this reform movement offered cooked meals to low-income Americans and poor immigrants across the city, but it did not cater to the needs of the Italian population.[23] In fact, immigrants from Italy were used to specific ingredients for preparing their meals, such as olive oil, and regarded cooking as a fundamental part of their tradition, a social event inside their family that also perpetuated gender roles and age hierarchy. The failure of American reformers to consider the characteristics of this immigrant community urged Italian American leaders and benefactors to organise their own welfare services and health centres, as Salvatore Cantoni had done with the Italian home at the end of the nineteenth century. This was also the case of the Italian Benevolent Institute and Hospital, founded in 1905 on 165 West Houston Street, very close to Little Italy, which moved to the East River on 83rd-84th Street in 1911.[24] Lionello Perera was among the promoters together with other prominent Italians, such as the import entrepreneur Antonio Zucca and law-firm founder Emanuel Gerli. The equipment and running expenses were funded by a mixture of individual donations, direct allowances from the Italian government, and charity performances at the Metropolitan Opera House. On January 8, 1927, the theatre held a performance of *La Gioconda* by Amilcare Ponchielli starring the Italian tenor Beniamino Gigli entirely for the benefit of the hospital, with boxes taken by patrons such as Mrs. Franklin D. Roosevelt.[25] Years later, Lionello was instrumental in the establishment of another hospital in 1922 that brought services nearer to the Italian American community. The East Harlem Health Center was initiated by the New York Chapter of the American Red Cross and was meant to provide services to the entire district. The choice of location was by no means accidental, since East Harlem was home to almost 120,000 people, predominantly Italian immigrants and Italian Americans, including at least 45,000 children.[26] In the late 1910s, residents of the district were in desperate need of better health services, since they suffered a much higher mortality rate as compared to the rest of the city, especially for infants.[27] Thus the American Red Cross promoted local chapters to establish community-based health centres that could deliver better services to specific districts, looking for the financial and organisational support of local leaders in business, philanthropy, and politics.[28] Interestingly, Lionello was made a treasurer of the East Harlem Health Center, while his wife and banking associates were involved as council members, including his nephews Guido and Mario Perera with their respective wives.[29]

The direct participation of Carolyn Allen Perera in the board of the latter hospital was not a matter of social prestige, but rather responded to a pattern of deep commitment toward the Italian American community. Since her marriage to Lionello she was involved in various philanthropic activities, including events for the benefit of the Italian Red Cross. First news of her efforts for Italian immigrants in New York is to be found in November 1911, when she sat among the Vice Presidents of the Italian Educational League, founded for the welfare of over 70,000 immigrant children scattered among various schools across the city.[30] In fact, soaring numbers of newly arrived immigrants around the turn of the century made single health care centres like the Italian Benevolent Institute or the East Harlem Health Center utterly insufficient to face the humanitarian challenge that was looming over New York.[31] Healthcare was not the only matter to be looked after to help Italians integrate in America and avert the peril of systemic discrimination. In the aftermath of World War I, it became even more obvious that immigrants needed a much broader range of services. Prompted by Lionello Perera and another Italian benefactor, Margherita De Vecchi, several women together with Carolyn formed the Italian Committee of the American Red Cross.[32] It was clear to them that the temporary emergency work of the Red Cross was not enough to permanently improve the welfare of thousands of immigrants across the many Italian neighbourhoods. Initially the committee's concerns were directed towards Italian American veterans and their families, so-called 'riservisti', who came back jobless after having left the United States to fight in the World War with the Kingdom of Italy. Even close relatives of Lionello were among them, including his cousin Guido Lopes Perera from Boston and his nephew Mario Perera, whose brother Decio had died early in the conflict.[33] In May 1920, it was decided to found the Italian Welfare League, which soon supported all Italian Americans, especially those that had just disembarked from ocean liners, to help them find civilian jobs, lodgings, medical care, groceries, and clothing.[34] The situation was very dire for Italians, with men mostly employed as labourers, factory hands, or petty tradesmen, while one-third of immigrant women had to supplement family income by various kinds of homework, from sewing to laundry services.[35] The Italian Welfare League came into being at the height of anti-immigrant and anti-Catholic feelings across the USA, particularly against Italians, when Federal legislation further limited the access to the country, thus mounting pressure on the foreign-born for speedy naturalisation.[36] Mrs. Lionello Perera, as Carolyn was called in her public activities, was elected first President of the Italian Welfare League. Organised as a non-partisan and non-sectarian organisation, she coordinated its activities from the headquarters at 345 Lexington Avenue for over two decades, helping people that struggled with poverty, language barriers, poor health conditions, and a lack of education.[37] Under her leadership the organisation was the first and only one to open an office directly at Ellis Island in 1924 to avoid unnecessary detention of Italians, while in the city they acted as a bureau for advice and information.[38] The league provided help of many sorts, such as old age care, assistance with immigration forms, food tickets, language help, translations, provisions for eye glasses, and basic domestic services. Funding for the charitable enterprise was obtained through donations at dinner parties that involved the Italian American elite of New York, including leaders such as Judge John J. Freschi, Senator Salvatore Cotillo, and public officer Edward Corsi.[39] It must also be noted that the Italian Welfare League was the only organisation of its kind managed entirely by women, which was definitely a unique feature at the time.[40] The reputation of Carolyn and Lionello with regard to immigrant assistance became paramount in the city, with Mayor Fiorello La Guardia appointing the banker to the New York Child Welfare Board in 1934.[41] A few years later, in 1939, Lionello Perera was selected to serve on the Advisory Council of the National Institute of Immigrant Welfare presided over by Harry Woodburn Chase.[42] That same year, the organisation was also present at the World's Fair in New York for a fundraising drive titled Italian Welfare League Day, showcasing its decade-long effort on behalf of Italian Americans and making this charity the Pereras most relevant achievement in the quest for immigrant assistance (Fig. 10.1).

Lionello Perera's appointment to the Child Welfare Board by Mayor La Guardia was no casual choice. The two leaders of the Italian American community were in a long-time relationship of collaboration that is well documented in the Perera family materials, in letters, newspaper clippings, and rally speeches.[43] Thanks to various reports in Italian American magazines, contacts between the Venetian banker and the New York mayor can be traced back to the period of World War I, though they probably knew each other from the beginning of La Guardia's political career earlier on. The magazine *Il Carroccio* mentioned that in 1919 a group of prominent Italian Americans founded the Italian Metropolis Club with headquarters at the prestigious Hotel Netherland on 5th Avenue.[44] The founding committee included banker Almerindo Portfolio as the president, entrepreneurs Giuseppe Di Giorgio and Emanuel Gerli as vice-presidents, Lionello Perera as treasurer, eventually with congressman Fiorello La Guardia, Senator Salvatore Cotillo, and Judge John J. Freschi as directors. Almost all the wives of the mentioned gentlemen were to found and lead the Italian Welfare League, demonstrating that in the 1920s, the Italian elite was employing a two-tier strategy: on the one side offering welfare services to immigrants, while on the other side constituting a political lobby to improve the acceptance of the Italian American community.[45] The Metropolis Club replaced the older Circolo

Nazionale Italiano, an elite club that included celebrities such as tenor Enrico Caruso and entrepreneur Guglielmo Marconi among its members, though it did not officially intervene in political matters.[46] It became clear that this group of prominent Italian Americans constituted the think-tank of the New York community, conveniently reformed on the occasion of La Guardia's run for Presidency of the New York City Board of Aldermen that year. Still in 1919, the banker and the congressman met at various ceremonies to honour the Italian reservists who came back from war, including La Guardia himself who had acted as an aviator commanding the second aerial squadron of the US Army in Italy.[47] This may explain why Lionello drew the caricatures of several Italian aviators, such as Guido Scelsi and Raul Lampugnani.[48] The meetings at which the two men were present in that period were abundant, such as in 1921 at the official dinner in honour of the new American ambassador to Italy, when even Attilio Giannini was present. It is evident that the banker and the politician had known each other for a very long time. It is further notable they both were of Italian and Jewish origins, since the mayor's mother was a Luzzatto Coen from the port city of Trieste. This proves that Lionello Perera openly supported the New York-born politician as the latter understood that, besides welfare and health services, Italian Americans needed their own representatives inside the US political system. Given the size of the Italian community in New York, as well as the increasing number of naturalisations, the vote of Italian Americans constituted a political launchpad for La Guardia, as well as offering an opportunity for the social and material improvement of immigrants.[49] Already in 1916, La Guardia was elected Member of the US House of Representatives with the support of the city's Italian community, and upon his return from the war he became President of the Board of Aldermen for the Republican Party.[50] From 1922 onwards he was continuously elected as a congressman for the Italian stronghold of East Harlem, where his political heir Vito Marcantonio would succeed him from 1932 to 1950.[51]

La Guardia's election as 99th Mayor of New York in 1933 was considered a remarkable achievement for the Italian community, although it did not necessarily prompt a period of city politics steered by Italian Americans, as he rather favoured people of Jewish descent in his Administration.[52] As a member of the City's Child Welfare Board appointed on February 14, 1934, it is thus significant that Lionello Perera was among the few Italian Americans chosen for relevant posts by the Mayor in his first term. The Venetian banker was particularly active in the first two election campaigns, in 1933 and 1937, as chairman of the Columbian League for La Guardia contributing with speeches and public appearances that fostered the participation of the Italian electorate. For example, Lionello opened a big rally at the New York Hippodrome on Sunday October 31, 1937, introducing New York's Deputy Commissioner, Edward Corsi, and the sitting Mayor Fiorello La Guardia.[53] His opening remarks were delivered in English and are preserved among family materials.[54] In his speech, the banker recalled that four years earlier Italian Americans had gathered in that same place to support La Guardia in his first mayoral campaign. Back then, he remarked, they were aware of the congressman's merits in Washington, thus Lionello called him "a man of action, a man of courage and integrity, an efficient and loyal official". However, they did not know, if he would be able to cope with the existing conditions of the city's administration and transform it for the better. In Lionello's opinion, La Guardia succeeded in this task and thus the banker asked the audience to give the mayor as many new councilmen as possible to "make his work smoother and better, eliminating any possibility of controversy and trouble". Many letters of gratitude from elected politicians are preserved in the Perera family archive, which disclose the respect several men of La Guardia's inner circle had for the banker's efforts in the 1937 campaign. One is a letter to Carolyn Allen Perera from Stanley M. Isaacs, who was elected President of the Manhattan Borough.[55] Also, Almerindo Portfolio, then treasurer for La Guardia, wrote to Carolyn thanking for her note of congratulations on the election results.[56] In his reply Portfolio acknowledged the great and discrete support of Lionello to the overall success of the campaign, stating: "I cannot rob your good husband of his share – his interest and cooperation helped so considerably". Edward Corsi wrote directly to Lionello in a heartfelt message on behalf of the entire Administration thanking him for his civic spirit in leading for the second time the election campaign of the "Italian community interested in the Mayor and the things for which he stands".[57]

This last comment by Corsi, referring to the Italians interested in the mayor's values, hints at the fact that not all Italians supported La Guardia, which reflected a wider schism in the Italian American community of New York during the 1930s, in particular with regard to the response toward Fascist Italy.[58] La Guardia's rule over the city consisted of twelve years at the intersection between the policies of the Republican Party and the American Labor Party, but in very close cooperation with Franklin D. Roosevelt.[59] The New York mayor was especially in line with the Democratic President's foreign policy, directed against fascism and later in favour of America's intervention in World War II against the Axis powers, which cost La Guardia a fall in the Italian electorate.[60] Lionello's affinity with the mayor certainly extended to his aversion to Mussolini and probably reflected the banker's general faith in democracy. Liberal Italian Americans were thus left with the only possibility to be committed to US politics, since Italy was by then in the grip of a totalitarian regime. Consequently, helping Italian immigrants to integrate in their new country became the banker's most urgent purpose in the interwar period. Lionello's activism in favour of La Guardia was consistent throughout the latter's entire career, as the banker evidently believed that the New York born politician could lead Italian Americans to their definitive integration in America, turning them into accepted citizens of twofold heritage. In Lionello's speech at the Hippodrome in 1937, speaking of Corsi, he highlighted how the young politician had been able to assimilate the noblest American traits, without losing the typical features of his Italian origins. Fiorello La Guardia and his acolytes evidently held the banker's opinion in high esteem, repeatedly involving him in various boards and events. In Lionello's view, his appointment to the Child Welfare Board in 1934 came as a confirmation of his personal commitment towards Italian immigrants, in which he saw continuity with the efforts of his late uncle Salvatore Cantoni (Fig. 10.2). In 1940 he was even included in the United States Conference of Mayors, when he was photographed together with La Guardia standing among convenors in the front row (Fig. 10.3). A year later, in April 1941, Lionello was also appointed to the Mayor's Committee for the "I Am An American Day", which was organised at the express desire of President Roosevelt. La Guardia himself communicated this appointment in a letter to Lionello, naming him an outstanding citizen, respected for his effort to uphold heritage, tradition, and good citizenship.[61] In the words of the Mayor, Lionello Perera was praised not just as any benefactor, but as one of the founding fathers of the Italian American community and a catalyst of civic spirit for the entire city of New York.

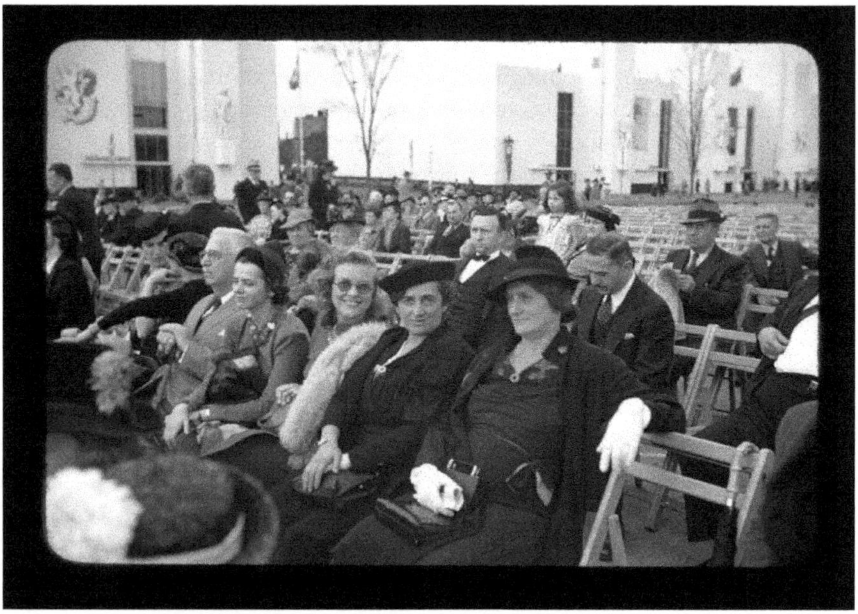

Figure 10.1: Italian Welfare League Day at the World's Fair (1939)
Photograph of the audience for the Italian Welfare League Day organised as a funding drive at the World's Fair in New York on September 19, 1939. The slide was shot by Mario Perera and shows, from left to right: Lionello Perera, his daughter Lydia, his daughter-in-law Dorothy Perera, Emma Pinto, Rose Perera, and behind them looking downwards Frank Pinto. (Courtesy of the Perera Family Archive)

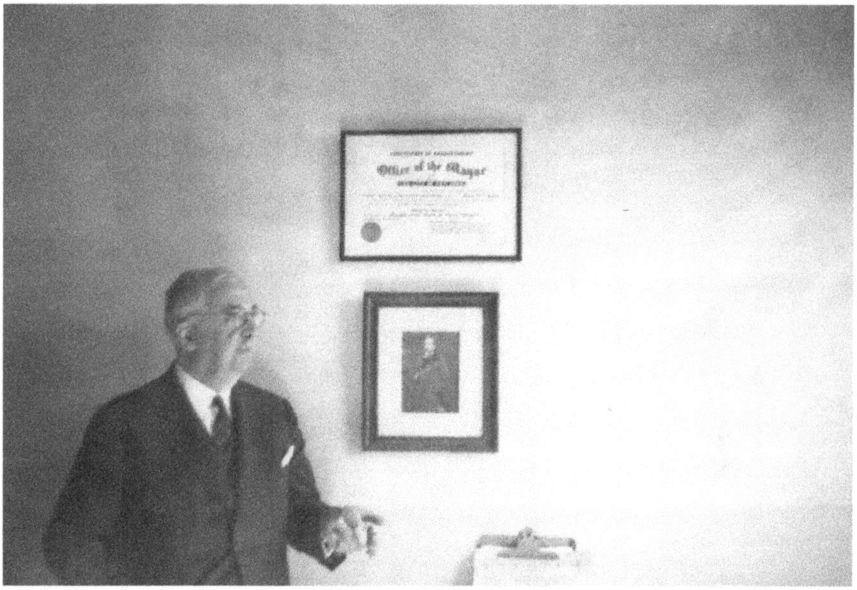

Figure 10.2: Lionello Perera appointed to Child Welfare Board (1934?)

Lionello Perera in his office standing proudly in front of a photograph of his uncle Salvatore Cantoni and displaying the certificate of his appointment to the New York Child Welfare Board, probably taken after 1934. (Courtesy of the Perera Family Archive)

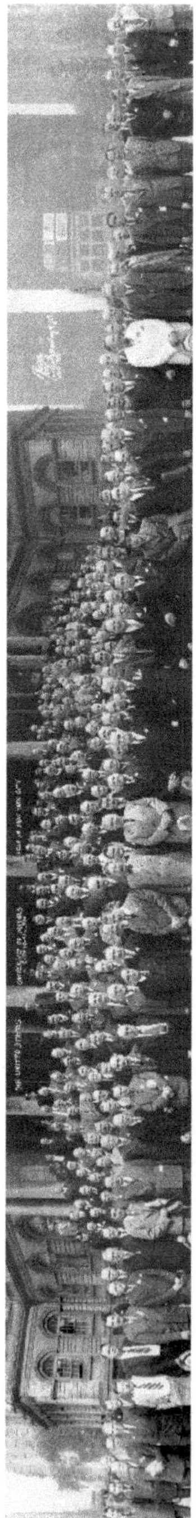

Figure 10.3: The United States Conference of Mayors (1940)

Group photograph of the mayors at the United States Conference of Mayors held in New York on September 19-21, 1940. Lionello Perera is standing in the front row (third to the right of the central man in light gray suit), while Fiorello La Guardia is just a few people away in the front row (third to the left of the central man in light gray suit). (Courtesy of the Perera Family Archive)

Part VI: Conclusions and Visual Traces

Chapter 11

A Gentle Italian American Legacy

In April 1920, Lionello Perera travelled on the Dante Alighieri Ocean Liner to Italy with his daughter Nina, who was thirteen years old. They were in good spirits, befriending the refined Italians lodged in the first class and even organising a concert on board. It starred the passenger Alessandro Dolci, a tenor in the Chicago Opera, accompanied at the piano by the banker's young daughter. In a letter to his wife Carolyn, who had stayed in New York, Lionello joked about the possibility of becoming a musical manager in case his banking activity should fail.[1] It was his last trip to Italy as an Italian citizen, since a few months later, in July 1920, he was finally granted naturalisation in the USA. His correspondence with Carolyn, however, reveals how much at ease he was about his double heritage. Travelling frequently between Italy and the United States, he evidently thought of himself as Italian and American. Especially after the watershed moment represented by World War I, the relationship between the two countries was cemented in his personal experience. After twenty-six years as an immigrant, he felt at home in both continents, although at the time he could not predict that the coming decades would prove extremely challenging for Italian Americans and the way they felt about their identity. He had contributed to the making of Italian Americans in New York, bringing together his kinsmen from various regional backgrounds into one coherent national group by means of philanthropic activities involving the entire Italian community. Indeed, immigrants arriving between the end of the nineteenth century and the inception of World War I had a strong sense of belonging to a specific region, province, or even village.[2] Nevertheless, in the United States they were confronted with discrimination and bigotry directed against Italians as a whole group. Despite the alliance between Italy and America against the powers of the Axis during World War I, in the aftermath life in the United States became even more difficult for people of Italian ancestry. Naming Italians as undesirable people, the Quota Acts of 1921 and 1924 heavily curbed immigration from Italy, thus reducing arrivals in the country from 222,260 in 1921 to 6,203 in 1925.[3] Such restrictive legislation made Italian immigrants understand that they could not move freely between the two countries anymore. As a consequence, naturalisation rates among the whole population of Italian descent soared from 28,1 percent in 1920 to 50 percent in 1930.[4] As far as Italian American identity is concerned, the interwar period was further complicated by the rise of fascism in Italy, as well as by the ambiguous relationship of the United States to Mussolini's regime.[5] In the 1920s, many Italian American magazines started to praise the Duce, or at least to highlight the general enthusiasm for his alleged improvements to the country's modernisation and international stance. Even fierce opponents of fascism who had escaped to the United States had to admit that immigrants eventually took pride in their Italian origin, especially because American public had shifted its view on Italy due to Mussolini's tough stance against communism.[6] Italian Americans visiting their country of origin were in general aware of the oppressive nature of the Fascist regime, expressing appreciation for democracy once they came back to America.[7] Nevertheless, most Italian Americans hoped Italy's international consideration under Mussolini's rule would free them of decade-long discrimination, as well as contrast ethnic prejudice motivated by Anglo-Saxon racial stances.[8] Inside the immigrant community, a faint amount of criticism grew by the day in the 1930s, but it must be said that Italian Americans mostly stood by their homeland even after Italy's global excommunication upon its imperialist aggression on Ethiopia.[9] The true watershed moment arrived only with the United States entering World War II against the Nazi Germany and Fascist Italy. Italian Americans thus started to regard the USA as the political entity they belonged to, while maintaining a mere emotional bond with their country of origin.[10] Italy's declaration of war against the United States on December 11, 1941, did not come as a surprise, as it was tied to the Japanese attack on Pearl Harbor. Nevertheless, it shook the immigrant community's political beliefs, with many disavowing the Fascist regime and getting closer to the American nation. On the other hand, it did not prompt Italian Americans to turn their back on their ethnic roots, which rather stayed with them as a self-conscious cultural heritage.[11] Angela Carlozzi, Secretary of the Italian Welfare League founded by the Pereras, commented publicly that she felt terrible to see her two countries at war, but she also stressed that she and fellow Italian Americans were first and foremost Americans.[12]

There is no doubt that Lionello and Carolyn shared the same view on the tragic clash between Italy and the United States. On one of his last nights, in April 1942, Lionello is recalled having sat in his studio with Arturo Toscanini after dinner, frantically searching radio stations for updates on the war in their homeland.[13] With close relatives still in Italy, and all of Jewish origin, the banker must have felt anxious during the entire interwar period. Furthermore, this might account for how he tackled the challenges to Italian American identity during the Fascist regime. In this regard, it is striking that Lionello Perera's opinions and persona were frequently featured in the Italian community of New York until the early 1920s, while no public comments by the banker about Italy can be found after Mussolini's rise to power. Furthermore, it must be noted that he earned his last official honour from Italy in 1924, a gold medal for his service to the Italian Red Cross bestowed by the King, not by the Duce.[14] After this recognition, Lionello's name cannot be found in Italian American magazines anymore, save for the bank run which occurred that same year in February. It appears that he progressively distanced himself from his homeland, leading his company instead towards a deeper integration in the United States. While he had built his success around the Italian community, with fascism Lionello set forth to consolidate his business within the American banking system of the United States. With regard to the immigrant community, he was evidently disillusioned with Italy's new course and understood that naturalisation was becoming the only viable option for Italian Americans in the interwar period.[15] Although he did not make public statements on the matter, his actions at the time were clear enough, as they described the kind of Italian heritage and Italian American identity he stood for. First and foremost, a closer look at the Italian Welfare League allows us to see the values he cherished and deemed necessary for a full integration in the United States. Interestingly, the charity was not religiously oriented, as was typical with many Italian benevolent organisations, which were steered or inspired by the Catholic Church. Nor was it politically oriented, resisting any links with the new Italian identity shaped by fascism. This gives the impression that Lionello Perera had a secular and liberal idea of nationhood in mind, one that was attuned with the Kingdom of Italy and compatible with the values of American democracy. In her memoirs, Carolyn notices two episodes that occurred during her Presidency of the Italian Welfare League, which further confirm the Pereras utter aversion to fascism.[16] The first one occurred in 1939, on their last trip together to Italy, where they used to travel every year on vacation and to visit relatives until the outbreak of World War II (Fig. 11.1). Lionello's wife made it her duty to flatter an Italian senator at the health resort of Salsomaggiore and convince him to give her a copy of a booklet with the names of all the leaders of the Fascist party, from the highest to the lowest ranks. She managed to smuggle the book through France and then delivered it to the FBI. A year later, at the headquarters of her charity in New York, she overheard a conversation among two Italian women about the Vulcania, a steamer departing for Italy. One of them was wondering about her former honeymoon cabin being shut, which led Carolyn to contact the FBI over the possibility that it had been filled with illegal ammunition for Germany. Sometime later, she was unexpectedly visited by the head of the British Intelligence, Sir Gerald Campbell, and the English Consul in New York, who congratulated her for helping them discover an illicit route of weapons to the Axis powers through Italian ports. All of this would not have happened, if Lionello had not back Carolyn and shared her view, as was the case with the paintings they secretly carried to the United States for Arturo Toscanini. Even the banker's continuous support for Fiorello La Guardia, which lasted throughout the 1930s by means of the Columbian League, is consistent with a worldview that was averse to fascism. It is noteworthy that Lionello used the term 'Columbian' as a synonym for 'Italian', which was common in the interwar period among Italian Americans that kept close to their immigrant heritage, though avoiding any direct reference to Italy because of the Fascist regime.[17] Not by chance, after America's declaration of war La Guardia became much more outspoken, explicitly encouraging Italians to revolt against fascism in a weekly radio show.[18]

From this perspective, one must also see the banker's involvement in the foundation of Casa Italiana at Columbia University in 1927, which was to become the first research centre for Italian studies based in a major American university. Critics at the time called this enterprise an inexcusable concession to Fascist Italy, allowing the creation of an institute for right-wing propaganda in America.[19] Among the founders of Casa Italiana there surely were prominent Italian Americans that did not conceal sympathy of Mussolini, but Lionello Perera rather participated out of the desire to see his heritage –not Italy's current ideology– recognised as a relevant study topic in American academia. Regarding Fascist Italy, Casa Italiana indeed emerged as a compromise solution between contrasting views. The plan to have a cultural centre for Italian studies at Columbia University predated the inception of the Fascist regime, as it involved the New York business elite already active through the Italy America Society.[20] Still in 1925, the plan was to create a centre for Italian cultural studies at a major university in New York, which would in turn allow the promotion of conferences, scholarships, and academic publications.[21] Despite Mussolini's coming to power, Casa Italiana received the backing of Chancellor of Columbia University, Nicholas Murray Butler, who believed such an enterprise could function for appeasement purposes, and foster a durable relationship between the United States and Italy.[22] The circumstances surrounding Casa Italiana reflect the complexity of positions towards fascism that characterised the Italian American community of the time, as well as the initial favour of the American elite. For those who had struggled for the ethnic and cultural recognition of Italian Americans, the research centre at Columbia definitively elevated Italian heritage into the highest ranks of academia, further consolidating it as an adjunct component of the overall American identity. For those who aimed at strengthening business relations between America and Italy, despite the latter's totalitarian regime, Casa Italiana offered a normalised image of the country, as stated by Guglielmo Marconi in the opening speech on October 12, 1927.[23] At this point, it is relevant to stress the fact that the centre was entirely funded by Italian American businessmen without any support of the Italian regime. The most relevant donation came from Anthony Campagna, Joseph and Michael Paterno, a group of property developers who constructed the building on a university spot between 117th Street and Amsterdam Avenue.[24] Lionello

Perera contributed with 10,000 dollars towards the library, thus expressly participating to the endowment fund for the research activities of scholars and students at Columbia.[25] He later took part in a dance on a steamboat to fund maintenance costs for Casa Italiana, which by then was directly managed by the university.[26] Soon after, however, the banker seems to have cut ties with Casa Italiana, probably because of its ambiguous position towards fascism. Although the centre was officially part of Columbia University and its cultural programme was supposed to be independent, rector Murray Butler like many in the American elite saw fascism as a valuable instrument against communism.[27] His view led to decisions regarding Casa Italiana that the Fascist regime could only but receive with delight, as with the appointment of the Italian journalist and intellectual Giuseppe Prezzolini as director in 1930. His name can be found among guests at the Pereras in the Upper East Side, on May 6, 1936, probably because Lionello showed respect for the director of such a centre, which represented Italian culture in America.[28] Furthermore, Prezzolini always denied being a member of the Fascist party and he publicly kept an ambiguous position towards the totalitarian regime. Far from being impartial though, he truly blocked access to the centre's cultural programme to any direct opponent of Mussolini, as harshly pointed out at the time by Anti-Fascist thinker Gaetano Salvemini.[29] The director of Casa Italiana was skilful enough to navigate a very difficult period for Italian American relations, in the 1930s, as well as through the turmoil of World War II. He even managed to conceal his membership in the Fascist party, which he acquired in 1935 according to a later investigation by the FBI.[30]

The case of Casa Italiana highlights the ambiguity of America's relationship to Fascist Italy, which was also reflected in the Italian American community. It shows how Fascist propaganda could make its way into the United States with the tolerance of the American elite. As far as Lionello Perera is concerned, he probably took part in the founding of the research centre, because he had been involved in the project since its inception before the Fascist regime took hold. Furthermore, he considered it a major accomplishment for people of Italian heritage that had struggled for recognition in America, though he underestimated the viciousness of fascism. Like many liberals of Italian descent living abroad, he probably thought that Mussolini did not constitute a real or direct threat, only to be shocked by the proclamation of the notorious Italian Racial Laws in 1938.[31] Like other Italian Jews, Lionello suddenly realised the violence Mussolini could unleash against his opponents. The banker and his relatives found themselves enemies of the Italian people because of their Judaism, while for his whole life he had been rather casual about his Jewish origins, seeing himself rather as a prominent Italian national in a foreign country. Evidence shows that the Fascist racial legislation found a fertile ground even in the Italian American community, particularly due to already strained relations between Jewish and Italian populations in the United States, caused by competition in the job and housing market.[32] A private letter dictated to Carolyn in early 1939, preserved among family materials in two typewritten draft copies and a page of handwritten notes, discloses Lionello's deep concern with the situation of Italian Jews.[33] Yet he was trying to be cautious and avoid public disapproval, mostly because of the backlash that could have hit his relatives in Italy. Fiorello La Guardia, who was also Jewish and took part in an Anti-Nazi league, also did not publicly oppose Italy's anti-semitic laws of 1938 until the declaration of war against the USA in 1941.[34] The banker's draft letters were typed by Carolyn on January 21, 1939, and stand as extraordinary documents to understand the mindset of prominent Jews of Italian descent at such a difficult time. They fully demonstrate the banker's anguish and disillusionment. By comparing the two draft versions it is possible to understand the editing process of the final letter, as well as the subsequent reconsiderations which were dictated by a deep state of fear, thus revealing that Lionello was perfectly aware of the tragedy looming over Europe's Jews. First, it is necessary to guess who the recipient of this letter was, since first name and address are missing. One draft letter directed to a Mr. Springer is probably the first version that was compiled, since it bares the longest text and many erasures. The second draft only has the initial S of the last name, so the recipient probably was an acquaintance of the Pereras, but not a close friend. As can be inferred from the content, it appears that the letter was written in response to a message by Mr. Springer, who had sent along the letter with a newspaper clipping earlier that week. The reason why Carolyn typed the reply in first person and quoting her husband was because Lionello was in bed with flu, which also accounts for the hesitant handwriting that can be found on a page of notes made directly by the banker.[35] Evidently, the old banker insisted answering immediately despite his health condition, thus considering it an urgent matter. The first typewritten draft is dated January 21, but the year is missing. The latter can be easily guessed as 1939, because the content referred to Mussolini's infamous speech in Trieste for the promulgation of racial laws on September 18, 1938. The letter further hints at the fact that the war in Europe had not yet begun, but there were serious threats that the situation would degenerate. The letter deals with the danger posed by fascism to the Jews of Italy, comparing their situation with the terrible fate that had already befallen German and Eastern European Jews. This detail may hint at the fact that Mr. Springer had sent an article on the detrimental progression of antisemitism and was wondering what the banker thought could be done by American Jews to prevent these dramatic events. His enquiry was directed to

Lionello as an Italian American Jew, asking explicitly for advice. It is thus likely that the person writing to the banker was M.R. Springer, who was an Orthodox Jewish adviser to the exiled Czechoslovak Government and State Council sheltering in the United States between 1938 and 1948.[36] In his reply, Lionello used harsh words such as "pogrom" and "extermination" to describe the unfolding of events against Jews in Europe. The banker's anguish was very personal too, since he insisted that the letter was confidential because his family in Italy was financially dependent on him and might suffer consequences. However, this remark was deleted in the second draft and may have been absent from the final version. The letter begins with Carolyn referring to her husband's worry that nothing could be done anymore to stop the persecution of Jews in Italy, since Mussolini had expressed the will to conduct the operation to its bitter end by inferring "tireremo diritto". It was Lionello's deepest conviction that Jews in Europe were systematically seized by Nazis and Fascists for economic exploitation, not because of an alleged plot by international Judaism against totalitarian regimes. Such remarks clearly referred to far-right propaganda of the time, like the infamous *Protocols of the Elders of Zion* that found widespread acceptance even among Italian Americans. Italian immigrants were thus led to believe that American Jews were pushing the United States to enter war against their own ancestral country.[37] To avoid fuelling such fallacy, the banker maintained that American Jews should better keep out of war talk. Furthermore, in his remarks Lionello clearly states that Italian Jews had been maliciously singled out as enemies of fascism, although he knew from direct experience that just as many non-Jewish Italians opposed fascism. He thus believed Mussolini embarked in the pogrom out of an opportunistic attitude to ensure a durable alliance with Adolf Hitler. In any case, the outcome would be detrimental for Jews all over Europe. Carolyn added her own remarks, stating she had read and archived dozens of Italian articles describing the progression of anti-semitism in Germany. To the Pereras, the tragic consequence of such criminal madness was by then irrevocable and self-evident. In her closing remarks, Carolyn sounds bitterly disillusioned about the dire prospect for people of Jewish descent under Nazi rule, though her husband is somehow more optimistic in the case of Italy: "I fear for all Jews in Germany, for their extermination is imminent, but it is my husband's firm opinion that the Italian[s] would not allow physical cruelty; I pray he may be correct."[38]

Even at such a tragic moment, Lionello Perera did not lose faith in the good nature of his nationals. Having spent a lifetime helping Italians in their homeland, as well as Italian immigrants in America, he could not believe they might turn on Jews like raging beasts. Unfortunately, history would prove him wrong, as it did with thousands of Italian Jews that could not escape the barbaric mass murder set in motion by the Nazis with the assistance of many Italian supporters.[39] His own beloved sisters, Clelia Perera Napoli and Olga Perera Pincherle, were chased by the SS across northern Italy in the aftermath of the country's occupation by German troops in 1943. Clelia went into hiding among the tortuous streets of Milan, changing constantly locations to avoid the Fascists coming regularly after her at the homes of various relatives across town.[40] Olga escaped from the city of Gorizia to the countryside near Udine, but was eventually arrested in Gemona del Friuli on January 22, 1944.[41] That same year, on February 26, she was deported to Auschwitz by train from Trieste with her daughter Emilia and her son Vittorio Samuele.[42] None of them survived, but Olga's other daughter Lea miraculously escaped being captured.[43] Fortunately, Lionello Perera did not witness the atrocities that affected his dear sister and her children. By then, he had already died of a stroke in New York on April 26, 1942, just after reaching Pennsylvania Station on the Congressional Limited from Washington.[44] He had visited his daughter Nina and her family there, before their departure to Bolivia on her husband's diplomatic mission. In his will, he had left provisions for his beloved wife Carolyn and their five children, all of which developed distinguished careers (Fig. 11.2). Charles became a renowned ophthalmologist, while George was the Dean of Columbia Medical School. Nina co-founded Young Audiences with her mother and Lydia was a well-known media performer with her own CBS show in the early days of television. Of the five siblings, Lionel was the one who continued the family tradition of banking business founding Perera, Manfra & Brookes, which specialised in foreign money exchange.[45] To Lionello and Carolyn's many grandchildren they were lovingly "Poppie" and "Nona", whose deeds and stories were cherished as amazing adventures that had offered a better life for them all, as they did for thousands of Italian Americans in New York.

Although memory has faded over time, Lionello Perera's legacy was one of great action, but few words. As an Italian American banker and patron in New York, who was proud of his Venetian and Jewish origins, his legacy is marked with passion and compassion. This book shall be of use, if it helps rediscovering such a remarkable and discreet Italian American biography. The words of farewell by Lionello's daughter Nina, spoken softly at the funeral, offer an intimate glimpse of the man behind this book, as well as coming as a perfect conclusion: "You gave all your life this deep sweetness, gentleness, compassion. You have gone but you have left a precious memory of love, and simplicity, and goodness. We must be better than we are, more worthy because of you".[46]

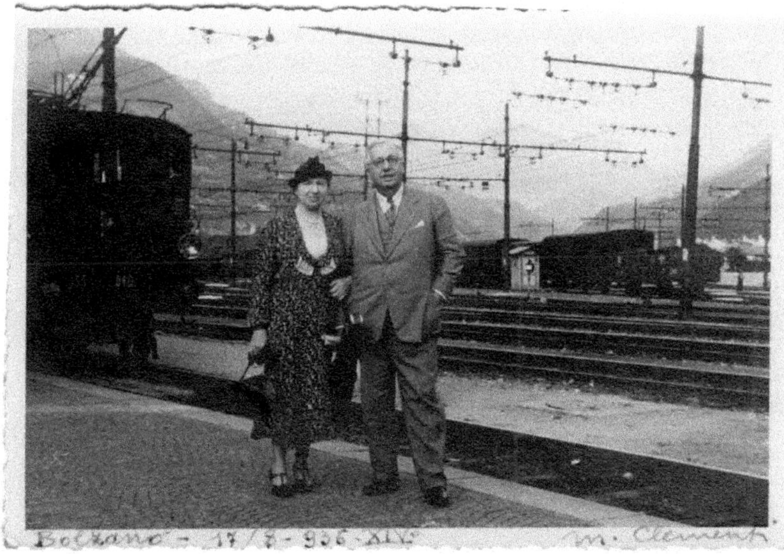

Figure 11.1: Lionello Perera and Carolyn Allen Perera in Italy (1936)
Lionello Perera and Carolyn Allen Perera at the train station of Bolzano on August 17, 1936, on vacation in the Alps in Northern Italy. (Courtesy of the Perera Family Archive)

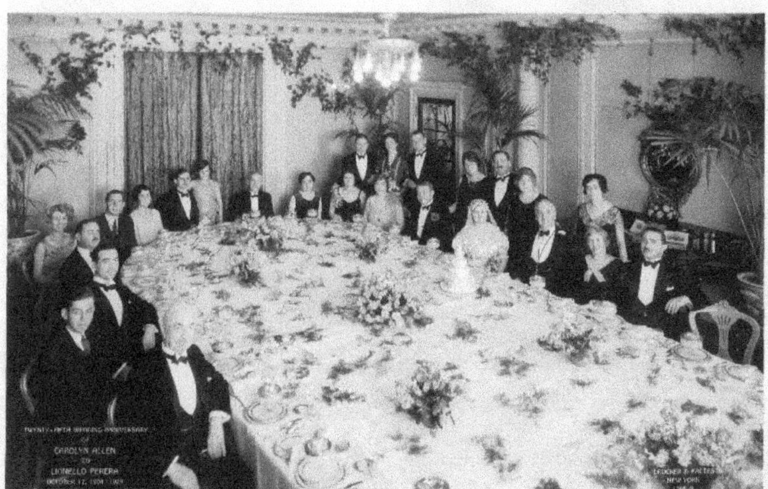

Figure 11.2: 25th wedding anniversary at Hotel Biltmore (1929)
Group photograph of the festive meal at the Hotel Biltmore, New York, for the 25th wedding anniversary of Lionello Perera and Carolyn Allen Perera on October, 17, 1929. Many relatives of the Pereras were present on this occasion, including their five children, as well as the banker's nephews Mario and Guido Perera with their respective families. (Courtesy of the Perera Family Archive)

Chapter 12

Plates from the Perera Collection

Plate 1

a. John Alfred Mohlte, *Portrait of Emilia Cantoni*, 1898-9, oil on canvas. (Courtesy of the Perera Family Archive)

b. John Alfred Mohlte, *Portrait of Cesare Lopes Perera*, 1898-9, oil on canvas. (Courtesy of the Perera Family Archive)

Plate 2

a. Lionello Perera, *Portrait of a young man (Brandon, Vt)*, September 12, 1931, coloured. (Courtesy of the Perera Family Archive)

b. Lionello Perera, *Caricature of a man (Lemonade not good!)*, no date. (Courtesy of the Perera Family Archive)

c. Lionello Perera, *Caricature of Ulderico Bellini (Eh! Huattro picche un sce l'aveva miha!!!)*, coloured, no date. (Courtesy of the Perera Family Archive)

d. Lionello Perera, *Nancy Dyson (Can't I come to luncheon, too?)*, no date. (Courtesy of the Perera Family Archive)

Plate 3

Lionello Perera, *Four caricatures of men with beards and moustaches*, no date. (Courtesy of the Perera Family Archive)

Plate 4

Lionello Perera, *Caricatures of Giulio Setti* (a), *Arturo Toscanini* (b), *Edward Phillips Oppenheim* (c), and *Harry Woodburn Chase* (d). (Courtesy of the Perera Family Archive)

Plate 5

Lionello Perera, *Four drawings of women attending concerts or playing music*, no date. (Courtesy of the Perera Family Archive)

Plate 6

a. Gino Lorenzo Perera, *Landscape (Countryside with hills)*, no date, oil on canvas. (Courtesy of the Perera Family Archive)

b. Gino Lorenzo Perera, *Landscape (Lake with Capitol Hill or Vatican?)*, no date, oil on canvas. (Courtesy of the Perera Family Archive)

Plate 7

Arturo Noci, *Sketch of Lionello Perera (Stamford 24 Ag 924)*, 1924, pencil on paper. (Courtesy of the Perera Family Archive)

Plate 8

Arturo Noci, *Study for the portrait of Lionello Perera*, 1933, pencil on paper. (Courtesy of the Perera Family Archive)

Plate 9

Arturo Noci, *Portrait of Lionello Perera*, 1933, oil on canvas. (Courtesy of the Perera Family Archive)

Plate 10

Arturo Noci, *Still life*, 1933, oil on canvas. (Courtesy of the Perera Family Archive)

Plate 11

Arturo Noci, *Landscape at Fiumarella di Canneto*, 1921, oil on canvas. (Courtesy of the Perera Family Archive)

Plate 12

Perera Home photograph series, *Sitting Room (fireplace with Arturo Noci portait)*, mid 1930s, 49 East 80th Street, New York. (Courtesy of the Perera Family Archive)

Plate 13

Eugène Feyen, *Two fisher girls sewing at the border of the sea in Brittany*, after 1860, oil on canvas. (Courtesy of the Perera Family Archive)

Plate 14

Antonio Ermolao Paoletti, *Peasant women going to the marketplace*, late nineteenth century, oil on canvas. (Courtesy of the Perera Family Archive)

Plates 15

a. Perera Home photograph series, *Library (writing desk with Bruegel painting)*, mid-1930s, 49 East 80th Street, New York. (Courtesy of the Perera Family Archive)

b. Perera Home photograph series, *Library (corner with Rosselli painting)*, mid-1930s, 49 East 80th Street, New York. (Courtesy of the Perera Family Archive)

Plate 16

Cosimo Rosselli, *Cristo in croce (Christ on the Cross)*, 1460-1507, tempera and oil on panel. (With the permission of Bryn Mawr College, photo credit James Schneck)

Plate 17

Lorenzo Lotto, *Self-Portrait (Portrait of a Gentleman)*; oil on canvas, 1500-1549. (Research purposes: © Museo Nacional Thyssen-Bornemisza, Madrid)

Plates 18

a. Perera Home photograph series, *Sitting Room (corner with three Longhi paintings)*, mid-1930s, 49 East 80th Street, New York. (Courtesy of the Perera Family Archive)

b. Perera Home photograph series, *Sitting Room (window side with piano)*, mid-1930s, 49 East 80th Street, New York. (Courtesy of the Perera Family Archive)

Plate 19

Pietro Longhi, *The Visit (The Game of Cards)*, ca. 1760, oil on canvas, Alte Pinakothek Munich, Germany. (With the permission of Fondazione Zeri)

Plate 20

Pietro Longhi, *The Quack Doctor (The Itinerant Charlatan)*, 1763-1770, oil on canvas, Los Angeles County Museum of Art, California, USA. (Public domain: www.lacma.org)

Plate 21

Pietro Longhi, *A Gentleman and his Wife*, ca. 1760, oil on canvas, private collection, St. Moritz, Switzerland. (Public domain: www.wikimedia.org)

Plate 22

Pietro Longhi, *Portrait of the Artist Sketching an Elegant Company (The Coffee Party)*, ca. 1760, oil on canvas, Norton Simon Museum, California, USA. (With the permission of Norton Simon Museum).

Plate 23

Pietro Longhi, *The Spinet Concert (A Musical Party)*, ca. 1760, oil on canvas. (With the permission of Fondazione Zeri)

Plate 24

Pietro Longhi, *The Dancer*, 1750-1760, oil on canvas. (With the permission of Fondazione Zeri)

Plate 25

Perera Home photograph series, *Facade on 80th Street*, mid-1930s, 49 East 80th Street, New York. (Courtesy of the Perera Family Archive)

Plate 26

Perera Home photograph series, *Garden Side*, mid-1930s, 49 East 80th Street, New York. (Courtesy of the Perera Family Archive)

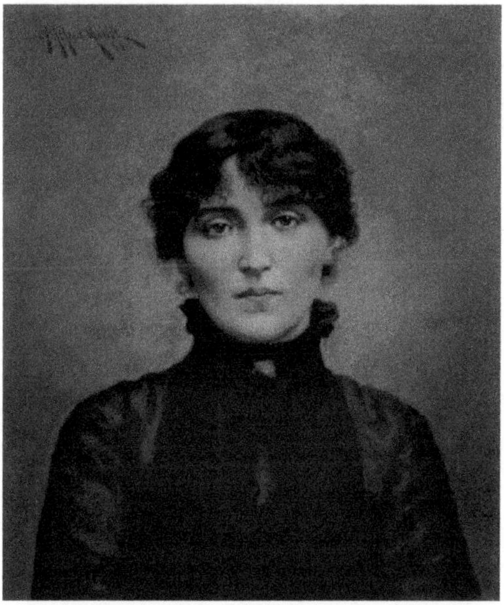

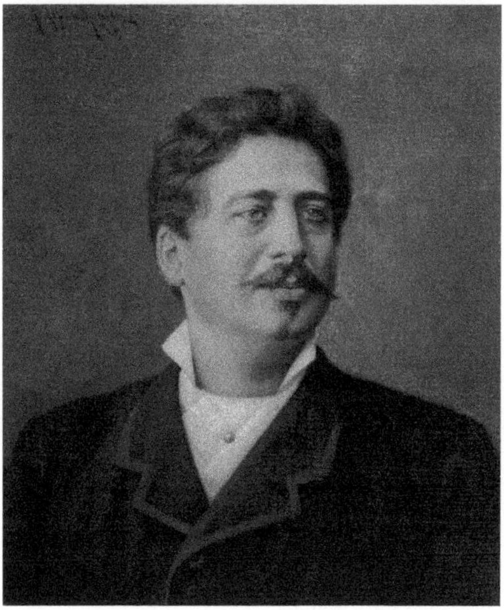

Plate 1

a. John Alfred Mohlte, *Portrait of Emilia Cantoni*, 1898-9, oil on canvas. (Courtesy of the Perera Family Archive)

b. John Alfred Mohlte, *Portrait of Cesare Lopes Perera*, 1898-9, oil on canvas. (Courtesy of the Perera Family Archive)

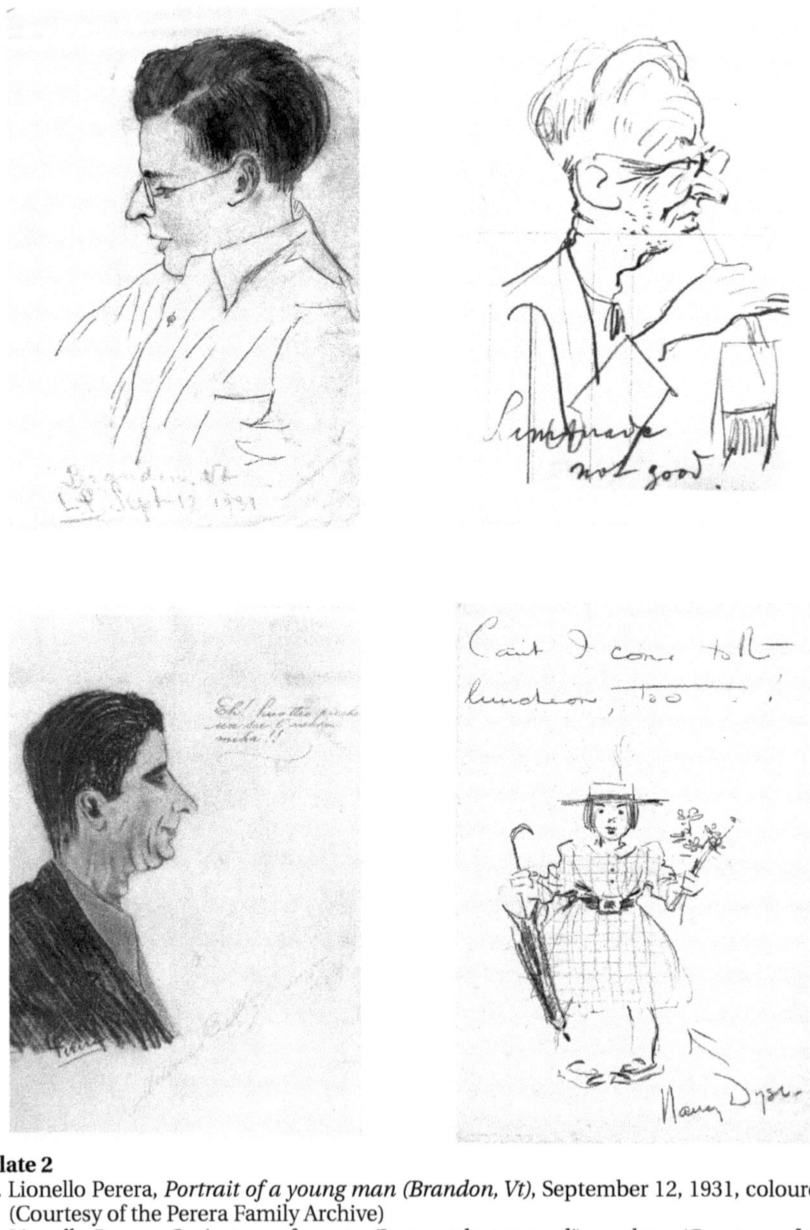

Plate 2

a. Lionello Perera, *Portrait of a young man (Brandon, Vt)*, September 12, 1931, coloured. (Courtesy of the Perera Family Archive)

b. Lionello Perera, *Caricature of a man (Lemonade not good!)*, no date. (Courtesy of the Perera Family Archive)

c. Lionello Perera, *Caricature of Ulderico Bellini (Eh! Huattro picche un sce l'aveva miha!!!)*, coloured, no date. (Courtesy of the Perera Family Archive)

d. Lionello Perera, *Nancy Dyson (Can't I come to luncheon, too?)*, no date. (Courtesy of the Perera Family Archive)

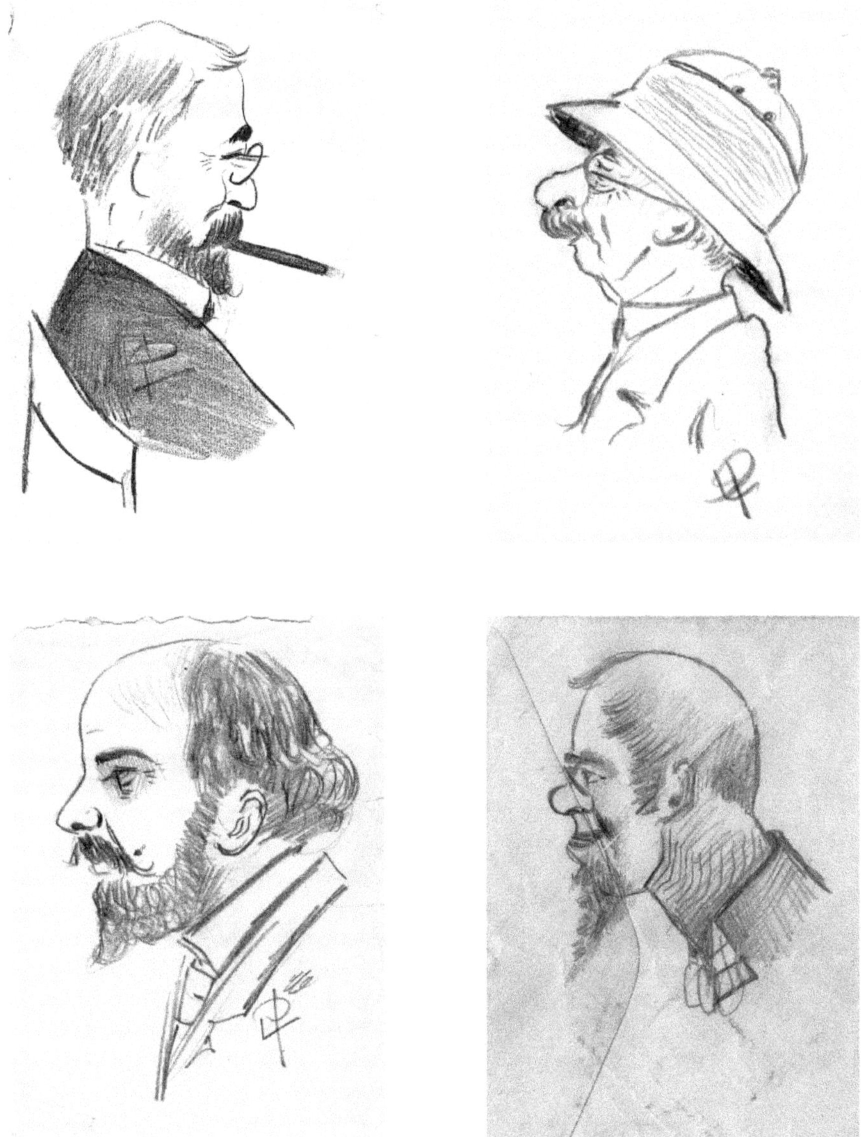

Plate 3
Lionello Perera, *Four caricatures of men with beards and moustaches*, no date. (Courtesy of the Perera Family Archive)

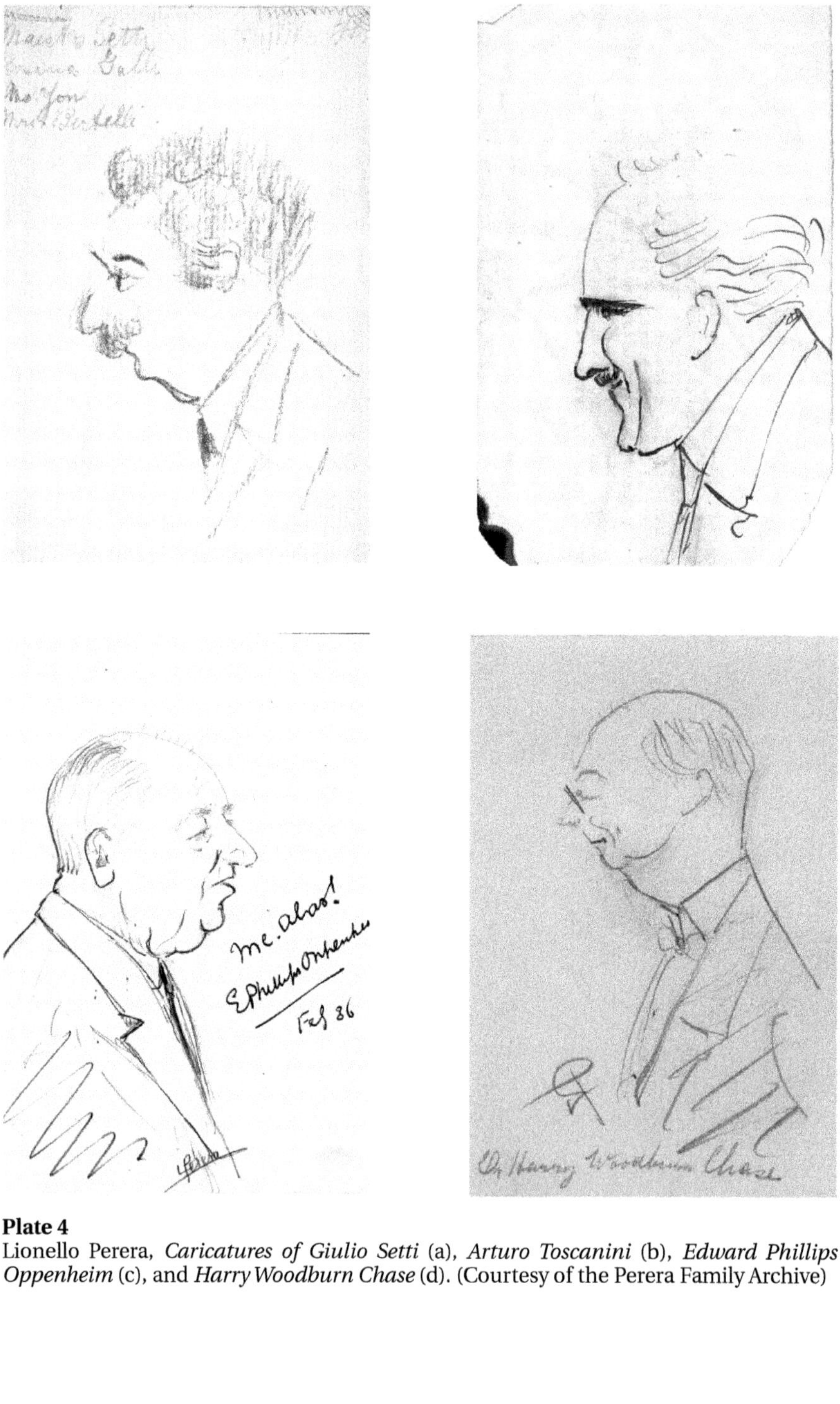

Plate 4
Lionello Perera, *Caricatures of Giulio Setti* (a), *Arturo Toscanini* (b), *Edward Phillips Oppenheim* (c), and *Harry Woodburn Chase* (d). (Courtesy of the Perera Family Archive)

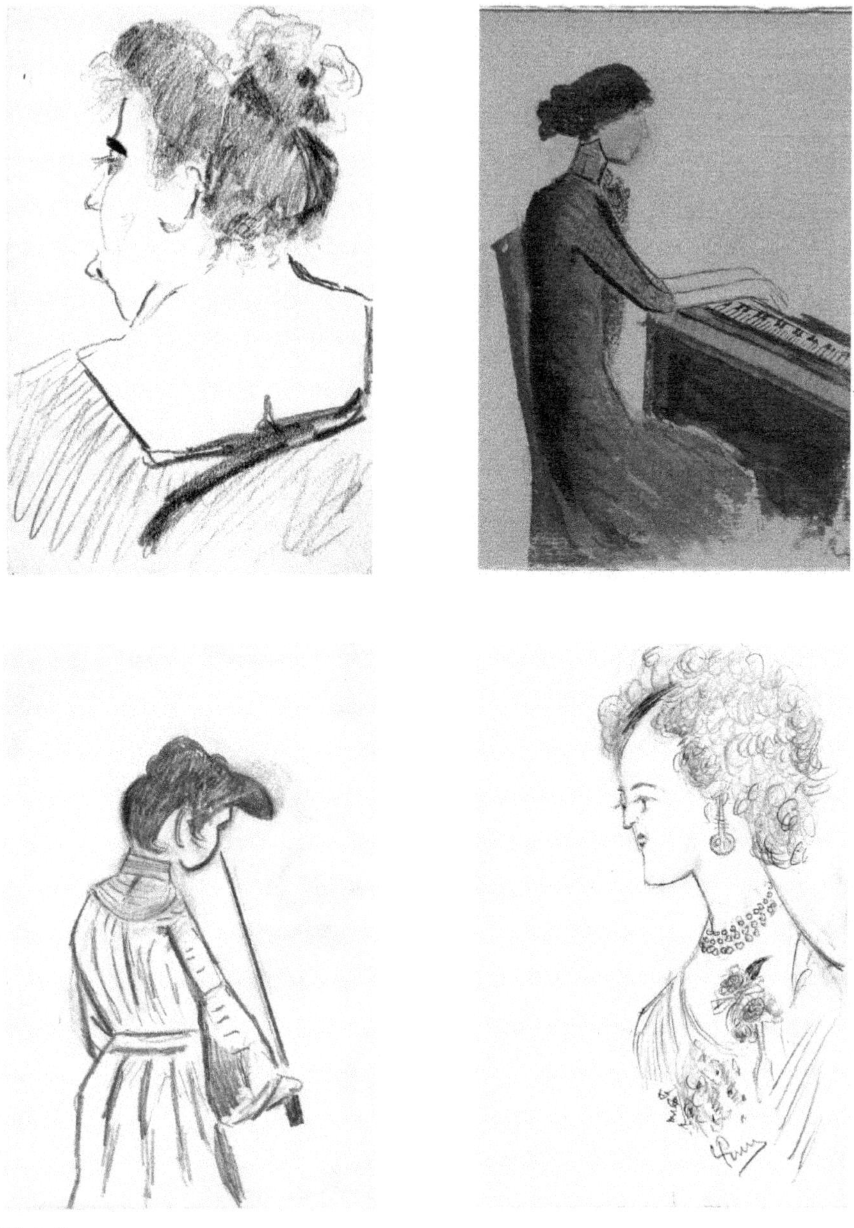

Plate 5
Lionello Perera, *Four drawings of women attending concerts or playing music*, no date. (Courtesy of the Perera Family Archive)

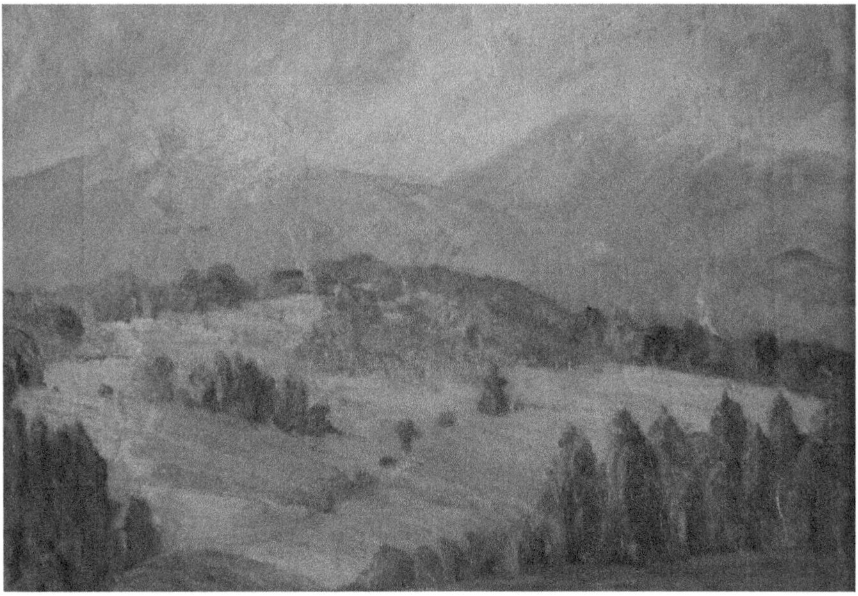

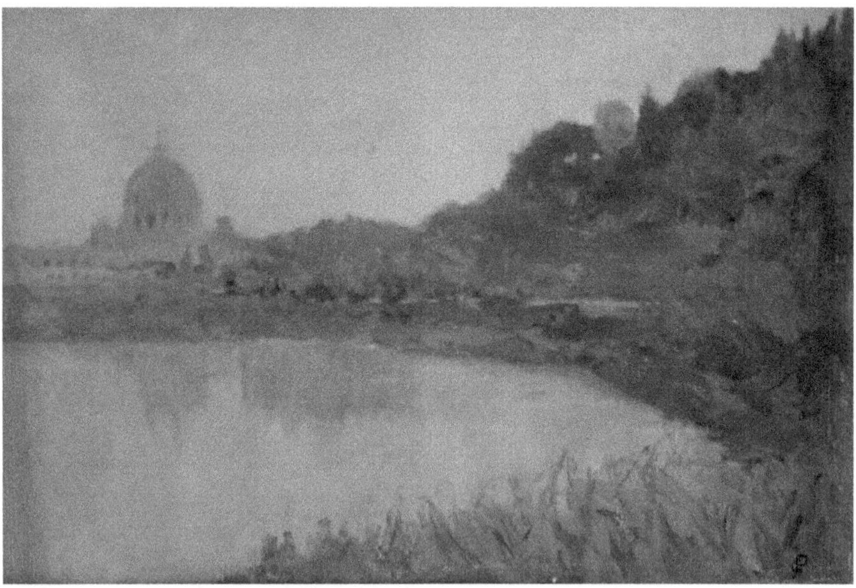

Plate 6

a. Gino Lorenzo Perera, *Landscape (Countryside with hills)*, no date, oil on canvas. (Courtesy of the Perera Family Archive)

b. Gino Lorenzo Perera, *Landscape (Lake with Capitol Hill or Vatican?)*, no date, oil on canvas. (Courtesy of the Perera Family Archive)

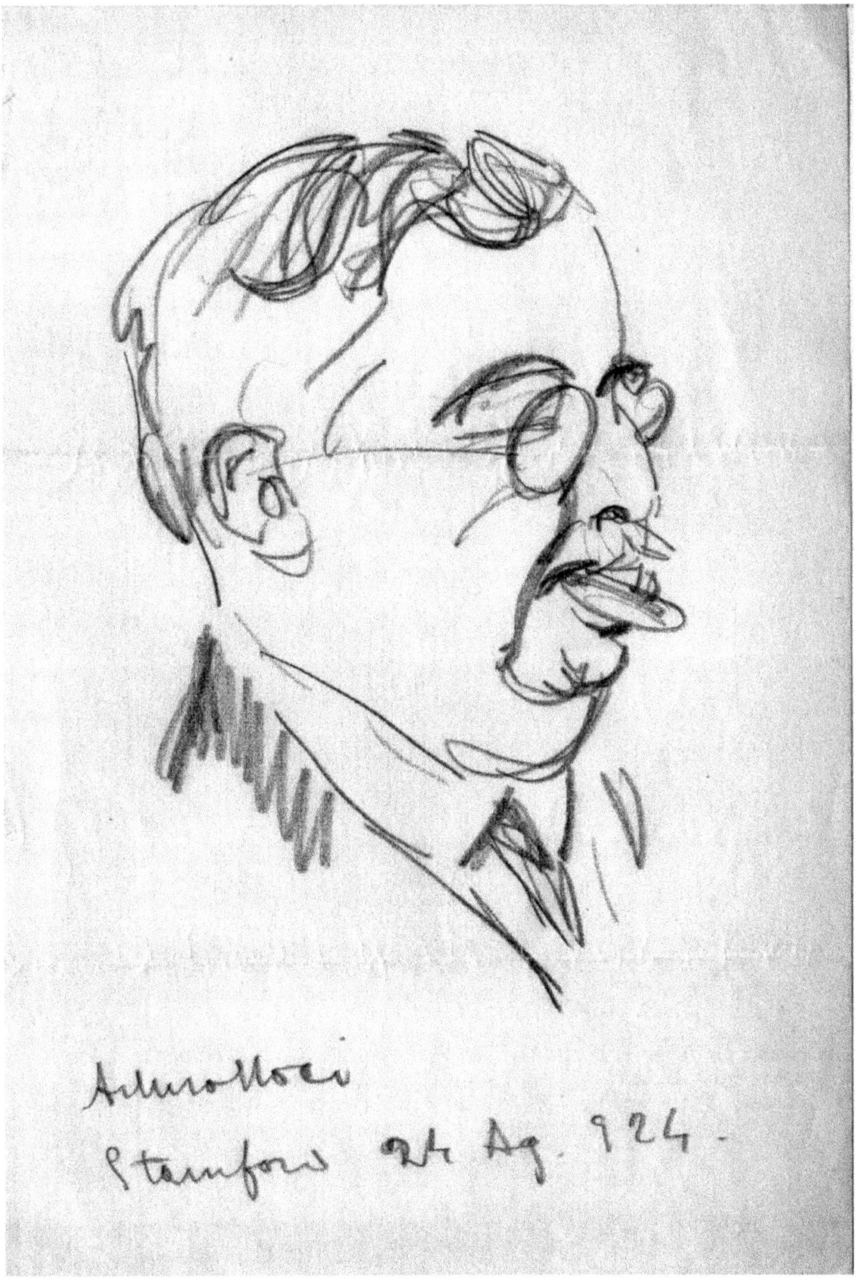

Plate 7
Arturo Noci, *Sketch of Lionello Perera (Stamford 24 Ag 924)*, 1924, pencil on paper. (Courtesy of the Perera Family Archive)

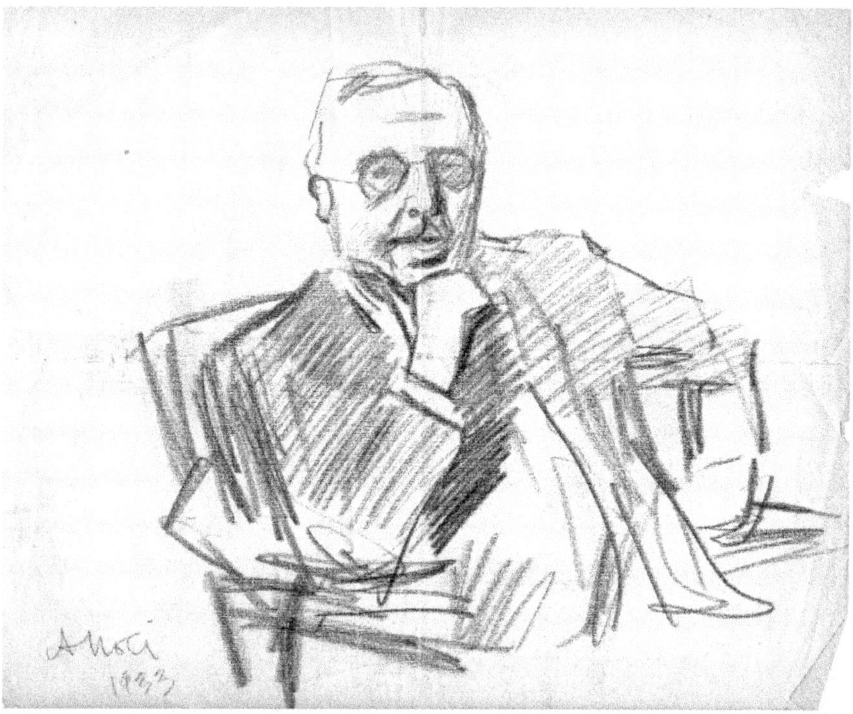

Plate 8
Arturo Noci, *Study for the portrait of Lionello Perera*, 1933, pencil on paper. (Courtesy of the Perera Family Archive)

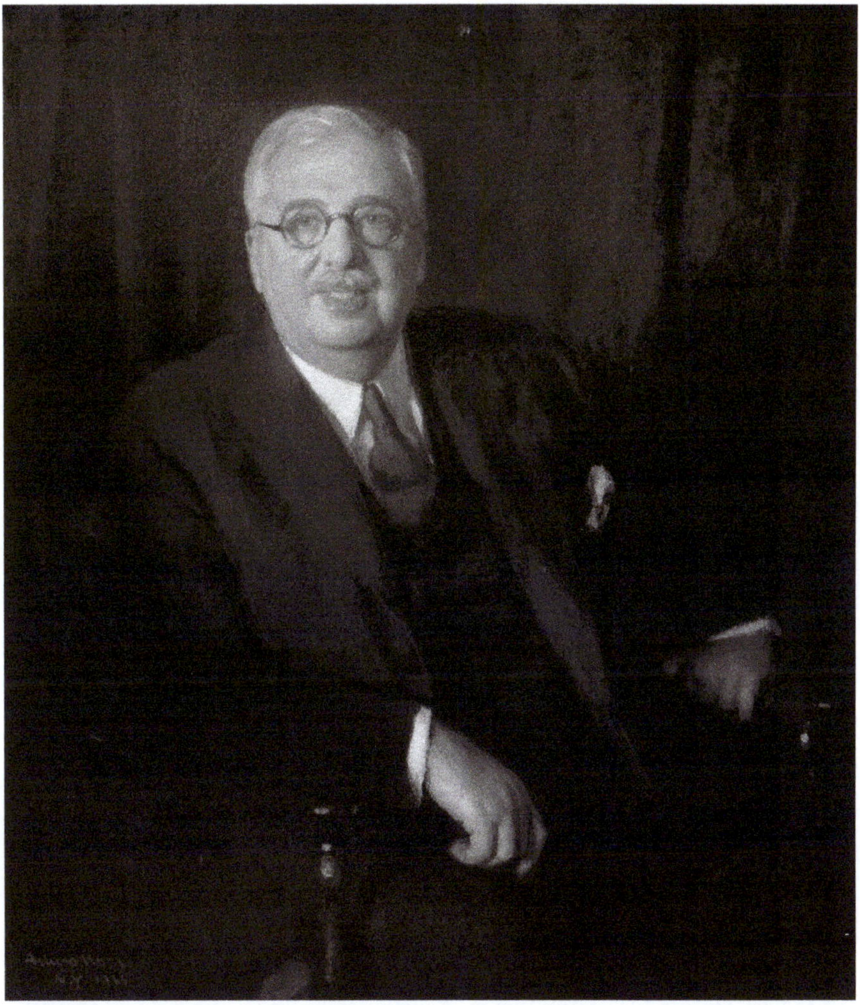

Plate 9
Arturo Noci, *Portrait of Lionello Perera*, 1933, oil on canvas. (Courtesy of the Perera Family Archive)

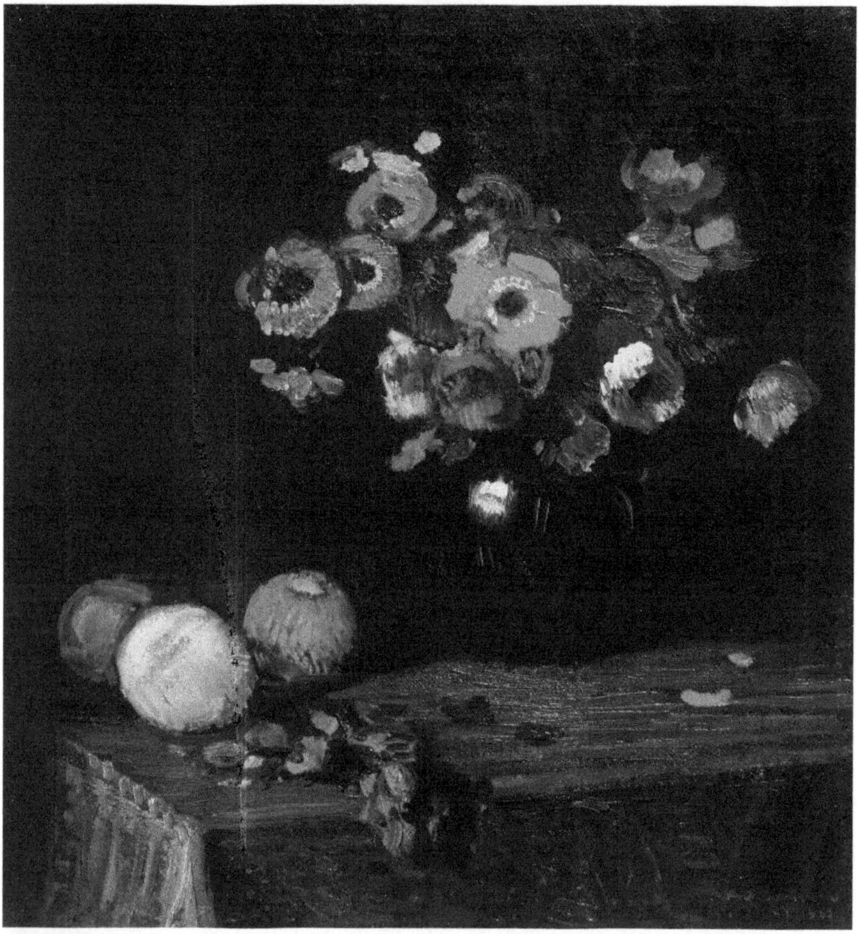

Plate 10
Arturo Noci, *Still life*, 1933, oil on canvas. (Courtesy of the Perera Family Archive)

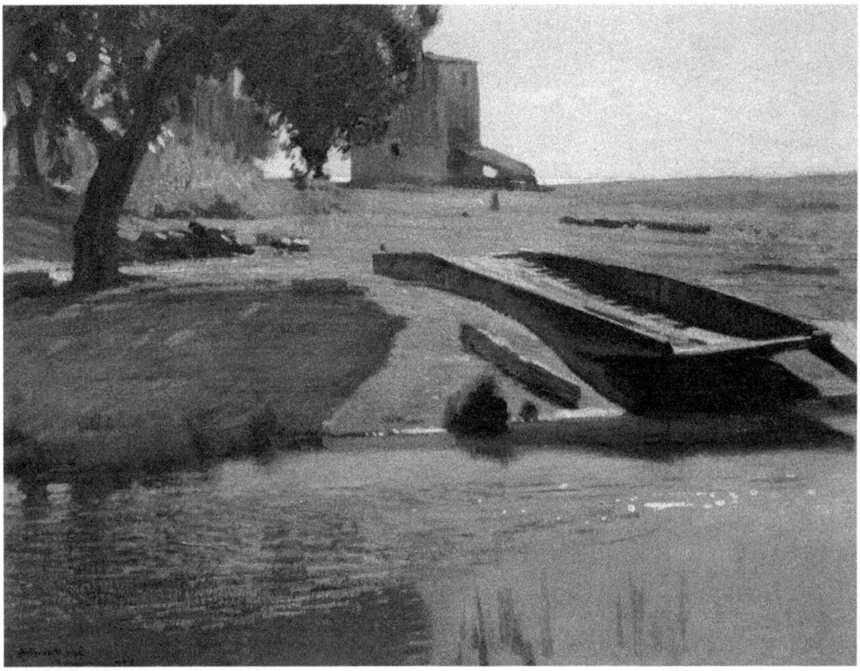

Plate 11
Arturo Noci, *Landscape at Fiumarella di Canneto,* 1921, oil on canvas. (Courtesy of the Perera Family Archive)

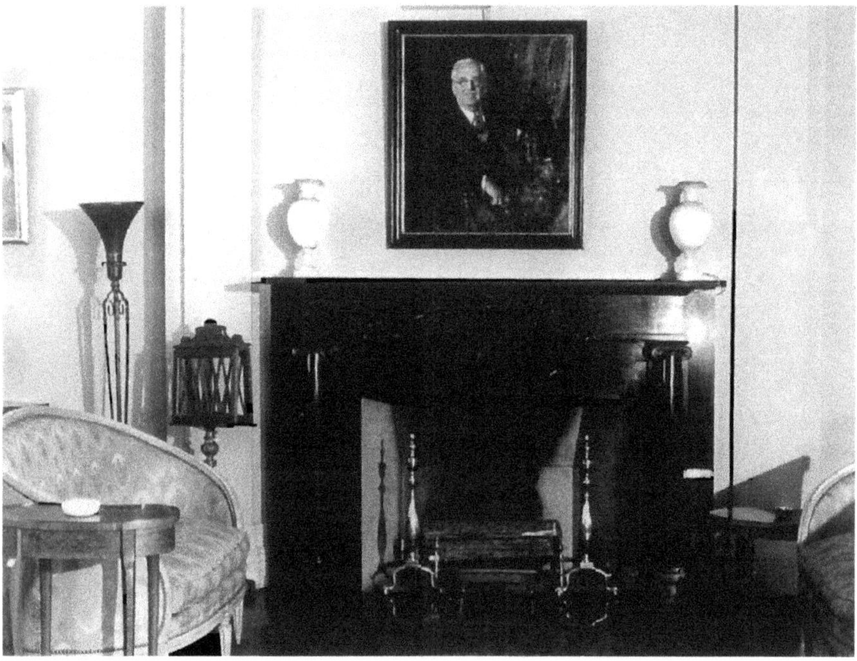

Plate 12
Perera Home photograph series, *Sitting Room (fireplace with Arturo Noci portait),* mid 1930s, 49 East 80th Street, New York. (Courtesy of the Perera Family Archive)

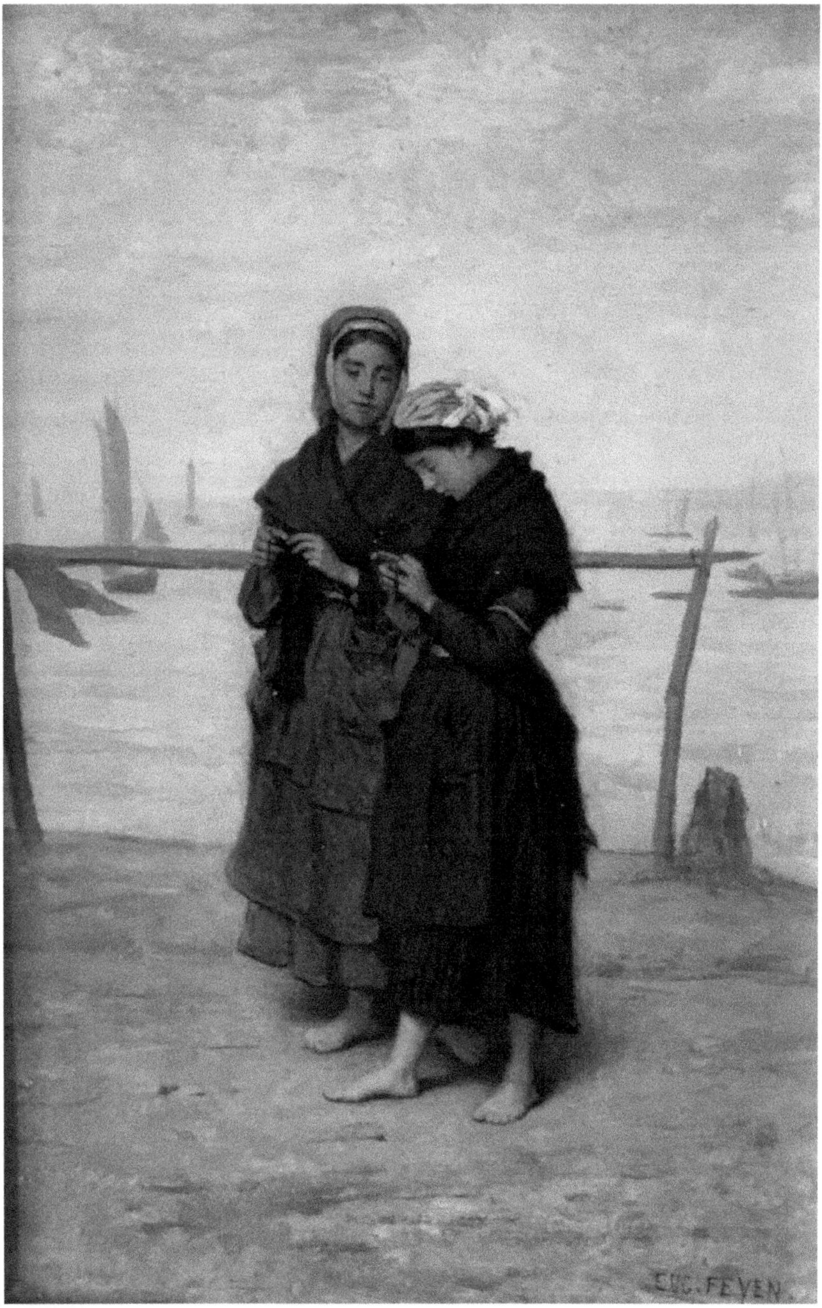

Plate 13
Eugène Feyen, *Two fisher girls sewing at the border of the sea in Brittany*, after 1860, oil on canvas. (Courtesy of the Perera Family Archive)

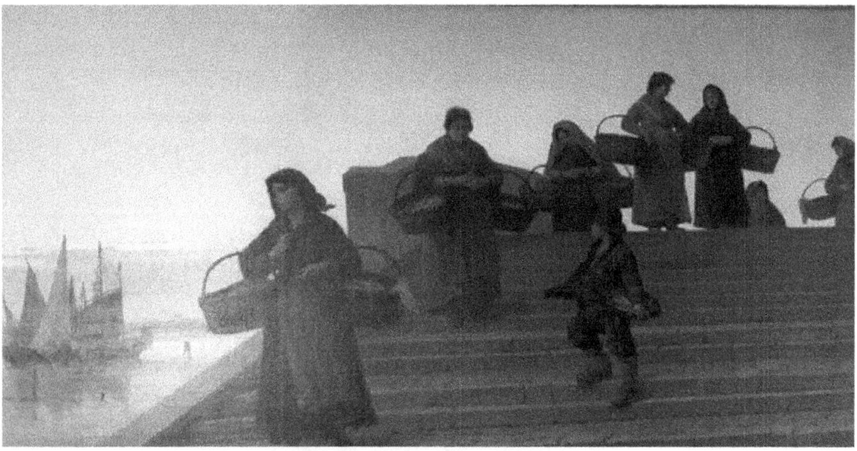

Plate 14
Antonio Ermolao Paoletti, *Peasant women going to the marketplace*, late nineteenth century, oil on canvas. (Courtesy of the Perera Family Archive)

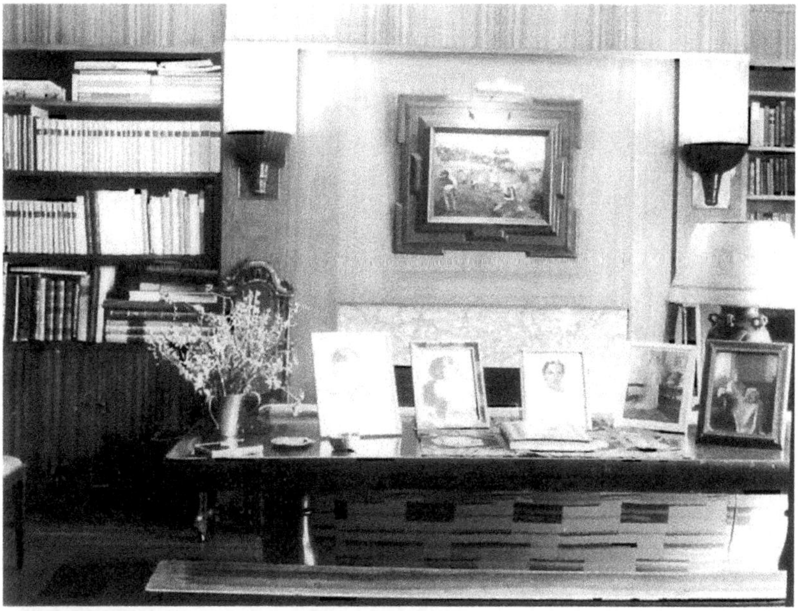

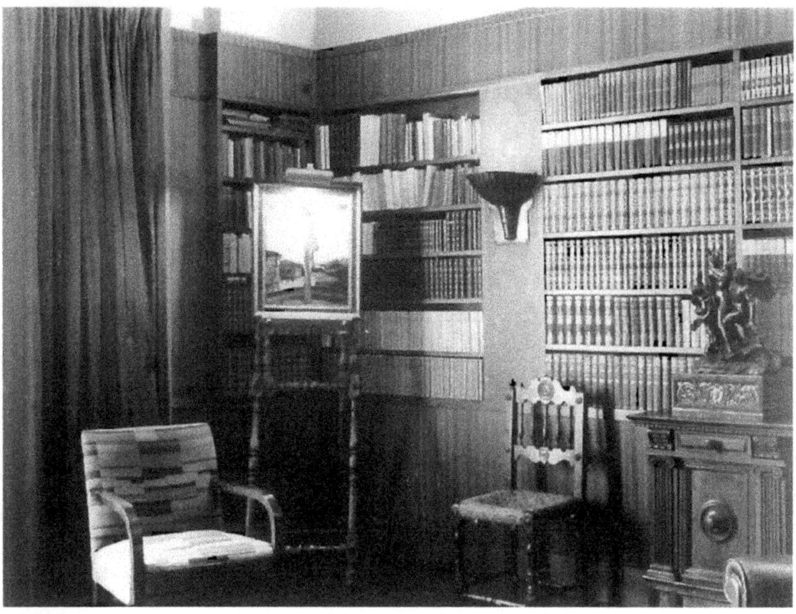

Plates 15

a. Perera Home photograph series, *Library (writing desk with Bruegel painting)*, mid-1930s, 49 East 80th Street, New York. (Courtesy of the Perera Family Archive)

b. Perera Home photograph series, *Library (corner with Rosselli painting)*, mid-1930s, 49 East 80th Street, New York. (Courtesy of the Perera Family Archive)

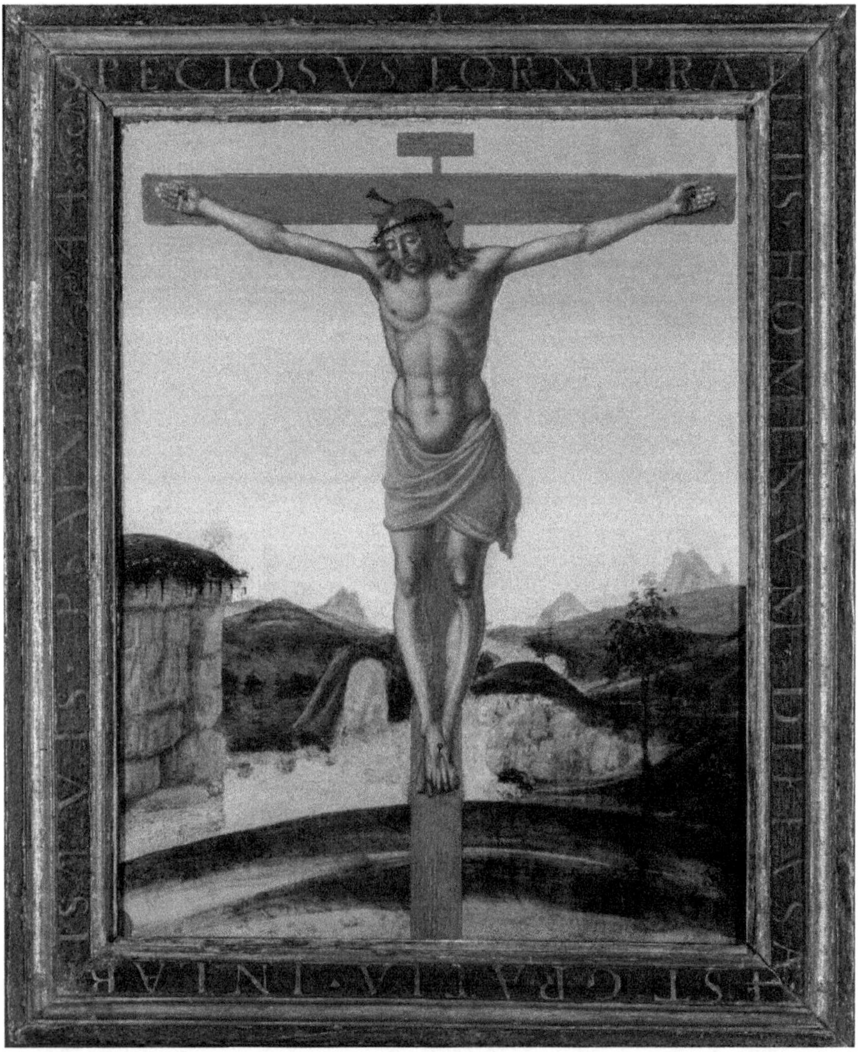

Plate 16
Cosimo Rosselli, *Cristo in croce (Christ on the Cross)*, 1460-1507, tempera and oil on panel. (With the permission of Bryn Mawr College, photo credit James Schneck)

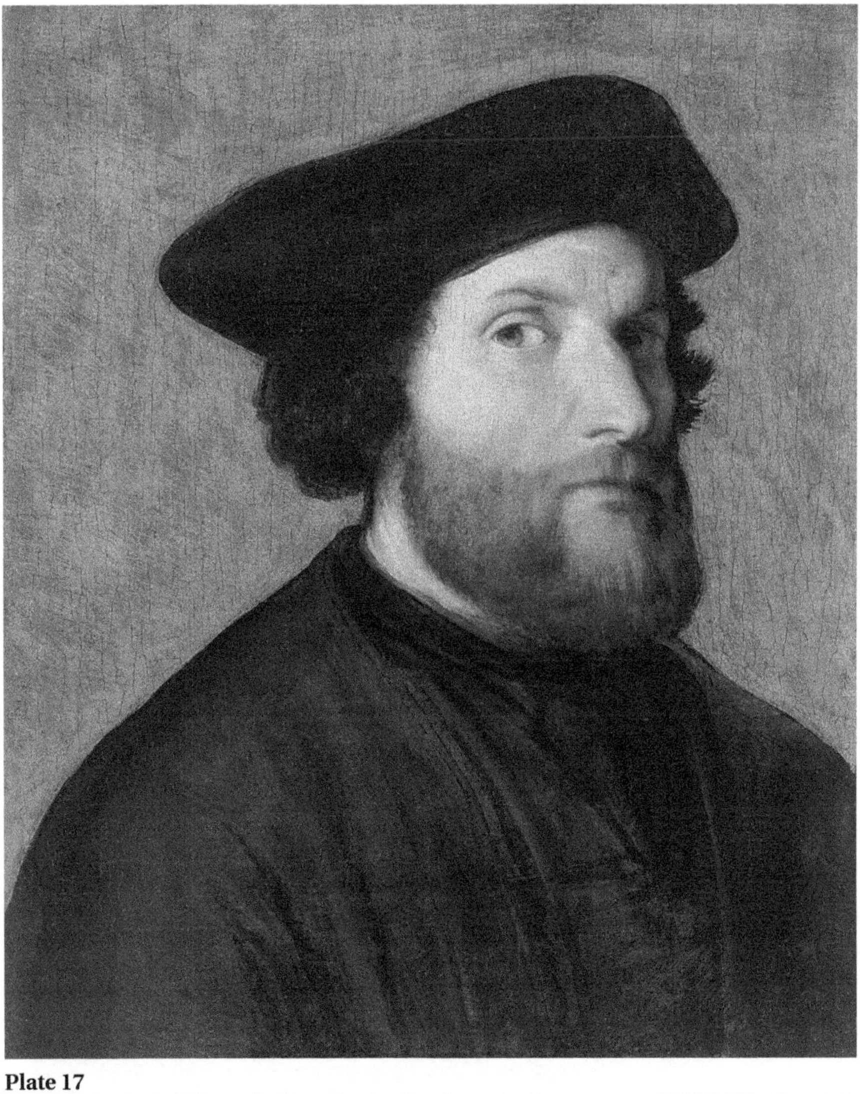

Plate 17
Lorenzo Lotto, *Self-Portrait (Portrait of a Gentleman)*; oil on canvas, 1500-1549. (Research purposes: © Museo Nacional Thyssen-Bornemisza, Madrid)

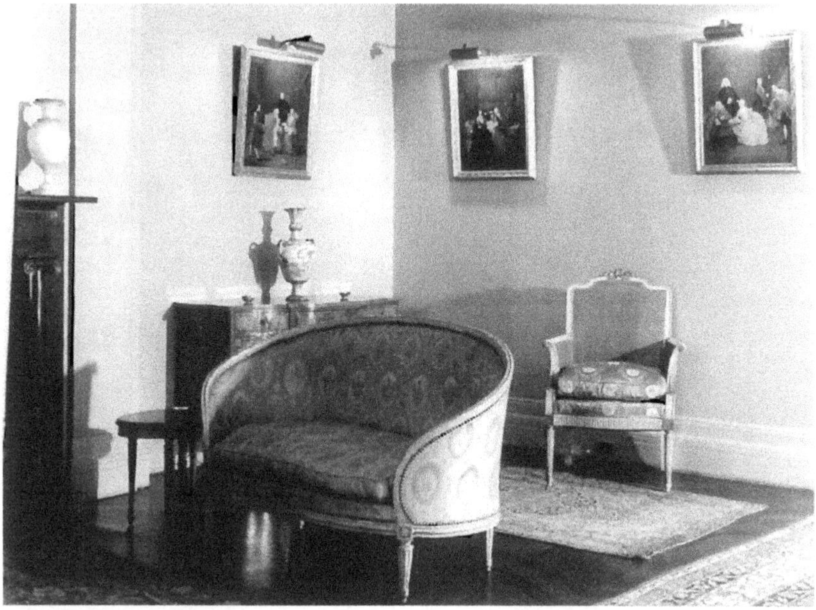

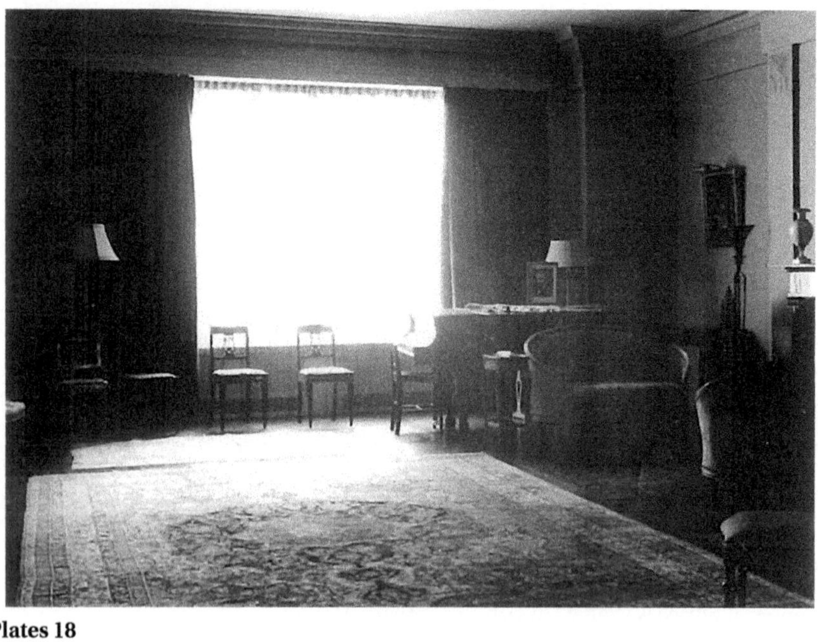

Plates 18
a. Perera Home photograph series, *Sitting Room (corner with three Longhi paintings)*, mid-1930s, 49 East 80th Street, New York. (Courtesy of the Perera Family Archive)
b. Perera Home photograph series, *Sitting Room (window side with piano)*, mid-1930s, 49 East 80th Street, New York. (Courtesy of the Perera Family Archive)

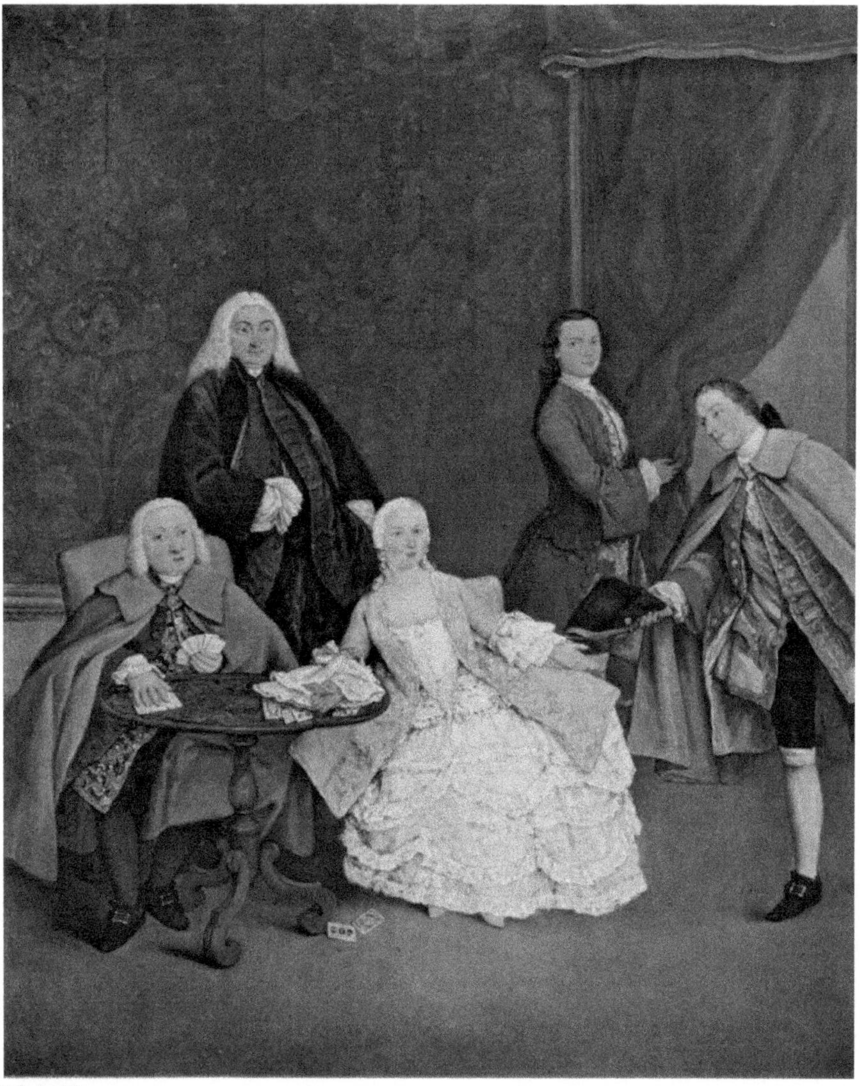

Plate 19
Pietro Longhi, *The Visit (The Game of Cards)*, ca. 1760, oil on canvas, Alte Pinakothek Munich, Germany. (With the permission of Fondazione Zeri)

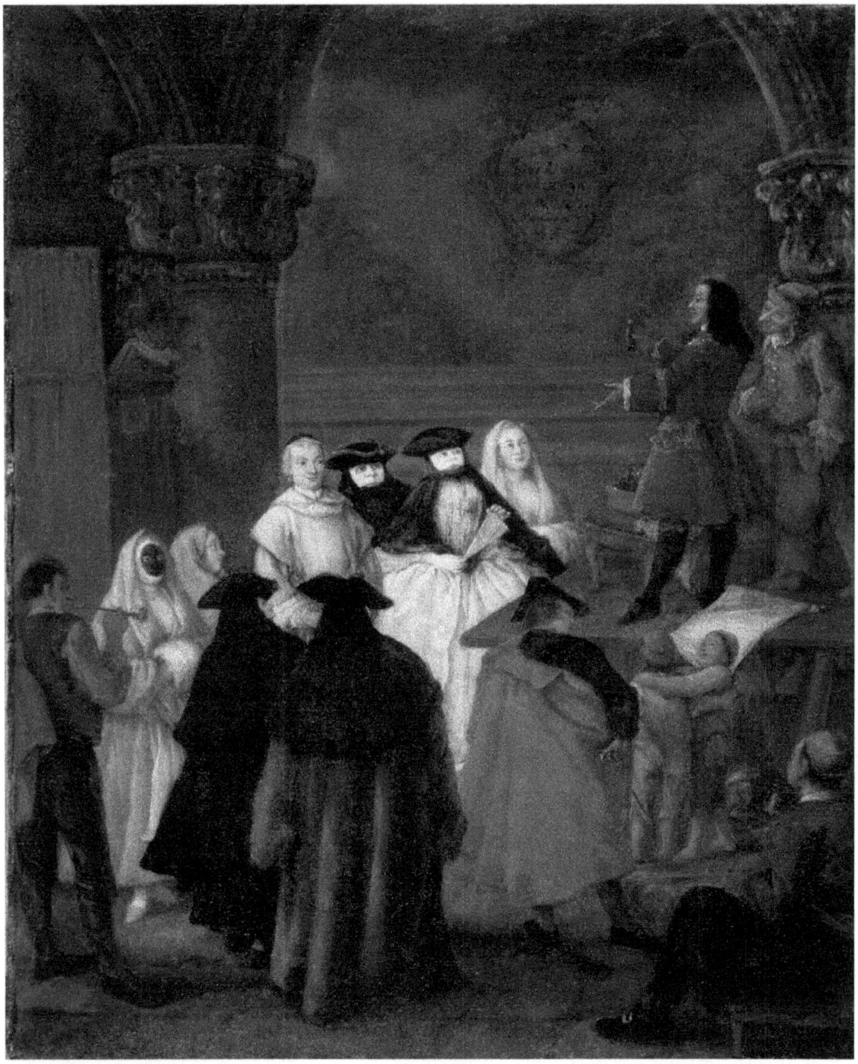

Plate 20
Pietro Longhi, *The Quack Doctor (The Itinerant Charlatan)*, 1763-1770, oil on canvas, Los Angeles County Museum of Art, California, USA. (Public domain: www.lacma.org)

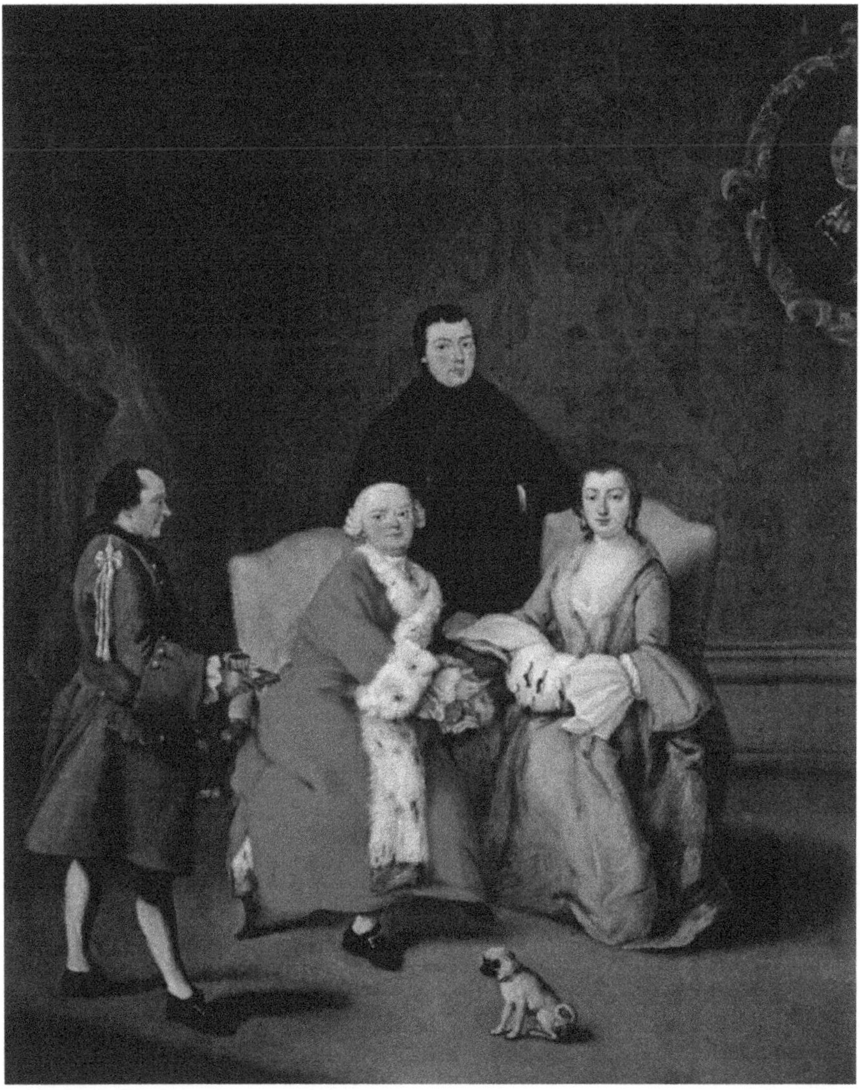

Plate 21
Pietro Longhi, *A Gentleman and his Wife*, ca. 1760, oil on canvas, private collection, St. Moritz, Switzerland. (Public domain: www.wikimedia.org)

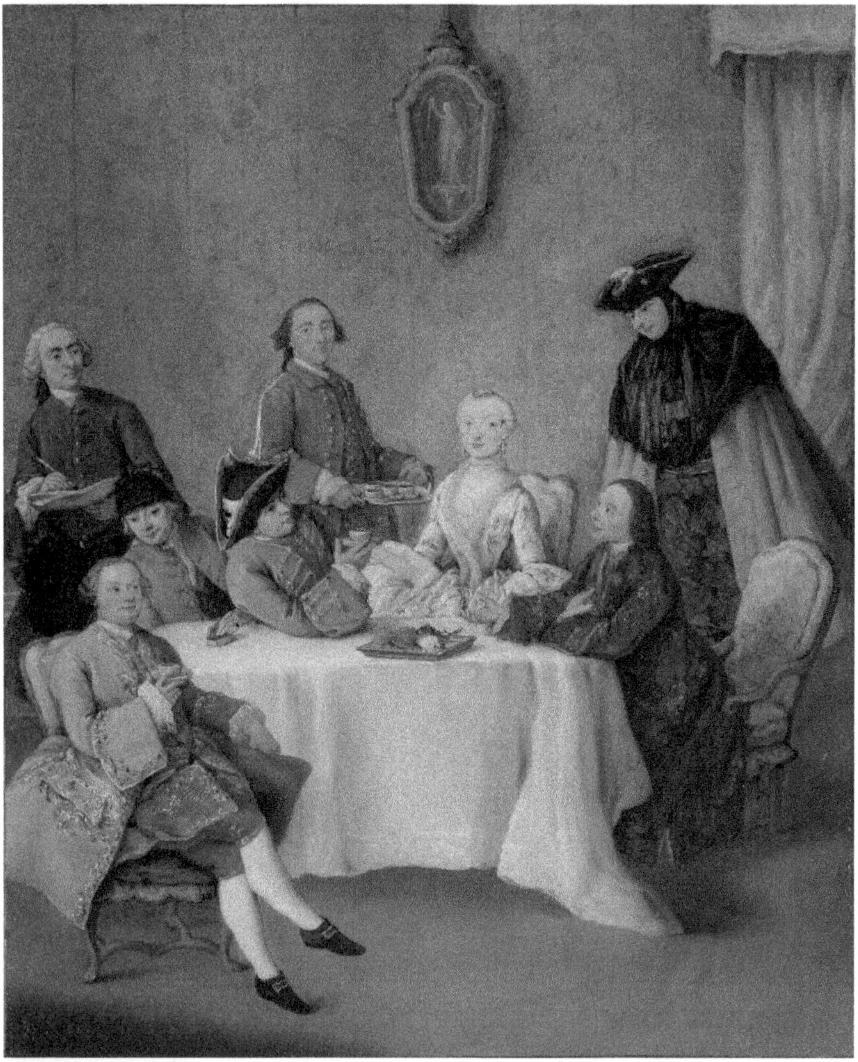

Plate 22
Pietro Longhi, *Portrait of the Artist Sketching an Elegant Company (The Coffee Party)*, ca. 1760, oil on canvas, Norton Simon Museum, California, USA. (With the permission of Norton Simon Museum).

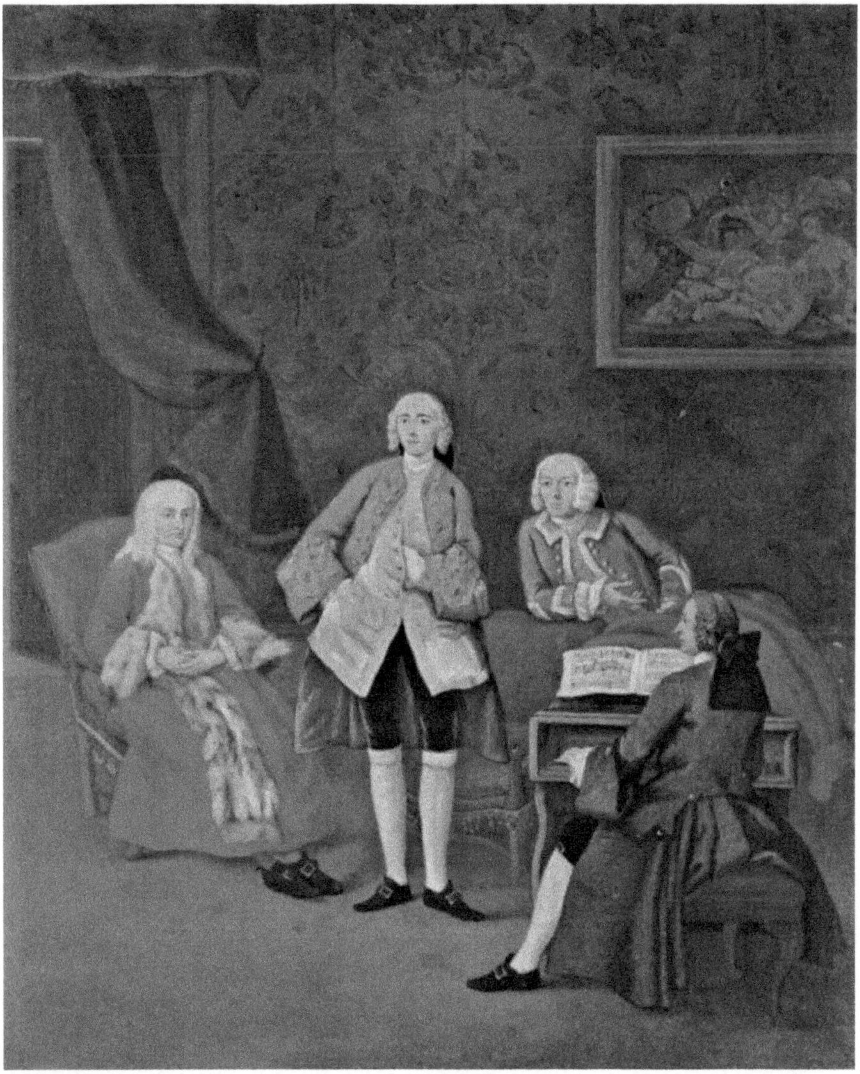

Plate 23
Pietro Longhi, *The Spinet Concert (A Musical Party)*, ca. 1760, oil on canvas. (With the permission of Fondazione Zeri)

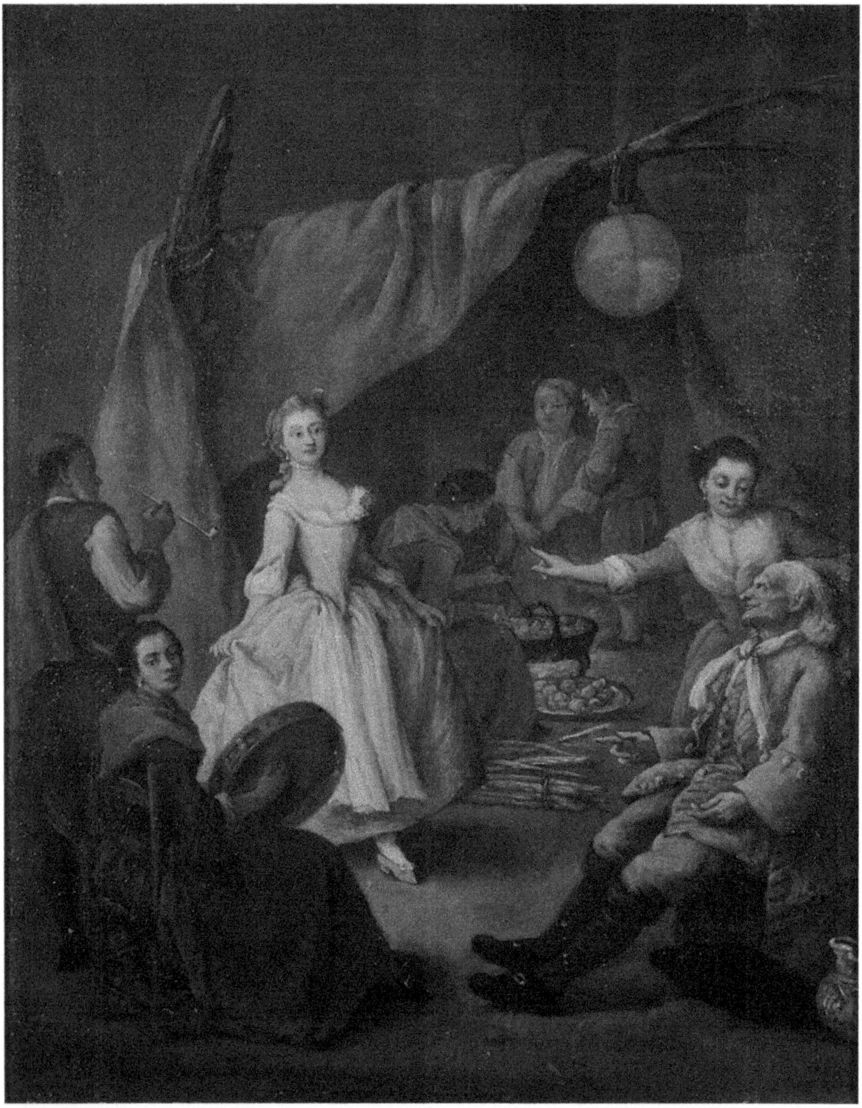

Plate 24
Pietro Longhi, *The Dancer*, 1750-1760, oil on canvas. (With the permission of Fondazione Zeri)

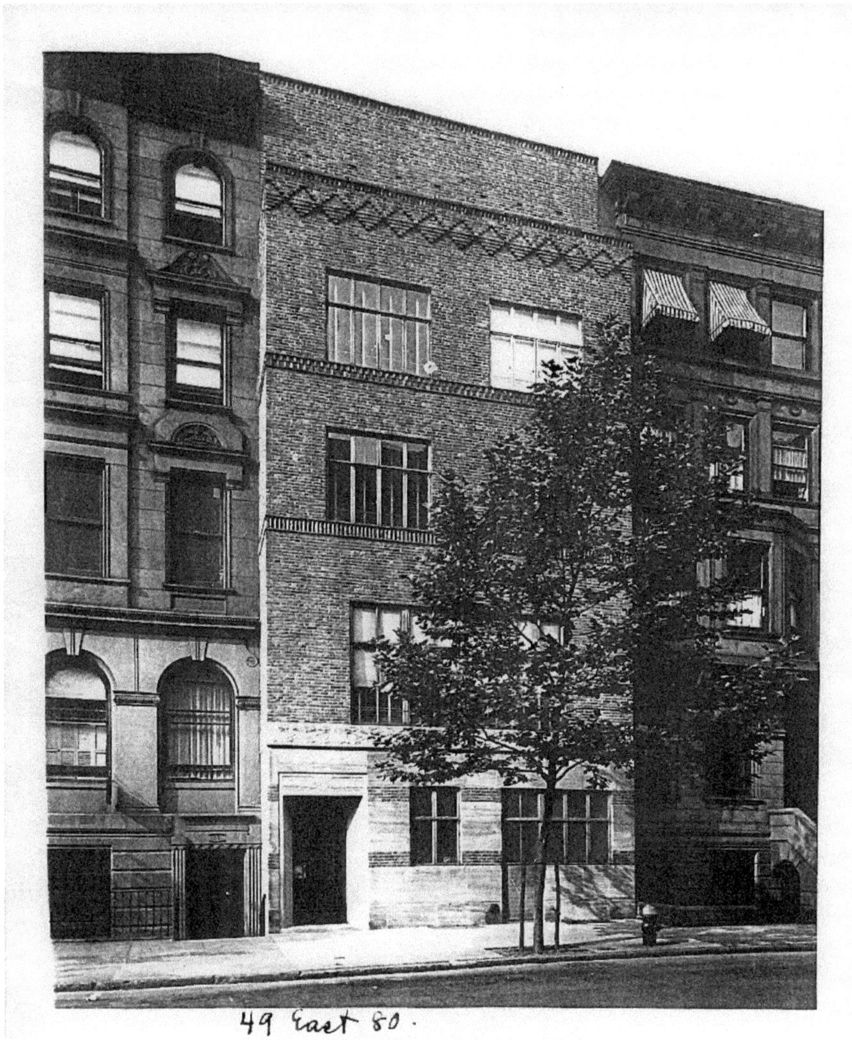

Plate 25
Perera Home photograph series, *Facade on 80th Street*, mid-1930s, 49 East 80th Street, New York. (Courtesy of the Perera Family Archive)

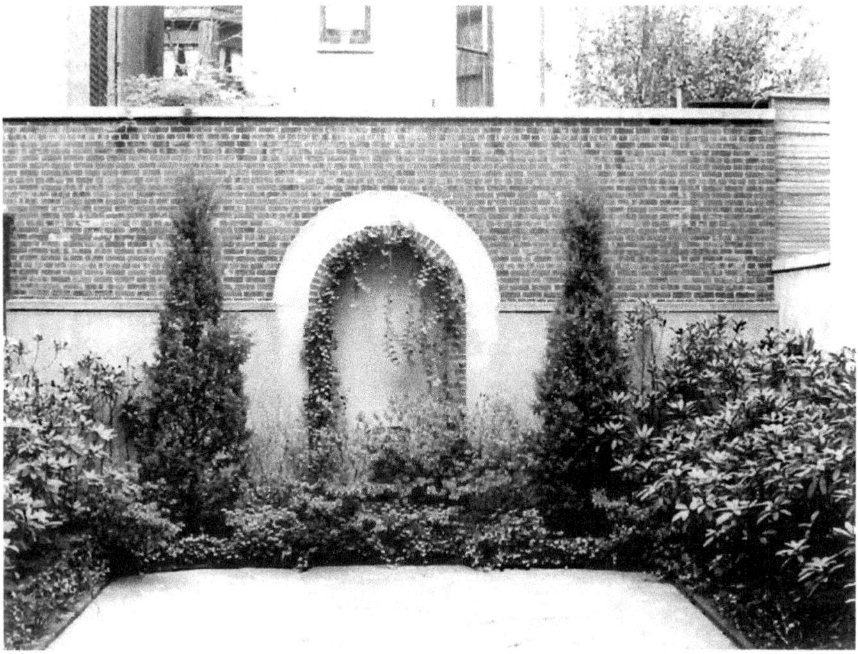

Plate 26
Perera Home photograph series, *Garden Side*, mid-1930s, 49 East 80th Street, New York. (Courtesy of the Perera Family Archive)

Notes

Chapter 2

[1] See: Mantoan, Bianchi 2015
[2] Sattin 2014, 134
[3] Bollettino 1902, March, 62
[4] See the official website of Teatro la Fenice and of the Ca' Foscari Alumni: http://archiviostorico.teatrolafenice.it/scheda_opera.php?ID=27494; and https://www.cafoscarialumni.it/eventi/ammmericanaria-alle-sale-apollinee-del-teatro-la-fenice (accessed on 2021/2/10)
[5] Find the podcast available at the online archive of RAI Radio3: https://www.raiplayradio.it/audio/2017/01/Toscanini-e-il-suo-amico-veneziano-15012017-2aa8b270-5933-410c-b87d-a07d9a077e09.html (accessed on 2021/2/10)
[6] Find the podcast available at the online archive of RAI Radio3: https://www.raiplayradio.it/audio/2017/02/La-Banca-Perera---Wikiradio-del-24022017-221f55ec-ab7d-49f1-a877-e02b4ffd09f4.html (accessed on 2021/2/10)
[7] Mangione, Morreale 1993
[8] Connell, Pugliese 2019
[9] Laurino 2014
[10] See: Marraro 1945 and 1946; and Schiavo [1957] 1992
[11] See: Luconi 2002, 2003, 2006, 2015 and 2016; Strazza 2004; and De Lucia 2008
[12] See: Ahamed 2009
[13] See: Calomiris 1995 and 2008; Calomiris, Gorton 1991; Calomiris, Mason 2004; Calomiris, Wheelock 1998; Jalil 2015

Chapter 3

[1] American Review 1959, 30
[2] Boytel, Leona 1943 (Correspondence)
[3] Regio Esercito Italiano 1891 (Document)
[4] Deputazione provinciale 1889 (Document)
[5] Leone XII and Leone XIII, the last one to carry this name in the Vatican.
[6] Rabbi Loew in Prague and the philosopher Leone Ebreo.
[7] Thanks to the engagement of the wider Perera family, particularly of Rosie Perera, Carol and Michele Weingeist, several genealogical efforts were made to reconstruct the exact ancestry of the family, as well as to claim Spanish citizenship. On behalf of Michele Weingeist, Michael Waas completed a historical study on the genealogy of the last name Perera (or Pereira) Lopes (or Lopez) in 2018, such that this chapter draws partially on his findings and on the genealogy reconstructed by the Perera relatives.
[8] Cassen 2014, 59-60
[9] Waas 2018, 3-4
[10] Studemund-Halévy 2019, 487-511

11 See: Kettubah of Moses Lopes Pereira to his wife Simha da Fonseca, dated 10 Ab 5486. Stadsarchief Amsterdam, Portugees-Israëlietische Gemeente 334, Inventory 391, page 19. (Waas 2018, 7)

12 The name is to be found in the book יצחק פחד, volume 2, written by Isaac, son of Samuel Lampronti, on page 44b. The letter, dated Thursday, 2 Adar II, 5502 (8 March 1742), from Livorno, is signed by the aforementioned Isaac as well as two other Dayyanim, David Meldola and Jacob Lusena. See: Waas 2018, 9-10

13 Waas 2018, 10

14 Melcer-Padon 2019, 346-380

15 Dimant 2019, 323-345

16 Bregoli 2010, 309-329

17 The ancestry of Lionello Perera has been reconstructed by Rosie Perera and Michele Weingeist departing from Abramo Lopes Perera, Lionello's paternal grandfather, over a period of several years and interrogating over a hundred living relatives. The places and dates of birth and death are quite accurate, although several doubts on single cases still remain. Full genealogical lists can be found online at the internet archive of the Lionello Perera Papers

18 Weingeist 2018, 34

19 Katz 2010, 127-153

20 Lang 2009, 116-117

21 Bergamin Barbato 2015, 48-49

22 American Review 1959, 30

23 Boytel, Leona 1943 (Correspondence)

24 American Numismatic Archaeological Society 1867 (Certificate)

25 American Review 1959, 30; Boytel, Leona 1943 (Correspondence)

26 Atti di morte 1882/1891 (Certificate)

27 Atti di morte 1892 (Certificate)

28 R. Scuola Superiore di Commercio 1886 (Certificate)

29 Registro matricolare 1886-1889 (Document)

30 Deputazione provinciale 1889 (Document)

31 Marriage Announcement 1892 (Document)

32 Ilari 1990, 298-300

33 In a note the document explicitly affirms that Lionello wouldn't need the preliminary permission of the military authority, in case he decided to expatriate. See: Regio Esercito Italiano 1891 (Document)

34 Passenger Record 1894 (Document)

35 Perera 1963, 8-9

36 Chicago Daily Tribune 1894/6/6, 2

37 Brooklyn Daily Eagle 1894/6/6, 1

38 Brooklyn Daily Eagle 1893/10/12, 9

39 These information and claims can be drawn from the obituary of Edward Francis' older brother Daniel Kingsland, who died in September 1919. See: New York Times 1919/9/11, 17; Brooklyn Life 1919/9/13, 3

40 See: De Beixedon 1921. Further information and comments on the Rogers' controversy can be found at the following anonymous website: https://www.wikitree.com/wiki/De_Beixedon-1#_note-6

[41] Beuka 2011, 1-21
[42] Brooklyn Daily Eagle 1896/7/1, 1
[43] New York Supreme Court 1897
[44] New York Journal 1897/1/20, 1; and New York Times 1897/11/24, 11
[45] New York Times 1897/10/16, 5; and New York Court of Appeals 1897
[46] Dubreuil 2018, 7
[47] Wyrwa 2016, 354-355
[48] See: Levis Sullam 2018

Chapter 4

[1] Favero 2015, 28
[2] Bergamin Barbato 2015, 49
[3] Donadon 2018, 15
[4] Morbiato 2014, 141-158
[5] Bergamin Barbato 2015, 148-150
[6] Favero 2015, 27-28
[7] Polese 1994, 36
[8] See: Berengo 1989
[9] Bergamin Barbato 2015, 48
[10] Pedani 2018, 18
[11] Deodati, Luzzatti 1868, 18-33
[12] Zucchello 2012, 28
[13] R. Scuola Superiore di Commercio 1886 (Certificate)
[14] Della statistica nei suoi rapporti coll'economia politica e colle altre scienze affini" (Of statistics in its relations with political economics and similar sciences). Berengo 1989, 20-25
[15] Boscaro 2018, 171
[16] The Doge was the highest political representative of the Venetian Republic. It was an elected post which lasted until his death.
[17] Bergamin Barbato 2015, 50-52
[18] See: Antinori 1994
[19] Conte 2018, 35-58
[20] That much was contained in the Royal legislation: D.M. April 13, 1871, n. 1807
[21] The third path was divided among these disciplines with different durations: Diritto, Economia e Statistica (Law, Economics and Statistics) – 5 years; Merceologia (Sciencs of goods and commodities) – 4 years; Computisteria, then Ragioneria (Accounting sciences) – 4 years; Lingue straniere (Foreign languages) – 5 years.
[22] Favero 2015, 31-32
[23] Boerio [1856] 1971, 60-61
[24] Tassini [1863] 1970, 51-52
[25] Favero 2015, 31-32
[26] Bergamin Barbato 2015, 47
[27] Registro matricolare 1886-1889 (Document)
[28] R. Scuola Superiore di Commercio 1886 (Certificate)
[29] Registro matricolare 1886-1889 (Document)

[30] R. Scuola Superiore di Commercio 1909 (Certificate)
[31] Jamet, Rossi 2018, 43-44
[32] Boscaro 2018, 173-174
[33] Donadon 2018, 15-16
[34] Pedani 2018, 16-18
[35] Ghersetti 2018, 65-70
[36] Perera 1963, 9-10
[37] Morbiato 2014, 144
[38] Bollettino 1899, January, 1
[39] Morbiato 2014, 145-146
[40] Sattin 2014, 130
[41] Morbiato 2014, 149-152
[42] Sattin 2014, 130-131
[43] Morbiato 2014, 152-154
[44] Sattin 2014, 134
[45] See: Bollettino 1900, November; and Bollettino 1901, March
[46] See: Bollettino 1899, January
[47] Bollettino 1902, March, 62
[48] See: Bollettino 1902, November

Chapter 5

[1] Schiavo 1957, 151
[2] Dubreuil 2018, 7
[3] Schiavo 1957, 152
[4] Luconi 2003, 89-90
[5] Cantoni, Leon Vita 1862 (Correspondence)
[6] Cantoni, Salvatore 1862 (Correspondence)
[7] Boytel, Leona 1943 (Correspondence)
[8] Cantoni, Perera 1907 (Calendar)
[9] Schiavo 1957, 311
[10] Campora 1924(?), 41-42
[11] Commercial and Financial Chronicle 1894, 1804
[12] Landmarks Preservation Commission 1978, 121
[13] Brooklyn Life, 1893/5/27, 17
[14] Brooklyn Daily Eagle 1893/10/12, 9
[15] Brooklyn Daily Eagle 1896/7/1, 1
[16] New York Times 1889/7/11, 3
[17] New York Times 1891/1/25, 11
[18] JAMA 1891, 284-285
[19] Oldrini 1918, 471
[20] Marraro 1946, 179-181
[21] Marraro 1945, 281
[22] Ibid, 188-191
[23] Faustini 2012, 202-204
[24] Alduino, Coles 2004, 47-48

[25] Luconi 2003, 88-89
[26] Aicardi, Cavaterra 1988, 204
[27] Particularly inspiring for Italian patriots were the memoires "Le mie prigioni" (My Prisons, 1832) of the poet Silvio Pellico, who was caught by the Austrians and condemned in Venice, later spending fifteen hard years in various Hapsburg prisons
[28] Cantoni, Salvatore 1862 (Correspondence)
[29] "… did I find a gold mine. No! it would be better if he [Leon Vita] said I ran away from Venice to avoid entering the [Austrian] army, as it did happen in fact." Quote: Cantoni, Salvatore 1862 (Correspondence)
[30] Cantoni, Leon Vita 1862 (Correspondence)
[31] American Review 1959, 30
[32] Pittston Gazette, 1905/9/13, 3
[33] Carroccio 1916 (August), 182-184
[34] Morais 1894, 245
[35] She was the daughter of Nathan and Caroline Loewi Sondheim. Singer 1904, 59
[36] Perera 1963, 8
[37] New York Times 1896/6/23, 4
[38] Brooklyn Daily Eagle 1896/7/1, 1
[39] Cantoni-Bomeisler 1890 (Document)
[40] See correspondence in Edison Papers 1900-1901 (accessed November 14, 2020)
[41] Perera 1963, 8-9
[42] Jalil 2015, 298-300
[43] Perera 1963, 9

Chapter 6

[1] See reports of condition in: Senate of New York 1917, 395; and Report of the Condition 1919 (Clipping)
[2] Bankers' Magazine 1896, 729
[3] Calomiris 2008, 11
[4] Davison, Ramirez 2014, 164-165
[5] King 2011
[6] Calomiris 2008, 10
[7] Commercial and Financial Chronicle 1918 (May), 1888
[8] See: Cantoni, Perera 1907 (Calendar)
[9] New York Times 1917/8/14, 20
[10] American Review 1959, 53
[11] Zerbe 1902, 345
[12] Fisher 1918, 922
[13] Griffin 1923, 882
[14] Smith, Underhill Moore 1923, 10
[15] Circuit Court of New York 1899 (certificate)
[16] Assembly of New York 1913, 254-257
[17] Ibid., 257
[18] New York Banking Department 1914 (Certificate)
[19] Mariano 1925, 61

[20] See reports of condition in: Senate of New York 1917, 395; and Report of the Condition 1919 (Clipping)
[21] For historical inflation rates see: https://www.usinflationcalculator.com/inflation/historical-inflation-rates/
[22] Senate of New York 1917, 395
[23] Report of the Condition 1919 (Clipping)
[24] Carroccio 1918 (May), 525
[25] Criscuolo 1918, 394
[26] Commercial and Financial Chronicle 1920 (May), 2025-2026
[27] Commercial and Financial Chronicle 1923 (August), 786
[28] Commerce and Finance 1922, 1484
[29] New York Times 1920/12/28, 24
[30] Evening Telegram 1917/3/11, 8
[31] For the kind of commercials and articles on Lionello Perera & Co. in Italian-American magazines see: Campora 1924(?); and various issues of *Il Carroccio*, such as Carroccio 1916 (August) and Carroccio 1918 (May)
[32] Dubreuil 2018, 53
[33] The exact translation is: "Bankers licensed by the State Banking Department"
[34] See advertisement on: Carroccio 1918 (May), XVI
[35] Among family materials there are several checks and memorabilia dating between 1896 and 1913 that hold this double denomination
[36] Basilicata nel mondo 1927, 52
[37] See the map of distribution of foreign-born Italians in Greater New York reproduced in Mariano 1921
[38] Calice 1982, 885
[39] Carroccio 1918 (May), 525
[40] Commercial and Financial Chronicle 1918 (May), 1888
[41] Carroccio 1921 (August), 237
[42] Calice 1982, 889
[43] Superintendent of Banks of New York, 1919, p. 540
[44] Three interesting examples in this regard are the still existing buildings of the Bowery Savings Bank on the Bowery, the Harlem Savings Bank on 125th Street, and the Brooklyn Trust Company in Montague Street
[45] Strazza 2004, 63-67
[46] Calice 1982, 888
[47] Strazza 2004, 31
[48] Carroccio 1919 (February), 179
[49] Mariano 1921, 55
[50] Strazza 2004, 32
[51] Ibid., 31
[52] Calice 1982, 891
[53] World War Foreign Debt Commission 1927, 222-26
[54] Luconi 2015, 7
[55] Perera 1918, 314-316
[56] Calice 1982, 889-890
[57] Luconi 2015, 12-13

Chapter 7

[1] Sunday News 1924/2/24, 1
[2] New York Times 1924/2/22, 21
[3] Sunday News 1924/2/24, 6
[4] New York Times 1924/2/22, 21
[5] Commercial and Financial Chronicle 1924 (March), 969
[6] American Review 1959, 30
[7] From a private conversation with Biancamaria Scaglia, grandniece of Lionello and Carolyn Perera, 2015/5/19 (Venice)
[8] New York Times 1924/2/24, 18
[9] American Review 1959, 31
[10] Commercial and Financial Chronicle 1924 (March), 969
[11] New York Times 1924/2/22, 21
[12] Sunday News 1924/2/24, 6
[13] Commercial and Financial Chronicle 1924 (March), 969
[14] Seward 1924, 11
[15] Calomiris 2008, 10
[16] Campora 1924(?), 41-42
[17] New York Times 1924/2/22, 21
[18] Superintendent of Banks of New York 1919, 386
[19] Strazza 2004, 31
[20] Jalil 2015, 295-296
[21] Calomiris, Gorton 1991, 109
[22] Ibid., 112
[23] Ibid., 114
[24] Jalil 2015, 327
[25] Ibid., 317
[26] Calomiris, Mason 2004, 393
[27] Calomiris 2008, 11
[28] Jalil 2015, 297
[29] Calomiris 1995, 305
[30] Calomiris, Gorton 1991, 109
[31] Posner 1958, 272
[32] Calomiris 2008, 12
[33] Calomiris 1995, 306
[34] California Historical Society 1964, 178
[35] Schweikart 1995, 800-801
[36] See: House of Representatives 1930
[37] Raschellà 2007, 114
[38] California Historical Society 1964, 178
[39] Saloutos, Immigrant in Pacific, 1975, p.196
[40] Giovinco 1968, 198-199
[41] California Historical Society 1964, 178

[42] "The Bank of Italy at the time held mortgages on 17,147 farms or on one of every 11 farms in the state, totaling $71,296,899 which was slightly less than 9 percent of the farm mortgages in California. These figures, however, did not include the millions of dollars held in mortgages by affiliates, loans to cooperative marketing associations, and seasonal loans to farmers, sometimes secured by crops". Quote: Saloutos 1975, 196
[43] California Historical Society 1964, 178
[44] Giovinco 1968, 208
[45] Posner 1958, 268
[46] Giovinco 1968, 210
[47] Posner 1958, 267-268
[48] Carroccio 1917 (June), 474
[49] Thomson Gartinhour 1931, 137
[50] Carroccio 1922 (October), 421-423
[51] Thomson Gartinhour 1931, 137
[52] Carroccio 1921 (June), 667-668
[53] Posner 1958, 271
[54] Ibid., 272-273
[55] See: House of Representatives 1930
[56] See: New York State, Dapartment of Financial Services: "An Institutional History of Banks Operating in New York State", url: https://www.dfs.ny.gov/system/files/documents/2020/05/inst_hist_list_20200520.txt (accessed 2020/11/3)
[57] New York Banking Department 1926 (Certificate)
[58] New York Times 1926/8/31
[59] Thomson Gartinhour 1931, 137-138
[60] Brooklyn Daily Eagle 1927/3/26
[61] Thomson Gartinhour 1931, 137-138
[62] Commercial Exchange National Bank 1928 (Document), 4
[63] New York Times 1926/7/16, 21
[64] New York Sun 1929(?)
[65] James, James [1954] 2002, 273
[66] Thomson Gartinhour 1931, 137
[67] James, James [1954] 2002, 273-274
[68] Thomson Gartinhour 1931, 138
[69] Commercial Exchange National Bank 1928 (Document), 1
[70] James, James [1954] 2002, 272
[71] Ibid., 293-296
[72] See: House of Representatives 1930
[73] James, James [1954] 2002, 323-326
[74] See note 54
[75] See: Perino 2010
[76] King 2011
[77] Melchiorre 1932, 68-69

Chapter 8

[1] Perera 2008, 4
[2] Perera 1963, 8
[3] Williams 1938, 61-66
[4] Trustees of the Metropolitan Museum of Art 1917, 33-39
[5] Information retrieved through family recollections reported by Rosie Perera: E-mail on 2021/1/1, 22:30
[6] Few biographic traces on John Aldred Mohlte can be found vetted on Swedish websites and on Artprice. See: https://sv.linkfang.org/wiki/Alfred_Mohlte; and https://www.artprice.com/artist/129285/john-alfred-mohlte/biography (accessed 2020/12/3)
[7] Académie Julian 2020 (Digital Archive)
[8] Yenişehirlioğlu 2015, 359
[9] Fehrer 1994, 752-753
[10] Académie Julian 2020 (Digital Archive), "Matisse": https://sites.google.com/site/academiejulian/m/matisse-1z<
[11] Burns 2019, 117
[12] American Art News 1905/12/16, 4
[13] American Art News 1906/12/8, 6
[14] Brush and Pencil 1907 (January), 5
[15] American Art News 1907/4/6, 2
[16] American Art News 1908/12/19, 6
[17] American Art News 1911/12/30, 2; and American Art News 1912/1/6, 2
[18] American Art News 1922/9/16, 3
[19] Brooklyn Museum Archives 1936 (Digital Archive)
[20] Shavit 2020, 77
[21] Miller 2009, 282
[22] Clayson 2016, 26
[23] Uidhir 2013, 147
[24] Campbell Coyle 2008, 16
[25] Katlan 1939, 4
[26] Uidhir 2013, 137
[27] Ndalianis 2011, 113
[28] Schorsch 1979, 57-59
[29] Simpson 2010, 11
[30] Puckett Sasser 2018, 157
[31] Progresso italo americano 1986
[32] American Review 1959, 30-31
[33] American Art News 1917/5/12, 3
[34] Perera 2008, 22-23
[35] On the Genealogies of Back Bay Houses in Boston it is reported that Gino Perera lived at 230 Commonwealth in the 1902-1903 winter season, then again in the 1904-1905 winter season, but moved thereafter. By the 1908-1909 season, Gino Perera and his wife were living at The Colonial at 382 Commonwealth. See: https://backbayhouses.org/230-commonwealth/ (accessed on 2020/12/4)

[36] See: "Wind-tossed Trees" in American Art News 1915/5/8, 6; and "Sunset in Jamaica" in American Art News 1916/12/23, 3
[37] American Art News 1921/12/17, 8
[38] See: Vasileos Kapousouz, *Head of Gino L. Perera* (1940); url: https://collections.mfa.org/objects/55290/head-of-gino-l-perera?ctx=37b48b40-89dd-466c-9c62-3137cdd3ac53&idx=0 (accessed on 2020/12/10)
[39] Carrera 2016, 25
[40] Fergonzi 1999, 34
[41] Carrera 2016, 51-52
[42] Ibid., 99-100
[43] Information retrieved through family recollections reported by Carol Weingeist: E-mail on 2020/12/1, 23:45
[44] Fig. 59 in: Carrera 2016, 106
[45] New York Tribune 1921/12/4, 5
[46] Ellsworth American 1918/9/25, 8
[47] Full materials are archived in the Records of the American Defense Society (1915-1942) at the New-York Historical Society, with this specific collection processed by Melissa Haley in 2011. See: http://dlib.nyu.edu/findingaids/html/nyhs/americandefsoc/bioghist.html
[48] Carroccio 1921 (April), 304
[49] Engineering and Mining Journal 1920, 684
[50] Italy-America Society 1927, 44
[51] Carrera 2016, 106
[52] Oldrini 1916, 123-124
[53] New York Times 1946/12/21, 19; and New York Times 1953/1/18, 93
[54] A picture of this caricature of Mario Perera is preserved in the archive of the Arturo Noci Estate and was accessed thanks to art historian Manuel Carrera, who oversees the painter's art historical legacy

Chapter 9

[1] See: Perera Guest Book 1930-1966 (Document)
[2] New York Times 1930/3/17, 19
[3] New York Times 1930/2/26, 22
[4] Williams 2004, 28-31, and 46
[5] Perera 1963, 13
[6] Among family materials there is a letter to Carolina (Carolyn) Perera from Arturo Toscanini (1952/4/3)
[7] Perera 1963, 13-14
[8] The mentioned medal is in the possession of Carol Weingeist
[9] See: Guide to the Mrs. Lionello Perera Papers, 1888-1966 (Bulk dates, 1930-1965): JPB 06-11, Music Division, The New York Public Library for the Performing Arts
[10] See: Brochure for the 60th Anniversary of Marlboro Music (2011), 39. Url: https://www.marlboromusic.org/wp-content/uploads/2015/07/60th-Reflections.pdf; and Manhattan School of Music Course Catalog (2017), 21-22. Url: https://silo.tips/download/manhattan-school-of-music-course-catalog

[11] Among family materials there are letters to Carolyn Allen Perera Isaac Stern (1963/5/20), Vladimir Horowitz (1965/6/1), and Yehudi Menuhin (1930/5/1)
[12] See letters to Carolyn Perera (1946/3/10 and 1952/8/9) in: The Paul Ben–Haim (Frankenburger) Archives, Mus. 55 Catalogue. The Israel National Library Department of Music: Jerusalem (2007)
[13] Bulletin of the New York Public Library 1966, 139
[14] Cincinnati Post and Times Star 1960/4/15, 25
[15] Perera 1963, 14
[16] Egelman, Gratzer, D'Angelo 2005, 94-95
[17] Gambino 1974, 185
[18] Kalmijn 1991: 786-800
[19] Egelman, Gratzer, D'Angelo 2005, 95-97
[20] Perera 1963, 9-10
[21] See: Vivaldi 2000, the auto-biography of Olga Lopes Perera Pincherle's niece Mariella Vivaldi, who recalls how she and her mother Lea Pincherle escaped the Nazis in northern Italy
[22] Luconi 2016, 40
[23] Puckett Sasser 2018, 157-159
[24] See: Photograph of Lionello Perera cheering with tenor Giovanni Martinelli in American Review 1959, 29
[25] According to the specialist magazine *Fruit Trade Journal*, Lionello Perera & Co. purchased several thousand boxes of lemons in the years of World War I. See for instance: *Fruit Trade Journal*, LVI/8, 1916/12/2: 15
[26] Gazzetta Ufficiale 1922, 2520
[27] Archival material, Bohemians Club list of members
[28] Musical America 1915/9/15, 6
[29] Musical Courier 1916/3/30, 61
[30] Musical America 1916/12/2, 41
[31] A black and white postcard of the time shows the mezzo soprano Nanà Genovese in her stage costume dressed as the tormented Spanish gypsy woman Carmen, the main character of the homonymous opera. See: https://www.ebay.com/itm/Nana-Genovese-Posing-with-Cigarette-Shawl-Opera-Singer-Postcard-/323999631543 (accessed on 2020/12/20)
[32] Musical America 1919/4/26, 18
[33] Musical America 1919/3/28, 44
[34] Musical Courier 1920/8/19, 1
[35] See: Carnagie Hall Icons. Url: https://www.carnegiehall.org/About/History/Carnegie-Hall-Icons/Arturo-Toscanini (accessed on 2020/12/16)
[36] The signature of Madame de Coppet appears on the second page of the Perera guestbook on the occasion of the very first concert they gave on March 16, 1930, when also Arturo Toscanini participated. See: Perera Guest Book 1930-1966 (Document), 1930/3/16; and Marcella Sembrich Collection 1790-1988 (Correspondence)
[37] See: Toscanini Legacy Papers 1686-1993 (Correspondence): Ara, Ugo 1920/7/21-27
[38] Perera 1963, p. 10-11
[39] New York Times 1938/1/6, 23

[40] Toscanini Legacy Papers 1686-1993 (Correspondence): Perera, Lionello and Carolyn 1938/3/9

[41] Toscanini Legacy Papers 1686-1993 (Correspondence): Perera, Carolyn 1952/4/3

[42] A postcard from Salzburg to Mrs. Frederick Muschenheim at Hotel Astor in NY was sent on August 16, 1938, with the signatures of the entire company, Carolyn and Lionello included. Lucerne instead is mentioned by Carolyn in her memoirs. See: Perera 1963, 12

[43] It is unclear where Alpino is exactly located, as it is not the name of a place, town or village. Given there is a photo of Lionello and Carolyn at the train station of Bolzano in South Tyrol dating to 1936, it is highly likely that Alpino was the name of a specific hotel, probably somewhere in the Gardena Valley.

[44] Perera 1963, 11

[45] Borgatta Dunnett 2007

[46] See: Miracco 2007

[47] The entire episode is told in: Perera 1963, 12-13

[48] Credit for finding the now dispersed painting goes to Prof. Milia Lorraine Khoury, who found the Guardi copy by Giovanni Grubacs (1929-1919) entitled The *Doge in the Pozzetto in Piazza San Marco, Venice* on auction records. See: http://www.artnet.com/artists/giovanni-grubas/the-doge-in-the-pozzetto-in-piazza-san-marco-oDkF4-EUkShswTP7peTLlg2 (accessed on 2022/2/7)

[49] The painting is now in the permanent collection of the Musée de Grenoble, France. See: https://www.museedegrenoble.fr/oeuvre/109/1922-le-doge-de-venise-porte-par-les-gondoliers-apres-son-election-sur-la-place-saint-marc.htm (accessed on 2021/2/7)

[50] Skalet 1975, 2

[51] Richardson 1969, 12-14

[52] See: Harris 1993, 13-28; Skalet 1975, 2-7; Dulaney 1979, 47-60; and Ake Sensabaugh, Matheson 2002, 30-49

[53] Trustees of the Metropolitan Museum of Art 1917, 39

[54] Richter 1941, 177

[55] Orfila 2011, 60

[56] The mentioned painting is now in the possession of Lucy Collier, granddaughter of Lionello Perera

[57] For comparison see the painting by Eugène Feyen, “Morning banter at the market”, sold at Christie’s on 2003/9/18. Url: https://www.christies.com/lot/lot-eugene-feyen-french-1826-1895-morning-banter-4151864/ (accessed on 2020/12/27)

[58] Scarce biographic and stylistic information are retrievable at: Paoletti 1865

[59] See Artwork Records on the Fondazione Zeri website, where the spelling of the last name of Lionello’s daughter is though spelt incorrectly (Pereira, instead of Perera): http://catalogo.fondazionezeri.unibo.it/entry/work/15366/Rosselli%20Cosimo%2C%20Cristo%20crocifisso

[60] When the banker died in 1942 his wife Carolyn Allen Perera inherited the painting and apparently gave it to their daughter Nina Perera Collier in December 1943. Upon Nina’s death in 1973, the painting was donated for educationl purpose to Bryn Mawr College where she had studied. See Artwork Records on the Bryn Mawr collection repository: https://triarte.brynmawr.edu/objects-1/info?query=mfs%20any%20%22rosselli%22&sort=0

[61] The translation in the New International Version of the Bible reads: "You are the most excellent of men, and your lips have been anointed with grace [, since God has blessed you forever]." (Psalm 45.2)
[62] Updated scientific data and restoration reports could be screened thanks to Marianne Weldon, Objects Conservator and Collections Manager for Art and Artifact Collections at Bryn Mawr College, and Joyce Hill Stoner, Edward F. and Elizabeth Goodman Rosenberg Professor of Material Culture at the University of Delaware and Paintings Conservator of the Winterthur Museum
[63] See Artwork Records on the Fondazione Zeri website, where the spelling of the last name of Lionello's daughter is again spelt incorrectly (Pereira, instead of Perera): http://catalogo.fondazionezeri.unibo.it/entry/work/48047/Lotto%20Lorenzo%2C%20Ritratto%20di%20gentiluomo
[64] See Artwork Record on the website of the Museo Nacional Thyssen-Bornemisza, Madrid, where it is hung in Room 6 and registered with Inv. no. 230 (1977.73): https://www.museothyssen.org/en/collection/artists/lotto-lorenzo/self-portrait
[65] See comments of Mar Borobia on the above Artwork Records
[66] See Ridolfi 1835, 189
[67] Massi 1990, 1–4
[68] See Artwork Record on the website of the Galleria Doria Pamphilj, Rome, where it is registered with Inv. no. FC 673: https://www.doriapamphilj.it/portfolio/lorenzo-lotto/
[69] See Artwork Page on the website of FAI Fondo per l'Ambiente Italiano: https://fondoambiente.it/luoghi/chiesa-di-santa-maria-in-telusiano?ldc
[70] Burroughs 1921, 96–99
[71] See: Orenstein 2001, and Artwork Record on the MET website: https://www.metmuseum.org/art/collection/search/338696 (accessed on 2020/12/23)
[72] See Artwork Record on the website of the National Museum of Art of Romania, Bucharest: http://mnar.arts.ro/en/?option=com_content&view=article&id=266&catid=113&Itemid=258; and the Sale Record on Christie's website: https://www.christies.com/en/lot/lot-6010101 (both accessed on 2020/12/23)
[73] In this regard, among the grandchildren of Lionello Perera, Sylvia Brinton Perera remembers that the painting went to George Allen Collier, selling it to cover a mortgage. (Private E-mail 2020/12/23)
[74] Report of the Trustees 1928, 239; and Journal of the American Museum of Natural History 1919, 225
[75] See Artwork Records on the Fondazione Zeri website: http://catalogo.fondazionezeri.unibo.it/ricerca.v2.jsp?locale=it&decorator=layout_resp&apply=true&percorso_ricerca=OA&filtroprovenienza_OA=8141%7C1014&sortby=LOCALIZZAZIONE&batch=10 (accessed 2020/12/18)
[76] The collection was later sold piece by piece, mostly through art dealers and auction houses. Carolyn Allen Perera herself sold four of the Longhis in 1964 through Christie's, while the remaining two were sold at later auctions in 1967. See: New York Times 19646/25, 30
[77] See: Volpi, Townsend, Kirby 1917, 251; Ravà 1909, pl.31b (called "Visite dopo cena"); and Pignatti 1968, p. 89
[78] These two paintings are now in the belongings of unknown private collections
[79] Shapley 1929, 6

[80] American Magazine of Art 1936, 266-267
[81] Bulletin of the City Art Museum of St. Louis 1936, 27
[82] Williams 1938, 61-66
[83] See: Fondazione Querini Stampalia 2018
[84] See: Cappellini, Goldhahn 2013; and Ferrazza 1993
[85] Volpi, Townsend, Kirby 1917, 250-261
[86] Herron Art Museum 1952, 40
[87] Metropolitan Museum of Art Bulletin 1914, 75–77
[88] Record and Guide 1910/9/10, 430
[89] New York Times 1920/8/20, 21
[90] See: Miller 2013
[91] Robins 2017, 172
[92] New York Times 1930/2/9, 1
[93] New York Times 1944/2/26, 24
[94] Robins 2007 (National Register), section 7
[95] New York Times 1970/6/5, 47

Chapter 10

[1] *L'Elisir d'Amore* (1832) was composed by Gaetano Donizetti on a libretto by Felice Romani, premiering in Milan
[2] Fox 1932, 62-64
[3] Hagaman Hall 1910, 476
[44] See information on the Verrazzano Monument Official Website of the New York City Department of Parks & Recreation: https://www.nycgovparks.org/parks/battery-park/monuments/1628
[5] Luconi 2016, 37-39
[6] Hudson-Fulton Celebration Commission 1909, 30
[7] Hagaman Hall 1910, 477
[8] See information on the Verdi Monument Official Website of the New York City Department of Parks & Recreation: https://www.nycgovparks.org/parks/verdi-square/monuments/1624 (accessed on 2020/12/17)
[9] Italy America Society 1920
[10] New York Times 1919/4/7, 1 and 4
[11] Perera 1918, 314-316
[12] The painting is registered in the catalogue of the Gallerie dell'Accademia, Venice, and hangs today in room 6. Url: https://www.gallerieaccademia.it/la-lezione-di-danza (accessed on 2021/12/12)
[13] The painting is registered in the catalogue of the Fondazione Giorgio Cini, Venice. Url: http://arte.cini.it/Opere/465957 (accessed on 2020/12/12). See also: Pignatti 1974, 91 (cat. 70, fig. 70); and Busetto 1995, 44 (cat. 8)
[14] The painting is registered in the catalogue of the Fondazione Giorgio Cini, Venice, and hangs today at the Museum of Ca' Rezzonico. Url: http://arte.cini.it/Opere/471714 (accessed on 2020/12/12). See also: Pignatti 1974, 91 (cat. 69, fig. 69); and Mariuz, Pavanello, Romanelli 1993, 80 (cat. 41)

[15] Volpi, Townsend, Kirby 1917, 260; and see entry in the database of the Fondazione Zeri: http://catalogo.fondazionezeri.unibo.it/scheda/fotografia/124680/Anonimo%20-%20Longhi%2C%20Pietro.%20The%20dance%20at%20the%20picnic%20-%20insieme (accessed on 2020/12/14)
[16] Pittston Gazette, 1905/9/13, 3
[17] Gazzetta Ufficiale del Regno d'Italia 1909, 393
[18] Consolato Generale d'Italia 1908 (Certificate)
[19] Re d'Italia 1909 (Certificate)
[20] Italian Red Cross 1911 (Correspondence)
[21] Hughes 1909, 66-68
[22] Perera 1916, 552-553
[23] Eula 2000, 90-91
[24] Walsh 1919, 791-792
[25] New York Times 1927/1/7, 19
[26] Widdemer 1924, 17
[27] In the period between 1916 and 1920, adults in East Harlem suffered a 15.3 (per 1000/year) mortality rate compared with 14.7 in the city; during the same period, the mortality rate for their babies was 100.6, versus 83.2 for the city as a whole. See: Widdemer 1932, 17
[28] D'Antonio 2013, 989-990
[29] Widdemer 1932, 16
[30] School 1911/11/9, 116
[31] Dubreuil 2018, 54-55
[32] Sorrentino 2003, 309-310; and Cavaioli 2000
[33] Oldrini 1916, 123
[34] For further information see the institute's website at: Italian Welfare League, History: https://www.italianwelfareleague.org/our-history (accessed on 2021/1/4)
[35] Leigh Harmon 2006, 25–28; and Widdemer 1932, 17.
[36] Luconi 2015, 6
[37] New York Times 1927/1/12, 26
[38] New York Sun 1940/1/11, 12
[39] New York Times 1936/1/27, 14; New York Times 1939/11/16, 13
[40] See: Dubreuil 2018
[41] Office of the Mayor 1934 (Certificate)
[42] United States Senate 1939, 141
[43] Federal Writers' Project 1939, 111 and 142
[44] Carroccio 1919 (July-August), 399
[45] Dubreuil 2018, 54-55
[46] Mariano 1921, 179-181
[47] Callegari 2012, 120
[48] Franz 2017, 37
[49] Pozzetta 1989, 79
[50] Zinn 2010, 7.
[51] Freeman 1993, 1658-1659
[52] Bayor 1972, 381

[53] Among archival material there is a ticket to the "Rally of New America for La Guardia" dated October 31, 1937, and an unspecified newspaper announcement in Italian that has Lionello Perera as a chairman of the rally
[54] Rally of New America 1937 (Document): all subsequent quotes are taken from this speech by Lionello Perera
[55] Perera Papers 1937 (Correspondence): Isaacs 1937/11/10
[56] Perera Papers 1937 (Correspondence): Portfolio 1937/11/10
[57] Perera Papers 1937 (Correspondence): Corsi 1937/11/19
[58] Luconi 2003, 97
[59] Costikyan 1993, 421
[60] Luconi 2002, 410
[61] Perera Papers 1941 (Correspondence): La Guardia 1941/4/26

Chapter 11

[1] Perera Papers 1920 (Correspondence): Perera 1920/4/13
[2] Luconi 2003, 91-92
[3] US Bureau of the Census 1957, 56
[4] Luconi 2015, 6
[5] De Lucia 2008, 84
[6] Luconi 2003, 94
[7] De Lucia 2008, 86
[8] Luconi 2015, 20
[9] Luconi 2006, 111
[10] De Lucia 2008, 94
[11] Luconi 2003, 97
[12] Mormino, Pozzetta 1999, 140
[13] American Review 1959, 31
[14] Italian Red Cross 1924 (Honour)
[15] Luconi 2015, 6
[16] Perera 1963, 17-18
[17] Luconi 2003, 97
[18] Luconi 2007, 9
[19] Calice 1982, 889
[20] Frezza Bicocchi 1970, 661-697
[21] Bacchin 2008, 243
[22] Calice 892-893
[23] New York Times 1927/10/13, 3
[24] New York Times 1927/3/13, 12
[25] New York Times 1927/9/4, 5
[26] Annual Report Columbia University 1928, 39 and 142
[27] Calice 894
[28] Perera Guest Book 1930-1966 (Document), 1936/5/6
[29] Calice, 895
[30] Bacchin 2008, 244-249
[31] See: Levis Sullam 2018

[32] Luconi 2006, 111
[33] Perera Papers 1942 (Correspondence), Springer 1939/1/21 (handwritten notes, first and second typewritten draft)
[34] Luconi 2006, 112
[35] Perera Papers 1942 (Correspondence), Springer 1939/1/21 (handwritten notes)
[36] Segal 1943, 253
[37] Luconi 2006, 115
[38] Perera Papers 1942 (Correspondence), Springer 1939/1/21 (second draft)
[39] See: Levis Sullam 2018
[40] See: Bianchi Scaglia 2013 (Testimony)
[41] Picciotto 2002, 66-71 and 77-80
[42] The records among victims of the Shoah of Olga Perera Pincherle and her children are retrievable on the digital archive of the CDEC Foundation: http://digital-library.cdec.it/cdec-web/persone/detail/person-5029/lopez-perera-olga.html; http://digital-library.cdec.it/cdec-web/persone/detail/person-6101/pincherle-vittorio-samuele.html; and http://digital-library.cdec.it/cdec-web/persone/detail/person-6095/pincherle-emilia.html (accessed on 2021/1/10)
[43] Declaration of absence 1946 (Document)
[44] New York Times 1942/4/27, 15
[45] New York Times 1964/1/31, 27
[46] Quote from Nina Perera Collier's remarks at the funeral of Lionello Perera, found on notes probably taken by Carolyn Allen in April 1942; no date, 3 pages

Bibliography

Bibliographical References and Scientific Literature

Ahamed 2009

Ahamed, Liaquat (2009): Lords of Finance: 1929, The Great Depression, and the Bankers who Broke the World. London: Penguin Group.

Aicardi, Cavaterra 1988

Aicardi, Cinzia Maria; Cavaterra, Alessandra (eds.) (1988): I fondi archivistici della legazione sarda e delle rappresentanze diplomatiche Italiane negli USA (1848-1901). Roma: Istituto Poligrafico e Zecca dello Stato.

Ake Sensabaugh, Matheson 2002

Ake Sensabaugh, David; Matheson, Susan B. (2002): "Ada Small Moore: Collector and Patron". Yale University Art Gallery Bulletin: 30-49.

Alduino, Coles 2004

Alduino, Frank W.; Coles, David J. (2004): "'Ye come from many a far off clime; And speak in many a tongue': The Garibaldi Guard and Italian-American Service in the Civil War". Italian Americana, 22/1 (Winter): 47-63.

American Magazine of Art 1936

Anon. (1936): "Seventeen Venetians at St. Louis". The American Magazine of Art, 29/4 (April): 266-267.

Annual Report Columbia University 1928

Var. Auth. (1928): Annual Report of the and Treasurer to the Trustees for year ending Jun 30, 1927. New York: Columbia University Publications.

Antinori 1994

Antinori, Carlo (1994): Luca Pacioli e la Summa de Arithmetica. Rome: Istituto Poligrafico e Zecca dello Stato.

Assembly of New York 1913

Var.Auth. (1913): Documents of the Assembly of the State of New York, 1/1-7. Albany (NY): Lyon Company.

Bacchin 2008

Bacchin, Elena (2008): "Prezzolini in America e il fascismo. Un memoriale". Contemporanea, 11/2 (April): 243-256.

Bankers' Magazine 1896

"New York City". The Bankers' Magazine, LIII, 1896 July-December: 729-730.

Bayor 1972

Bayor, Ronald H. (1972): "Italians, Jews and Ethnic Conflict". The International Migration Review, 6/4 (Winter): 377-391.

Berengo 1989

Berengo, Marino (1989): La fondazione della Scuola Superiore di commercio di Venezia. Venice: Poligrafo.

Bergamin Barbato 2015

Bergamin Barbato, Maria (2015): "La fondazione di Ca' Foscari e il corso di Laura in economia aziendale. Due tappe fondamentali nel percorso della cultura manageriale". In Mantoan, Diego; Bianchi, Stefano (eds.): 30+ anni di aziendalisti in Laguna. Gli studi manageriali a Venezia. Venice: Edizioni Ca' Foscari: 43-68.

Beuka 2011
Beuka, Robert (2011): American Icon: Fitzgerald's 'The Great Gatsby' in Critical and Cultural Context. Literary Criticism in Perspective. Rochester (NY): Boydell & Brewer.

Boerio [1856] 1971
Boerio, Giuseppe [1856] 1971. Dizionario del dialetto veneto. Venice: Cecchini Editore.

Bollettino 1899, January
Bollettino degli Antichi Studenti (1899), 1 (January). Venice: Ca' Foscari.

Bollettino 1900, November
Bollettino degli Antichi Studenti (1900), 6 (November). Venice: Ca' Foscari.

Bollettino 1901, March
Bollettino degli Antichi Studenti (1901), 7 (March). Venice: Ca' Foscari.

Bollettino 1902, March
Bollettino degli Antichi Studenti (1902), 10 (March). Venice: Ca' Foscari.

Bollettino 1902, November
Bollettino degli Antichi Studenti (1902), 12 (November). Venice: Ca' Foscari.

Boscaro 2018
Boscaro, Adriana (2018): "Japanese Teachers at the Royal School of Commerce (1873-1923)". In De Giorgi, Laura; Greselin, Federico (eds.): 150 Years of Oriental Studies at Ca' Foscari. Venice: Edizioni Ca' Foscari: 171-191.

Bregoli 2010
Bregoli, Francesca (2010): "'Two Jews walk into a Coffeehouse': the 'Jewish question,' utility, and political participation in late eighteenth-century Livorno". Jewish History, 24/3-4, Special issue on Tradition and Transformation in Eighteenth-Century Europe: Jewish Integration in Comparative Perspective: 309-329.

Bulletin of the City Art Museum of St. Louis 1936
Var. Auth. (1936): "Special Loan Exhibition: Venetian Painting of the Eighteenth Century". Bulletin of the City Art Museum of St. Louis, 21/2 (March): 15-48.

Bulletin of the New York Public Library 1966
Var. Auth. (1966): "Front Matter". Bulletin of the New York Public Library, 70/3 (March): 138-140.

Burns 2019
Burns, Emily C. (2019): "Spectral figures: Edward Hopper's empty Paris". In Campbell, Courtney J.; Giovine, Allegra; Keating, Jennifer (Eds.): Empty Spaces: perspectives on emptiness in modern history. London: University of London Press: 111–132.

Burroughs 1921
B[urroughs], B[ryson] (1921): "The Harvesters by Pieter Brueghel the Elder". Metropolitan Museum of Art Bulletin, 16 (May): 96–99, 102–103.

Busetto 1995
Busetto, Giorgio (ed.) (1995): Cento scene di vita veneziana. Pietro Longhi e Gabriel Bella alla Querini Stampalia. Milan: Bompiani.

Calice 1982
Calice, Nino (1982): "Il fascismo e l'emigrazione lucana negli USA". Studi Storici, 23/4 (October-December): 881-896.

California Historical Society 1964
"Histories of Associate Members". California Historical Society Quarterly, 43/2 (June 1964), 177-180.

Callegari 2012
Callegari, Renato (2012): Il Fronte del Cielo: Guida all'Aviazione nel Veneto durante la Grande Guerra, 1915-1918. Treviso: Istituto per la Storia del Risorgimento Italiano and Comune di Istrana.

Calomiris 1995
Calomiris, Charles (1995): "The Costs of Rejecting Universal Banking: American Finance in the German Mirror, 1870-1914". In Lamoreaux, Naomi R.; Raff, Daniel M. (eds.): Coordination and Information. Historical Perspectives on the Organisation of Enterprise. Chicago: University of Chicago Press: 257-322.

Calomiris 2008
Calomiris, Charles (2008): "Banking Crises". NBER Reporter, 4: 10-14.

Calomiris, Gorton 1991
Calomiris, Charles; Gorton, Gary (1991): "The Origins of Banking Panics: Models, Facts, and Bank Regulation". In Hubbard, R. Glenn (ed.): Financial Markets and Financial Crises. Chicago: University of Chicago Press: 109-174.

Calomiris, Mason 2004
Calomiris, Charles; Mason, Joseph (2004): "How to Restructure Failed Banking Systems: Lessons from the United States in the 1930s and Japan in the 1990s". In Ito, Takatoshi; Krueger, Anne O. (eds.): Governance, Regulation, and Privatization in the Asia-Pacific Region, NBER East Asia Seminar on Economics, 12. Chicago: University of Chicago Press: 375-423.

Calomiris, Wheelock 1998
Calomiris, Charles; Wheelock, David (1998): "Was the Great Depression a Watershed for American Monetary Policy?". In Bordo, Michael D.; Goldin, Claudia; White, Eugene N. (eds.): The Defining Moment: The Great Depression and the American Economy in the Twentieth Century. Chicago: University of Chicago Press: 23-66.

Campbell Coyle 2008
Campbell Coyle, Heather (2008): "Caricature and Criticism in Art Academies". American Art, 22/1 (Spring): 15-18.

Carrera 2016
Carrera, Manuel (ed.) (2016): Arturo Noci (1874-1953) - Tra Roma e New York: dal divisionismo aristocratico al ritratto borghese (Exhibition Catalogue). Rome: Galleria Berardi.

Cassen 2014
Cassen, Flora (2014): "The Last Spanish Expulsion in Europe: Milan 1565—1597". AJS Review, 38/1, April: 59-88.

Cavaioli 2000
Cavaioli, Frank J. (2000): Salvatore Primeggia and Joseph A. Varacalli. New York: Garland Publishing.

Clayson 2016
Clayson, Hollis (2016): "Bright Lights, Brilliant Wits.: Caricature and Electric

Light in Later Nineteenth-Century Paris". In Beltran, Alain; Laborie, Léonard; Lanthier, Pierre; Le Gallic, Stéphanie (eds.): Electric Worlds / Mondes électriques: Creations, Circulations, Tensions, Transitions (nineteenth–21st C.). Bern: Peter Lang AG: 17-38.

Connell, Pugliese 2019
Connell, William J.; Pugliese, Stanislao G. (eds.) (2019): The Routledge History of Italian Americans. London: Routledge.

Conte 2018
Conte, Alessio (2018): "Tra Dalmazia e Balcani. Imperialismo adriatico a Ca' Foscari durante il fascismo". In Casellato, Alessandro; Favero, Giovanni (eds.): Ca' Foscari e il Novecento, VENETICA, XXXII, 55/2: 35-58.

Costikyan 1993
Costikyan, Edward N. (1993): "Politics in New York City: A Memoir of the Post-War Years". New York History, 74/4 (October): 414-434.

D'Antonio 2013
D'Antonio, Patricia (2013): "Cultivating Constituencies: The Story of the East Harlem Nursing and Health Service, 1928–1941". American Journal of Public Health, 103/6 (June): 988–996.

Davison, Ramirez 2014
Davison, Lee K.; Ramirez, Carlos D. (2014): "Local banking panics of the 1920s: Identification and determinants". Journal of Monetary Economics, Elsevier, 66(C), 164-177.

De Beixedon 1921
De Beixedon Jr., Edward Francis Frémaux (1921): The ancestors and descendants of Dr. David Rogers. New York: New York Public Library.

De Lucia 2008
De Lucia, Francesca (2008). "The Impact of Fascism and World War II on Italian-American Communities". Italian Americana, 26/1 (Winter): 83-95.

Deodati, Luzzatti 1868
Deodati, Edoardo; Luzzatti, Luigi (1868): "Ordinamento della regia Scuola superiore di commercio in Venezia: R. D. 6 agosto 1868 n. 4530". Ministero d'agricoltura, industria e commercio. Florence: G. Barbera, 1868.

Dimant 2019
Dimant, Mauricio (2019) "Sephardic Community and Social Practices in the Circuit of Money: Social Implications of Payment Networks in the Context of the Livorninas". In Kaplan, Yosef (ed.): Religious Changes and Cultural Transformations in the Early Modern Western Sephardic Communities. Leiden: Brill: 323-345.

Donadon 2018
Donadon, Marco (2018): "Il ritorno del leone. Ca' Foscari e il colonialismo italiano". In Casellato, Alessandro; Favero, Giovanni (eds.): Ca' Foscari e il Novecento, VENETICA, XXXII, 55/2: 13-34.

Dubreuil 2018
Dubreuil, Catherine (2018): Le rôle de l'Italian Welfare League dans le processus d'intégration des italiens aux États-Unis – 1920-1965 (Doctoral thesis). Université Bretagne Loire: April 21.

Dulaney 1979
Dulaney, William L. (1979): "Wallace Nutting: Collector and Entrepreneur". Winterthur Portfolio (American Furniture and Its Makers), 13: 47-60.

Egelman, Gratzer, D'Angelo 2005
Egelman, William; Gratzer, William; D'Angelo, Michael (2005): "Italian-Jewish Intermarriage: The Italian-American Spouse". Italian Americana, 23/1 (Winter): 94-105.

Eula 2000
Eula, Michael J. (2000): "Failure of American Food Reformers Among Italian Immigrants in New York City, 1891-1897". Italian Americana, 18/1 (Winter): 86-99.

Faustini 2012
Faustini, Giuseppe (2012): "L'Unità d'Italia: gli Stati Uniti e un garibaldino americano". Italica, 89/2 (Summer): 202-218.

Favero 2015
Favero, Giovanni (2015): "L'insegnamento delle discipline aziendali a Venezia dalla Scuola Superiore di Commercio all'Università Ca' Foscari". In Mantoan, Diego; Bianchi, Stefano (eds.): 30+ anni di aziendalisti in Laguna. Gli studi manageriali a Venezia. Venice: Edizioni Ca' Foscari: 27-42.

Federal Writers' Project 1939
Workers of the Federal Writers' Project (1939): The Italians of New York: A Survey. New York: Random House.

Fehrer 1994
Fehrer, Catherine (1994): "Women at the Académie Julian in Paris". The Burlington Magazine, 136/1100 (November): 752-757.

Fergonzi 1999
Fergonzi, Flavio (1999): "Auguste Rodin e gli scultori italiani (1889-1915)". Prospettiva, 2/95-96 (July-October): 24-50.

Ferrazza 1993
Ferrazza, Roberta (1993): Palazzo Davanzati e le Collezioni di Elia Volpi. Florence: Cassa di Risparmio di Firenze, Centro DI.

Fisher 1918
Fisher, Jerome B. (1918): Reports of Cases heated and determined in the Appellate Division of the Supreme Court of the State of New York (vol. 182). Albany (NY): Lyon Company.

Fondazione Querini Stampalia 2018
Var. Auth. (2018): Fondazione Querini Stampalia (Museum Catalogue). Venice: Fondazione Querini Stampalia.

Franz 2017
Franz, Fabio (2017): Il campo d'aviazione di Gonars, 1915-17. Udine: Aviani & Aviani Editori.

Freeman 1993
Freeman, Joshua B. (1993): "Reviewed Work: Vito Marcantonio: Radical Politician, 1902-1954. by Gerald Meyer". The Journal of American History, 79/4 (March): 1658-1659.

Frezza Bicocchi 1970
Frezza Bicocchi, Daria (1970): "Propaganda fascista e comunità italiane in Usa: la Casa Italiana della Columbia University". Studi storici, 4: 661-697.
Gambino 1974
Gambino, Richard: (1974): Blood of my Blood: The Dilemma of the Italian Americans. New York: Doubleday.
Gazzetta Ufficiale 1922
Var. Auth. (1922): "Ordine della Corona d'Italia". Gazzetta Ufficiale del Regno d'Italia, 237 (October 9): 2520.
Gazzetta Ufficiale del Regno d'Italia 1909
Var. Auth. (1909): Gazzetta Ufficiale del Regno d'Italia, 19, 1909/1/23.
Ghersetti 2018
Ghersetti, Antonella (2018): "A 'Cafoscarino' in the World: Arturo De Luciano". In De Giorgi, Laura; Greselin, Federico (eds.): 150 Years of Oriental Studies at Ca' Foscari. Venice: Edizioni Ca' Foscari: 65-70.
Giovinco 1968
Giovinco, Joseph (1968): "Democracy in Banking: The Bank of Italy and California's Italians". California Historical Society Quarterly, 47/3 (September): 195-218.
Griffin 1923
Griffin, Austin B. (1923): Reports of Cases heated and determined in the Appellate Division of the Supreme Court of the State of New York (vol. 205). Albany (NY): Lyon Company.
Hagaman Hall 1910
Hagaman Hall, Edward (1910): The Hudson-Fulton Celebration 1909. Albany (NY): Lyon Company.
Harris 1993
Harris, Neil (1993): "William Preston Harrison: The Disappointed Collector". Archives of American Art Journal, 33/3: 13-28.
Herron Art Museum 1952
Var. Auth. (1952): Venice 1700-1800: An Exhibition of Venice and the Eighteenth Century (Exhibition catalogue). The Detroit Institute of Arts, John Herron Art Museum.
House of Representatives 1930
House of Representatives, seventy-first Congress (1930): Hearings before the Committee on Banking and Currency: Branch, Chain, and Group Banking, 2/11, H. Res. 141 (May 6-8). Washington: United States Government Printing Office.
Hudson-Fulton Celebration Commission 1909
Hudson-Fulton Celebration Commission (1909): Official Program: Hudson-Fulton Celebration. New York: Redfield Bros.
Ilari 1990
Ilari, Virgilio (1990): Storia del servizio militare in Italia, vol.II. Rome: Collana del Centro Militare di Studi Strategici: 219-517.
Italy America Society 1920
Italy America Society (1920): "Officers". Addresses delivered at the banquet in

honour of H.E. the Royal Italian Ambassador Baron Romano Avezzana (February 24). New York: Hotel Astor.

Jalil 2015
Jalil, Andrew J. (2015): "A New History of Banking Panics in the United States, 1825–1929: Construction and Implications". American Economic Journal: Macroeconomics, 7/3 (July): 295-330.

James, James [1954] 2002
James, Marquis; James, Bessie R. [1954] (2002): The Story of Bank of America: Biography of a Bank. Washington: Beard Books.

Jamet, Rossi 2018
Jamet, Marie-Christine; Rossi, Giuliano (2018): "150 anni della 'lingua di Molière' a Ca' Foscari". In Cardinaletti, Anna; Cerasi, Laura; Rigobon, Patrizio (eds.): Le lingue occidentali nei 150 anni di storia di Ca' Foscari. Venice: Edizioni Ca' Foscari: 44-64.

Johnson, Taylor 1953
Johnson, Lee E.; Taylor, C. W. (1953): Eminent Californians 1953. Palo Alto (CA): C.W. Taylor Publishing.

Journal of the American Museum of Natural History 1919
Var. Auth. (1919): Natural History. Journal of the American Museum of Natural History, XIX/1, (January): 239.

Kalmijn 1991
Kalmijn, Matthijs (1991): "Shifting Boundaries: Trends in Religious and Educational Homogamy". American Sociological Review, 56 (December): 786-800.

Katlan 1939
Katlan, Alexander W. (1939): The Salmagundi Club Painting Exhibition Records 1889 to 1939: A Guide to the American Exhibition of Oil Paintings and the Annual Exhibition and Auction Sale of Pictures. New York: Salmagundi

Katz 2010
Katz, Dana A. (2010): "'Clamber not you up to the casements': On ghetto views and viewing". Jewish History, 24/2: 127-153.

King 2011
King, Gilbert (2011): "The Man Who Busted the 'Banksters'". Smithsonian Magazine, November 29.

Landmarks Preservation Commission 1978
Landmarks Preservation Commission (1978): Fort Greene Historic District Designation Report. Dasignation List-119 LP-0973. New York 1978/9/26.

Lang 2009
Lang, Ariella (2009): "The Double Edge of Irony in Simone Luzzatto's Discorso". Jewish Social Studies, 15/3, Spring/Summer: 114-133.

Laurino 2014
Laurino, Maria (2014): The Italian Americans: A History. New York: W.W. Norton & Co.

Leigh Harmon 2006
Leigh Harmon, Russell (2006): The Tenants of East Harlem. Berkeley (Ca): University of California Press.

Levis Sullam 2018
Levis Sullam, Simon (2018): The Italian Executioners. The Genocide of the Jews of Italy. Princeton (NJ): Princeton University Press.

Luconi 2002
Luconi, Stefano (2002): "The Impact of World War II on the Political Behavior of the Italian-American Electorate in New York City". New York History, 83/4 (Fall): 404-417.

Luconi 2003
Luconi, Stefano (2003): "Forging an Ethnic Identity: The Case of Italian Americans". Revue française d'études américaines, 96 (May): 89-101.

Luconi 2006
Luconi, Stefano (2006): "The Venom of Racial Intolerance": Italian Americans and Jews in the United States in the Aftermath of Fascist Racial Laws". Revue française d'études américaines, 107 (Politique étrangère et société civile) (March): 107-119.

Luconi 2007
Luconi, Stefano (2007): "Italian Americans and the Invasion of Sicily in World War II". Italian Americana, 25/1: 5–22.

Luconi 2015
Luconi, Stefano (2015): "Fascism and Italian-American Identity Politics". Italian Americana, 33/1 (Winter): 6-24.

Luconi 2016
Luconi, Stefano (2016): "Opera as a Nationalistic Weapon: The Erection of the Monument to Giuseppe Verdi in New York City". Italian Americana, 34/1 (Winter): 37-61.

Mangione, Morreale 1993
Mangione, Jerre; Morreale, Ben (1993): La Storia: Five Centuries of the Italian American Experience. New York: Harper Perennial.

Mantoan, Bianchi 2015
Mantoan, Diego; Bianchi, Stefano (eds.) (2015): 30+ anni di aziendalisti in Laguna. Gli studi manageriali a Venezia. Venice: Edizioni Ca' Foscari

Mariano 1921
Mariano, John H. (1921): The Italian Contribution to American Democracy. Boston: The Cristopher Publishing House.

Mariano 1925
Mariano, John H. (1925): The Italian Immigrant and Our Courts. Boston: The Cristopher Publishing House.

Mariuz, Pavanello, Romanelli 1993
Mariuz, A.; Pavanello, G.; Romanelli, Giandomenico (eds.) (1993): Pietro Longhi (exhibition catalogue). Milan: Mondadori Electa.

Marraro 1945
Marraro, Howard R. (1945): "Italians in New York during the first half of the nineteenth century". New York History, 26/3 (July): 278-306.

Marraro 1946
Marraro, Howard R. (1946): "Garibaldi in New York". New York History, 27/2 (April): 179-203.

Massi 1990
Massi, Norberto (1990): "The Self-Portrait of Lorenzo Lotto in the 'Crucifixion? Of Monte San Giusto". Source: Notes in the History of Art, 9/4: 1–4.

Melcer-Padon 2019
Melcer-Padon, Nourit (2019): "Charity Begins at Home: Reflections on the Dowry Society of Livorno". In Kaplan, Yosef (ed.): Religious Changes and Cultural Transformations in the Early Modern Western Sephardic Communities. Leiden: Brill: 346-380.

Metropolitan Museum of Art Bulletin 1914
Anon. (1914): "New Acquisitions of Pictures." The Metropolitan Museum of Art Bulletin, 9 (March).

Miller 2009
Miller, Henry J. (2009): "John Leech and the Shaping of the Victorian Cartoon: The Context of Respectability". Victorian Periodicals Review, 42/3 (Fall): 267-291.

Miracco 2007
Miracco, Renato (ed.) (2007): La musica segreta del maestro: La collezione d'arte di Arturo Toscanini (Exhibition Catalogue). Milano: Mazzotta.

Morais 1894
Morais, Henry Samuel (1894): The Jews of Philadelphia. Philadelphia: The Levytype Company.

Morbiato 2014
Morbiato, Anna (2014): "Ca' Foscari vista dagli occhi dei suoi ex allievi. Una prima ricognizione di episodi e vicende dell'associazionismo fra ex studenti dell'Ateneo veneziano". In Mantoan, Diego; Quaino, Otello (eds.): Ca' Dolfin e i Cadolfiniani. Storia di un collegio universitario a Venezia. Venice: Edizioni Ca' Foscari: 141-158.

Mormino, Pozzetta 1999
Mormino, Gary R.; Pozzetta, George E. (1999): "Italian Americans and the 1940s". In Cannistraro, Philip V. (ed.): The Italians of New York: Five Centuries of Struggle and Achievement. New York: New York Historical Society: 139-153.

Ndalianis 2011
Ndalianis, Angela (2011): "Why Comics Studies?". Cinema Journal, 50/3 (Spring): 113-117.

Orenstein 2001
Orenstein, Nadine M. (ed.) (2001): Pieter Bruegel the Elder: Drawings and Prints. New York: MET Publications.

Orfila 2011
Orfila, Jorgelina (2011): "Art Collecting in America during the Interwar Period: The Chester Dale Collection of Modern French Art". Archives of American Art Journal. 50/1-2 (Spring): 48-61.

Paoletti 1865
Paoletti, Antonio (1865): Orazione di Antonio Paoletti pittore storico recitata il giorno 18 giugno 1865 in una delle sale del municipio di Venezia prima della estrazione del quadro da lui dipinto. Venice: Tipografia del Commercio.

Pedani 2018
Pedani, Maria Pia (2018): "Teaching Asian and African Languages in Ca'

Foscari (1868-1929)". In De Giorgi, Laura; Greselin, Federico (eds.):150 Years of Oriental Studies at Ca' Foscari. Venice: Edizioni Ca' Foscari: 17-26.

Perera 1963
Perera, Carolyn Allen (1963): Now It Should Be Told. Some reminiscences in the life of Carolyn Allen Perera. North Conway (NH): The Reporter Press.

Perera 2008
Perera, Ronald C. (2008): 'I Tell You Facts!' The Life of Gino L. Perera (1872-1961). Northampton (MA): Impress Inc.

Perino 2010
Perino, Michael (2010): The Hellhound of Wall Street: How Ferdinand Pecora's Investigation of the Great Crash Forever Changed American Finance. London: Penguin Books.

Picciotto 2002
Picciotto, Liliana (2002): Il libro della memoria: gli ebrei deportati dall'Italia, 1943-1945.Ricerca della Fondazione Centro di documentazione ebraica contemporanea. Milano: Mursia.

Pignatti 1968
Pignatti, Terisio (1968): Pietro Longhi. Venice: Alfieri.

Pignatti 1974
Pignatti, Terisio (ed.) (1974): L'opera completa di Pietro Longhi. Milan: Rizzoli.

Polese 1992
Polese, Bruno (1992): "Un modello funzionale: la Scuola superiore di commercio di Venezia (1868)". In Massa Piergiovanni, Paola (ed.), Dalla scuola superiore di commercio alla facoltà di economia: un secolo di elaborazione scientifica e di attività didattica al servizio dell'economia genovese, 1884-1986. Genoa: Università degli Studi di Genova: 33-77.

Posner 1958
Posner, Russell M. (1958): "The Bank of Italy and the 1926 Campaign in California". California Historical Society Quarterly, 37/3 (September): 267-275.

Pozzetta 1989
Pozzetta, George E. (1989): "Immigrants and Ethnics: The State of Italian-American Historiography". Journal of American Ethnic History, 9/1 (Fall): 67-95.

Puckett Sasser 2018
Puckett Sasser, Patricia (2018): "A Recording Artist: Enrico Caruso and his Scrapbooks". Fontes Artis Musicae, 65/3 (July–September): 157-169.

Ravà 1909
Ravà, Aldo (1909): Pietro Longhi. Bergamo: Istituto Italiano d'Arti Grafiche.

Report of the Trustees 1928
Var. Auth. (1928): "Building the American Museum (1869-1927)". Fifty-ninth Annual Report of the Trustees for the Year 1927. New York: The American Museum of Natural History: 225.

Richardson 1969
Richardson, E. P. (1969): "Allen Smith, Collector and Benefactor". The American Art Journal, 1/2 (Autumn): 5-19.

Richter 1941
Richter, G. M. (1941): "The New National Gallery in Washington". The Burlington Magazine for Connoisseurs, 78/459 (June): 174-83.

Ridolfi 1835
Ridolfi, Carlo (1835): Le maraviglie dell'arte ovvero le vite degli illustri pittori Veneti e dello stato. Vol.1. Padova: Cartallier. doi:10.11588/diglit.33473

Robins 2017
Robins, Anthony W. (2017): New York Art Deco: A Guide to Gotham's Jazz Age Architecture. State University of New York: Excelsior Editions.

Saloutos 1975
Saloutos, Theodore (1975): "The Immigrant in Pacific Coast Agriculture, 1880-1940". Agricultural History, 49/1 (January), 182-201.

Sattin 2014
Sattin, Antonella (2014): "Fonti documentarie sugli Alumni nell'Archivio Storico di Ca' Foscari. Un ideale percorso di ricerca sugli ex studenti dell'Ateneo veneziano". In Mantoan, Diego; Quaino, Otello (eds.): Ca' Dolfin e i Cadolfiniani. Storia di un collegio universitario a Venezia. Venice: Edizioni Ca' Foscari: 123-140.

Schiavo [1957] (1992)
Schiavo, Giovanni [1957] (1992): Four Centuries of Italian American History. New York: Center for Migration Studies.

Schorsch 1979
Schorsch, Anita (1979): "A Key to the Kingdom: The Iconography of a Mourning Picture". Winterthur Portfolio, 14/1 (Spring): 41-71.

Segal 1943
Segal, Simon (1943): "Bohemia-Moravia". The American Jewish Year Book, 44/ 5703 (September 12, 1942 to September 29, 1943): 250-253.

Senate of New York 1917
Var. Auth. (1917): Documents of the Senate of the State of New York, 3/7-12. Albany (NY): Lyon Company.

Shapley 1929
Shapley, John (1929): "Art Activities in New York". Parnassus, 1/3 (March 15): 3-6.

Shavit 2020
Shavit, Zohar (2020): "Cultural translation and the recruitment of translated texts to induce social change: The case of the Haskalah". In Van Coillie, Jan; McMartin, Jack (eds.): Children's Literature in Translation Book: Texts and Contexts. Leuven: Leuven University Press: 73-91.

Simpson 2010
Simpson, Marc (2010): "Caricatures for ye Broadway Lily". Archives of American Art Journal, 49/3-4 (Fall): 4-13.

Singer 1904
Singer, Isidore (ed.) (1904): Jewish Encyclopedia, vol.8. New York: Funk and Wagnalls Company.

Skalet 1975
Skalet, Linda (1975): "Thomas B. Clarke, American Collector". Archives of American Art Journal, 15/3: 2-7.

Smith, Underhill Moore 1923
Smith, Howard L.; Underhill Moore, William (1923): Cases on the Law of Bills & Notes selected from decisions of English and American Courts. St. Paul: West Publishing Company.

Sorrentino 2003
Sorrentino, Frank M. (2003): "Italian Welfare League". In LaGumina, Salvatore J.; et al. (eds.): The Italian American Experience: An Encyclopedia. London: Routledge: 309–310.

Strazza 2004
Strazza, Michele (2004): Emigrazione e fascismo in Basilicata. Gli emigrati lucani negli Stati Uniti e l'appoggio al fascismo. Melfi: Tarsia Editore.

Studemund-Halévy 2019
Studemund-Halévy, Michael (2019): "Sea Is History, Sea Is Witness: The Creation of a Prosopographical Database for the Sephardic Atlantic". In Kaplan, Yosef (ed.): Religious Changes and Cultural Transformations in the Early Modern Western Sephardic Communities. Leiden: Brill: 487-511.

Superintendent of Banks of New York 1919
Var.Auth. (1919): Annual Report of the Superintendent of Banks of the State of New York for the Year Ending December 31, 1918. Albany (NY): Lyon Company.

Tassini [1863] 1970
Tassini, Giuseppe [1863] (1970). Curiosità Veneziane: Ovvero origini delle denominazioni stradali di Venezia. Venice: Filippi Editore.

Thomson Gartinhour 1931
Thomson Gartinhour, Gaines (1931): Branch, Group and Chain Banking. New York: The Macmillan Company.

Trustees of the Metropolitan Museum of Art 1917
Var. Auth. (1917): "The Pierpont Morgan Collection". Annual Report of the Trustees of the Metropolitan Museum of Art, 48: 33-39.

Uidhir 2013
Uidhir, Christy Mag (2013): "Epistemic Misuse and Abuse of Pictorial Caricature". American Philosophical Quarterly, 50/2 (April): 137-151.

United States Bureau of the Census 1957
United States Bureau of the Census (1957): Historical Statistics of the United States, Colonial Times to 1957. Washington, DC: GPO.

United States Senate 1939
United States Senate, seventy-sixth Congress (1939): Hearings before a Subcommittee of the Committee on Immigration, S. 407-411 (March 21-23). Washington: United States Government Printing Office.

Vivaldi 2000
Vivaldi, Mariella (2000): La porta della salvezza: una donna e sua figlia in fuga dai nazisti. Venice: Marsilio.

Volpi, Townsend, Kirby 1917
Volpi, Elia; Townsend, Horace; Kirby, Thomas E. (1917): Italian Art Treasures and Antiquities acquired by Prof. Elia Volpi (Auction Catalogue). New York: American Art Galleries. DOI: https://doi.org/10.5479/sil.89395.39088002210516

Waas 2018
Waas, Michael (2018): "Lopes Perera Report". Prepared on behalf of Michele Jackson Weingeist.

Walsh 1919
Walsh, James J. (1919): History of Medicine in New York, vol.3. New York: National American Society.

Weingeist 2018
Weingeist, Michele (2018): "Our Efforts to Reclaim Spanish Citizenship". Avatoyanu: The International Review of Jewish Genealogy, XXXIV/4, Winter: 32-36.

Widdemer 1924
Widdemer, Kenneth (1924): The House That Health Built. New York: East Harlem Health Center.

Widdemer 1932
Widdemer, Kenneth (1932): A Decade of Health Center Pioneering. New York: East Harlem Health Center and the American Red Cross.

Williams 1938
Williams, Hermann W. (1938): "Tiepolo and His Contemporaries". The Metropolitan Museum of Art Bulletin, 33/3 (March): 61-66.

Williams 2004
Williams, Amedee Daryl (2004): Lillian Fuchs, First Lady of the Viola. Bllomington (IN): Iuniverse.

World War Foreign Debt Commission 1927
World War Foreign Debt Commission (1927). Combined Annual Reports. Washington, DC: GPO.

Wyrwa 2016
Wyrwa, Ulrich (2016): "The Language of Anti-Semitism in the Catholic Newspapers 'Il Veneto Cattolico / La Difesa' in Late Nineteenth-Century Venice". Church History and Religious Culture, 96/3: 346-369.

Yenişehirlioğlu 2015
Yenişehirlioğlu, Filiz (2015): "Whiter Art History? How Global Is Ottoman Art and Architecture?". The Art Bulletin, 97/ 4 (December): 359-363.

Zinn 2010
Zinn, Howard (2010): La Guardia in Congress. Ithaca (NY): Cornell University Press.

Zucchello 2012
Zucchello Paola (2012): La Ragioneria a Ca' Foscari nell'Ottocento (MA thesis). Venice: Università Ca' Foscari Venezia.

Newspapers and Periodicals

American Art News 1905/12/16
American Art News, 4(10), 1905/12/16: 1-8.

American Art News 1906/12/8
American Art News, 5(8), 1906/12/8: 1-8.

American Art News 1907/4/6
American Art News, 5(25), 1907/4/6: 1-8.

American Art News 1908/12/19
American Art News, 7(10), 1908/12/19: 1-8.

American Art News 1911/12/30
American Art News, 10(12), 1911/12/30: 1-8.
American Art News 1912/1/6
American Art News, 10(13), 1912/1/6: 1-8
American Art News 1915/5/8
American Art News, 13(31), 1915/5/8: 1-8.
American Art News 1916/12/23
American Art News, 15(11), 1916/12/23: 1-8.
American Art News 1917/5/12
American Art News, 15(31), 1917/5/12: 1-10
American Art News 1921/12/17
American Art News, 20(10), 1921/12/17: 1-10.
American Art News 1922/9/16
American Art News, 20(40), 1922/9/16: 1-10.
American Review 1959
Anon.: "Tradition of International Banking Carried on in the Perera Family". American Review, 1(4), Winter 1959: 29-31.
Basilicata nel mondo 1927
La Basilicata nel mondo, 4(3), March-April 1927.
Borgatta Dunnett 2007
Borgatta Dunnett, Emanuela: "Toscanini tra note e colori". Foglidarte.it, 2007/9/15.
Brooklyn Daily Eagle 1893/10/12
"Marriage Announcement: De Beixedon-Cantoni". The Brooklyn Daily Eagle, 1893 October 12: 9.
Brooklyn Daily Eagle 1894/6/6
"Mrs. Forster Sues Cantoni". The Brooklyn Daily Eagle, 1894 June 6: 1.
Brooklyn Daily Eagle 1896/7/1
"Salvatore Cantoni's Will". The Brooklyn Daily Eagle, 1896/7/1: 1.
Brooklyn Daily Eagle 1927/3/26
"Approve Sessa Banks Merger". Brooklyn Daily Eagle, 1927/3/26.
Brooklyn Life 1893/5/27, 17
"Mrs. Salvatore Cantoni: Society Column". Brooklyn Life, 1893/5/27: 17.
Brooklyn Life 1919/9/13
"Obituary: De Beixedon, Daniel Kingsland". Brooklyn Life, 1919/9/13: 3.
Brush and Pencil 1907 (January)
"Exhibitions: Past and to Come". Brush and Pencil, 19(1), January 1907: 2-6.
Campora 1924(?)
Campora, Vincenzo: "Da Ca' Foscari a Wall Street. Un signore della finanza italo-americana: il comm. Lionello Perera". Columbus, 1924(?): 41-42.
Carroccio 1916 (August)
"Pagine della Croce Rossa". Il Carroccio, IV(2), August 1916: 182-184.
Carroccio 1917 (June)
Il Carroccio, III(6), June 1917.
Carroccio 1918 (May)
"Gl'italiani negli Stati Uniti". Il Carroccio, VII(5-6), May 1918: 521-527.

Carroccio 1919 (February)
Il Carroccio, IX/2, February 1919.

Carroccio 1919 (July-August)
Il Carroccio, IX(7), July-August 1919.

Carroccio 1921 (April)
Il Carroccio, "Cinquant'anni di vita italiana in America, April 1921.

Carroccio 1921 (June)
Il Carroccio, XIII(6), June 1921.

Carroccio 1921 (August)
"Il nuovo edificio della banca Perera in Harlem". Il Carroccio, XVI(2), August 1921: 237.

Carroccio 1922 (October)
Il Carroccio, XIV(4), October 1922.

Chicago Daily Tribune 1894/6/6
"She Sues for $170,000 Damages". The Chicago Daily Tribune, 1894 June 6: 2.

Cincinnati Post and Times Star 1960/4/15
"A Gift from Toscanini Opened a New World". Cincinnati Post and Times Star, 1960/4/15: 25.

Commerce and Finance 1922
"Italy". Commerce and Finance, 11(40), 1922/10/4: 1484.

Commercial and Financial Chronicle 1894
"Bond Subscription Larger than Reported". The Commercial and Financial Chronicle. Hunt's Merchant's Magazine, 59(1539), 1894/12/22: 1804-1806.

Commercial and Financial Chronicle 1918 (May)
"Current Notice". The Commercial and Financial Chronicle, 1918/5/4: 1888.

Commercial and Financial Chronicle 1920 (May)
"Luigi Criscuolo on necessity of campaign of education in floating Italian bonds". The Commercial and Financial Chronicle, 1920/5/15: 2025-2026.

Commercial and Financial Chronicle 1923 (August)
"Italian submarine cable". The Commercial and Financial Chronicle, 1923/8/18: 786.

Commercial and Financial Chronicle 1924 (March)
The Commercial and Financial Chronicle, 118(3062), 1924/3/1: 969.

Criscuolo 1918
Criscuolo, Luigi (1918): "Italians in the Liberty Loan". Il Carroccio, VII(5-6), May 1918: 393-396.

Ellsworth American 1918/9/25
"Advertisement: The Crimes of Germany". Ellsworth American, 1918/9/25: 8.

Engineering and Mining Journal 1920
"Men you should know about". Engineering and Mining Journal, 110(14), 1920.

Evening Telegram 1917/3/11
"Case bancarie". The Evening Telegram New York, 1917/3/11: 8.

Fox 1932
Fox, Ann: "The 'Dumy Show': Italian marionettes in New York". Atlantica, XIII/3, May 1932: 62-64, 86-87.

Hughes 1909
Hughes, Charles E. (1909): "How New York Raised Funds for Italy". American Red Cross Bulletin, IV/2, April: 66-68.
Italy-America Society 1927
Italy-America Society Bulletin, 1-2, 1927.
JAMA 1891
"Letter from New York: Domestic Correspondence". JAMA (Journal of the American Medical Association), XVI(8), 1891/2/21: 284-285.
Melchiorre 1932
Melchiorre, Matthew A. (1932): "The Man Who Came Back: Giannini Regains Control of Transamerica". Atlantica, XIII/2, April: 68-69.
Musical America 1915/9/15
Musical America, XII(18), 1915/9/15.
Musical America 1916/12/2
Musical America, 1916/12/2.
Musical America 1919/3/28
Musical America, XXIX(18), 1919/3/28.
Musical America 1919/4/26
Musical America, XXIX(26), 1919/4/26.
Musical Courier 1916/3/30
Musical Courier, 1916/3/30.
Musical Courier 1920/8/19
Musical Courier, LXXXI(8), 1920/8/19.
New York Journal 1897/1/20
"Is Against Mrs. Forster". New York Journal, 1897/1/20: 1.
New York Sun 1929(?)
"Sale Was Due to Bank Merger". New York Sun, 1929(?).
New York Sun 1940/1/11
"Mrs. Perera is a Good Friend to the Italians of New York". New York Sun, 1940/1/11: 12.
New York Times 1889/7/11
"City and Suburban News: New York". The New York Times, 1889/7/11: 3.
New York Times 1891/1/25
"The Italian Home". The New York Times, 1891/1/25: 11.
New York Times 1896/6/23
"Obituary Record: Salvatore Cantoni". The New York Times, 1896/6/23: 4.
New York Times 1897/10/16
"The Forster-Cantoni Case". The New York Times, 1897/10/16: 5.
New York Times 1897/11/24
"Elsa Forster Beaten". The New York Times, 1897/11/24: 11.
New York Times 1917/8/14
"At Bay in a Bank, Leaps an Airshaft". The New York Times, 1917/8/14: 20.
New York Times 1919/4/7
"$430,000 Is pledged at rally for Victory Loan". The New York Times, 1919/4/7: 1, 4.

New York Times 1919/9/11
"Obituary: De Beixedon, Daniel Kingsland". The New York Times, 1919 September 9: 17.

New York Times 1920/12/28
"New Wall Street Bonuses". The New York Times, 1920/12/28: 24.

New York Times 1920/8/20
"Apartment House Buyers". The New York Times, 1920/8/20: 21.

New York Times 1924/2/22
"Bank Meets Run Caused by Rumor". The New York Times, 1924/2/22: 21.

New York Times 1924/2/24
"Bank Meets Run; Redeposits Start". The New York Times, 1924/2/24: 18.

New York Times 1926/7/16
"Bancitaly enters Wall Street field". The New York Times, 1926/7/16: 21.

New York Times 1926/8/31
"Perera heads new bank". The New York Times, 1926/8/31: 28.

New York Times 1927/1/12
"Italian Welfare League Outlines Work in This City With Second Largest Italian Population in the World". The New York Times, 1927/1/12: 26.

New York Times 1927/1/7
"Opera in Aid of Italian Hospital". The New York Times, 1927/1/7: 19.

New York Times 1927/10/13
"Columbia receives the Casa Italiana". The New York Times, 1927/10/13: 3.

New York Times 1927/3/13
"Furniture of the age of Dante". The New York Times, 1927/3/13: 12.

New York Times 1927/9/4
"$10,000 to Casa Italiana". The New York Times, 1927/9/4: 5.

New York Times 1930/2/26
"Pizzetti, composer, sees opera secure". The New York Times, 1930/2/26: 22.

New York Times 1930/2/9
"Manhattan Private Home Plans at a Low Record". The New York Times, 1930/2/9: 1.

New York Times 1930/3/17
"Ildebrando Pizzetti is Guest". The New York Times, 1930/3/17: 19.

New York Times 1936/1/27
"Italian Group Gives Dinner". The New York Times, 1936/1/27: 14.

New York Times 1938/1/6
"Toscanini to offer Beethoven Works". The New York Times, 1938/1/6: 23.

New York Times 1939/11/16
"$13,125 for Italian League". The New York Times, 1939/11/16: 13.

New York Times 1942/4/27
"Lionello Perera, Banker, dies at 69". The New York Times, 1942/4/27: 15.

New York Times 1944/2/26
"Town House Sold". The New York Times, 1944/2/26: 24.

New York Times 1946/12/21
"Mario Perera: Retired Official of the City Bank Farmers Trust Company Dies". The New York Times, 1946/12/21: 19.

New York Times 1953/1/18
"Guido Perera, expert in foreign currency". The New York Times, 1953/1/18: 93.
New York Times 1964/6/25
"Two Rembrandts sold at auction". The New York Times, 1964/6/25: 30.
New York Times 1964/1/31
"Lionel C. Perera Is Dead At 54". The New York Times, 1964/1/31: 27.
New York Times 1970/6/5
"Barbra Streisand's 5-Story Compromise". The New York Times, 1970/6/5: 47.
New York Tribune 1921/12/4
"Italian Welfare League to Give Dance Saturday: Benefit Supper and Ball Will Take Place at the Biltmore Hotel". New York Tribune, 1921/12/4: III-5.
Oldrini 1916
Oldrini, Alessandro (1916): "Morti e viventi eroi italici". Il Carroccio, IV(2), (August): 123-124.
Oldrini 1918
Oldrini, Alessandro (1918): "Lincoln e Garibaldi". Il Carroccio, VII(5-6), May: 470-471.
Perera 1916
Perera, Lionello (1917): "Pagine della Croce Rossa Italiana". Il Carroccio, IV(6), December 1916: 552-553.
Perera 1918
Perera, Lionello (1918): "Quarto prestito della libertà". Il Carroccio, VIII(4), October 1918: 314-316.
Pittston Gazette, 1905/9/13
"Soliciting Aid". Pittston Gazette, 1905/9/13: 3.
Progresso italo americano 1986
"Il banchiere che portò Caruso negli USA". Il Progresso italo americano, sezione B - Due Mondi. New York, 1986/7/27.
Raschellà 2007
Raschellà, Damiano M. (2007): "Vino e finanza: Amadeo Peter Giannini". Porthos, 26: 113-128.
Record and Guide 1910/9/10
"Real Estate Records". Record and Guide, LXXXVI(2217), 1910/9/10 (New York): 429-438.
School 1911/11/9
"Fifty Thousand Members Wanted". School, 1911/11/9: 116.
Schweikart 1995
Schweikart, Larry E. (1995): "Review: A. P. Giannini. Banker of America, by Felice A. Bonadio". The Journal of American History, 82(2), (September): 800-801.
Seward 1924
Anne Seward (1924): "Bank runs rare now owing to federal reserve law". The New York Times, 1924/3/2: IX-11.
Sunday News 1924/2/24
"Stream of gold revives faith in bank hit by run". Sunday News, 1924/2/24: 1, 6.

Zerbe 1902
Zerbe, Farran (1902): "Slugs and Stellas". Numismatis, XV/1, 344-345.

Archival Materials

Académie Julian 2020 (Digital Archive)
- Liste établie d'après les documents déposés aux archives nationales et référencés: 63 AS, Fonds de l'Académie Julian (accessed 2020/12/5).

American Numismatic Archaeological Society 1867 (Certificate)
- American Numismatic Archaeological Society (1867): Certificate on electing Leon Vita Cantoni a Corresponding Member, 1867/11/14.

Atti di morte 1882/1891 (Certificate)
- Atti di Morte, Venice, n.65 (1882/1891): Lopez Perera, Cesare, death occured on 1882 January 10, register entry updated in 1891.

Atti di morte 1892 (Certificate)
- Atti di Morte, Venice, n.1452 (1892): Cantoni, Emilia (Vedova Lopez Perera), death occured on 1892/7/3.

Bianchi Scaglia 2013 (Testimony)
- Bianchi Scaglia, Biancamaria (2013): "Il mio 25 aprile". Testimony as blog entry on bartesaghi-verderio-storia, 2013/4/22: http://bartesaghiverderio storia.blogspot.ca/2013/04/il-mio-25-aprile-di-biancamaria-bianchi.html (accessed on 2021/1/13).

Boytel, Leona 1943 (Correspondence)
- Biographical sketch of Lionello Perera;
- Draft notes on biography of Lionello Perera;
- Letter from Town Hall Inc. to Mrs. Lionello Perera, 1943/3/16.

Brooklyn Museum Archives 1936 (Digital Archive)
- Brooklyn Museum Archives (1936): "Press releases, 1931-36. 01-03_1936, 008". Records of the Department of Public Information.

Cantoni-Bomeisler 1890 (Document)
- Wedding invitation (1890): Natalie Cantoni to Louis Edwin Bomeisler to be held at home of bride's parents at 56 South Portland Avenue [Brooklyn], June 11.

Cantoni, Leon Vita 1862 (Correspondence)
- Letter from Leon Vita Cantoni to Luogotenenza in Venezia (military officials in Venice),1862/8/8.

Cantoni, Perera 1907 (Calendar)
- Banca Cantoni, Lionello Perera & Co. Page from company calendar (New York), 1907 December.

Cantoni, Salvatore 1862 (Correspondence)
- Letter from Salvatore Cantoni to his parents and siblings, Hotel de Russie (Paris), 1862/7/16 (Correspondence).

Cappellini, Goldhahn 2013
Cappellini, Patrizia; Goldhahn, Almut (2013): Fotografien eines Kunsthändlers: Die Sammlung Elia Volpis (Online exhibition). Photothek des Kunsthistorischen

Instituts in Florenz, Max-Planck-Institut (online from 2013/4/22). Url: http://photothek.khi.fi.it/documents/oau?set_language=de (accessed on 2020/12/05).

Circuit Court of New York 1899 (Certificate)

- Circuit Court of the United States for the southern district of New York: intention of Lionello Perera to become US citizen, 1899/02/01.

Commercial Exchange National Bank 1928 (Document)

- Commercial Exchange National Bank in New York: Minutes of Proceedings at Special Meeting, 1928/4/26 (44 Wall Street, New York).

Consolato Generale d'Italia 1908 (Certificate)

- Certificate from R. Consolato Generale d'Italia to Lionello Perera (Italian Consulate), New York, 1908/5/7.

Declaration of absence 1946 (Document)

- Dichiarazione di assenza di Olga Lopez Perera e Sami Pincherle (Declaration of absence), Lea Pincherle at Tribunale di Gorizia (courtroom), 1946/2/22.

Deputazione provinciale 1889 (Document)

- Decree n.190 by the Deputazione provinciale di Venezia (University Scholarship), 1889/1/9.

Edison Papers Digital Edition 1900-1901

Thomas A. Edison Papers Digital Edition:

- Letter from Thomas Alva Edison to Louis Edwin Bomeisler, 1900: http://edison.rutgers.edu/digital/document/D0015AAT;
- Letter from Thomas Alva Edison to Louis Edwin Bomeisler, April 6th, 1900: http://edison.rutgers.edu/digital/document/LB064515;
- Letter from Thomas Alva Edison to Louis Edwin Bomeisler, February 1901: http://edison.rutgers.edu/digital/document/D0103AAF.

Italian Red Cross 1911 (Correspondence)

- Letter from Rinaldo Taverna, President of the Italian Red Cross, regarding the appointment of Lionello Perera as Ufficiale (Italian Honorary Official), Rome, 1911/3/11.

Italian Red Cross 1924 (Honour)

- Gold Medal from Croce Rossa Italiana to Lionello Perera, issued by President of the Italian Red Cross President in the name of the King and Queen of Italy, Rome, 1924/1/7.

Marcella Sembrich Collection 1790-1988 (Correspondence)

- The Marcella Sembrich Collection (1790-1988), JPB 91-94. Music Division, The New York Public Library for the Performing Arts.

Marriage Announcement 1892 (Document)

- Marriage Announcement (1892): Olga Lopez Perera and Eugenio Pincherle, oggi Sposi, Venice, 1892/6/26.

Miller 2013

Miller, Tom (2013): "The 1930 Perera House: No. 49 E. 80th Street". Daytonian in Manhattan (Independent blog), 2013/1/29. Url: http://daytoninmanhattan.blogspot.ca/2013/01/the-1930-perera-house-no-49-e-80th.html (accessed on 2019/11/21).

New York Banking Department 1914 (Certificate)
- State of New York Banking Department: permission for Lionello Perera to conduct private banking business, 1914/10/26.

New York Banking Department 1926 (Certificate)
- State of New York Banking Department: permission for Commercial Exchange Bank to conduct private banking business, 1926/10/14.

New York Court of Appeals 1897
- Court of Appeals of the State of New York (1897): “Bomeisler v. Forster”. 154 N.Y. 229, November 23.

New York Supreme Court 1897
- New York Supreme Court (1987): 19 Misc. 222. "Forster v. Cantoni", January.

Office of the Mayor 1934 (Certificate)
- Certificate of appointment of Lionello Perera to the Child Welfare Board (signed by Fiorello La Guardia), Office of the Mayor, The City of New York, 1934/2/14.

Passenger Record 1894 (Document)
- American History Immigration Center at Ellis Island: Lionello Perera, passenger record, 1894 April 19.

Perera Guest Book 1930-1966 (Document)
- Lionello and Carolyn Perera's Guest Book, 49 East 80th Street, New York (1930-1966).

Perera Papers 1920 (Correspondence)
- Perera, Lionello: Dante Alighieri (ocean liner), to [Mrs. Carolyn Allen Perera], n.p.; 1920/4/13. Autograph letter, signed. Description of journey with daughter Nina.

Perera Papers 1937 (Correspondence)
- Isaacs, Stanley M. (elected President of the Manhattan Borough): New York, to [Mrs. Lionello Perera], n.p.; 1937/11/10. Typewritten and autograph letter, signed. Thanking for support in election.
- Portfolio, Almerindo (treasurer for Mayor La Guardia): New York, to [Mrs. Lionello Perera], n.p.; 1937/11/10. Typewritten letter, signed. Thanking for support in election.
- Corsi, Edward (Deputy Commissioner of Public Welfare): New York, to [Mrs. Lionello Perera], n.p.; 1937/11/19. Typewritten letter, signed. Thanking for support in election.

Perera Papers 1941 (Correspondence)
- La Guardia, Fiorello (Mayor of New York): New York, to [Mr. Lionello Perera], n.p.; 1941/4/26. Typewritten letter, signed. Appointment to the Mayor's Committee for the “I Am An American Day”.

Perera Papers 1942 (Correspondence)
- Perera, Carolyn and Lionello (first draft): New York, to [Mr. Springer], n.p.; 1939/1/21. Handwritten draft for letter. Response on situation of Jews in Europe.
- Perera, Carolyn and Lionello (second draft): New York, to [Mr. Springer], n.p.; 1939/1/21. Typewritten draft for letter. Response on situation of Jews in Europe.

R. Scuola Superiore di Commercio 1886 (Certificate)

- R. Scuola Superiore di Commercio (1886): Certificato dell'esame di ammissione di Leonello Perera (admission certificate), academic year 1886-1887, signed by F.Ferrara, 1886/10/31.

R. Scuola Superiore di Commercio 1909 (Certificate)

- R. Scuola Superiore di Commercio (1909): Diploma di Laurea (Master's Degree), granted by Nicolò Papadopoli Aldrovandi, 1909/2/10.

Rally of New America 1937 (Document)

- Speech by Lionello Perera at La Guardia campaign event, probably the Rally of New America for La Guardia, (New York Hyppodrome), 1937/10/31.

Re d'Italia 1909 (Certificate)

- Certificate of appointment of Lionello Perera as Cavaliere from Vittorio Emanuele III, Re d'Italia (Order of the Crown of Italy), Rome, 1909/1/24.

Regio Esercito Italiano 1891 (Document)

- Foglio di congedo illimitato di IIIa categoria (Military Leave), Venice, 1891/9/10.

Registro matricolare 1886-1889 (Document)

- R. Scuola Superiore di Commercio (1886-1889): Registro matricolare, academic years 1886-1889, page 42, n. 425, Perera Leonello, di Cesare.

Report of the Condition 1919 (Clipping)

- Report of the Condition of Lionello Perera & Co., 1919/02/21 (from unknown newspaper).

Robins 2007 (National Register)

Robins, Anthony W. (2007): "National Register of Historic Places: House at 49 East 80th Street". United States Department of the Interior: National Park Service, 2007/9/27.

Toscanini Legacy Papers 1686-1993 (Correspondence)

Toscanini Legacy Papers (1686-1993), JPB 90-1. Music Division, The New York Public Library:

- Ara, Ugo. Letter: New York, to [Lionello Perera], n.p.; 1920/7/21. Autograph letter, signed, with enclosure; ink (3 p.) Includes a list of persons pledging money towards bringing AT to the U.S.;
- Ara, Ugo. Letter: New York, to [Lionello Perera], n.p.; 1920/7/27. Autograph letter, signed; ink (2 p.) Acknowledges receipt of $2,000 towards bringing AT to the U.S. to perform.";
- Toscanini, Arturo and Carla. Telegram: New York, to Lionello and Carolyn Perera, New York; 1938/3/9. (1 p.) Gratitude for their contribution to the Casa di Riposo per Musicisti in Milan, Italy;
- Toscanini, Arturo. Letter: n.p., to Caroline Perera, n.p.; 1952/4/3. Photocopy of autograph letter, signed, with envelope; 5 p. (2 copies). Thanks her for a book and for her contribution to the Casa di Riposo per Musicisti.

Index

G

H

I

J

K

L

M

N

O

www.ingramcontent.com/pod-product-compliance
Ingram Content Group UK Ltd.
Pitfield, Milton Keynes, MK11 3LW, UK
UKHW020800290926
15470UKWH00008B/1833/J

9 781648 894411